SEQUENCE OF EVENTS

The weather "bomb" created by a rapidly deepening depression traveled south-southeast from Fiji at about 15 knots. Its hurricane-force winds and steep, 50-foot waves severely battered yachts taking part in the 1994 cruising regatta from New Zealand to Tonga. (Note: Times are given in New Zealand Standard Time.)

THURSDAY, JUNE 2

1500: *Destiny*, farthest north of the affected yachts, receives weatherfax giving first hint of storm about to form.

FRIDAY, JUNE 3

1200: Tropical depression starts to form between Vanuatu and Fiji. Central pressure 1,001 mb. *Destiny* heaves-to. Wind increases to 50 knots.
1600: *Destiny* runs under bare poles with drogue.

SATURDAY, JUNE 4

0841: *Destiny* sends Pan message alerting Kerikeri Radio to the extreme conditions.
0911: In 70-knot winds, *Destiny* pitchpoles. Distress beacon (EPIRB) switched on.
1030: RCC (Rescue Centre) activated. NZ Naval ship *Monowai* diverted to rescue *Destiny*.
1145: First Orion P3 search-and-rescue plane departs.
1200: Barometric pressure now 986 mb, creating an official weather "bomb."
1220: *Mary T* sends Pan call. *Monowai* diverted to *Mary T*.
1440: Orion contacts *Destiny*; merchant ship *Tui Cakau III* goes to rescue yacht's crew.
1548: *Quartermaster* sends Mayday after knockdown, but quickly cancels it.
2211: *Sofia* sets off EPIRB.

SUNDAY, JUNE 5

0035: *Quartermaster* reports another knockdown.
0204: Last call from *Quartermaster*.
0440: Another EPIRB detected— probably from *Quartermaster*.
0500: *Ramtha* asks *Monowai* for help.
0745: *Tui Cakau* rescues *Destiny*'s crew.
0750: *Heart Light* activates EPIRB.
0800: A Hercules rescue plane reports *Sofia* in distress.
1000: *Monowai* rescues *Ramtha*'s crew. French Naval vessel *Jacques Cartier* sent to aid *Sofia*.
1210: Hercules finds *Silver Shadow* dismasted.
1446: *Quartermaster*'s life raft found empty.
1738: Fishing vessel *San Te Maru* sent to *Heart Light*.
1800: Low-pressure system bottoms out at 978 mb. Swell estimated at 30 to 50 feet.
2000: Orion finds *Pilot* in distress.

MONDAY, JUNE 6

0020: *San Te Maru* locates *Heart Light*.
0810: *Waikiwi II* activates EPIRB.
0838: *Monowai* rescues *Pilot*'s crew.
1000: *San Te Maru* rescues *Heart Light*'s crew, then recovers *Quartermaster*'s life raft.
1445: Merchant ship *Nomadic Duchess* diverts from course to rescue *Waikiwi II*.
1745: *Monowai* rescues crew of *Silver Shadow*.
2009: *Jacques Cartier* rescues *Sofia*'s crew.
2104: *Mary T*, in improving weather, cancels her Pan message.

TUESDAY, JUNE 7

0955: Orion aircraft and Wasp helicopter from *Monowai* continue search for *Quartermaster*'s crew.
1503: *Nomadic Duchess* rescues crew of *Waikiwi II*.

WEDNESDAY, JUNE 8

1755: Search for *Quartermaster*'s crew suspended.

FROM THE LIBRARY OF

Larry Lee

RESCUE
in the
PACIFIC

RESCUE
in the
PACIFIC

A True Story of Disaster and

Survival in a Force 12 Storm

TONY FARRINGTON

INTERNATIONAL MARINE   CAMDEN, MAINE

McGRAW-HILL BOOK COMPANY AUSTRALIA   SYDNEY

McGRAW-HILL BOOK COMPANY NEW ZEALAND   AUCKLAND

International Marine/
Ragged Mountain Press

A Division of The **McGraw·Hill** Companies

10   9   8   7   6   5   4   3

Copyright © 1996 International Marine®, a division of The McGraw-Hill Companies. All rights reserved. The publisher takes no responsibility for the use of any of the materials or methods described in this book, nor for the products thereof. The name "International Marine" and the International Marine logo are trademarks of The McGraw-Hill Companies. Printed in the United States of America.

Library of Congress Cataloging-in-Publication Data
Farrington, Tony.
 Rescue in the Pacific : a true story of disaster and survival in a force 12 storm / Tony Farrington.
   p.   cm.
  Includes index.
  ISBN 0-07-021367-4 (alk. paper)
   1. Shipwrecks — South Pacific Ocean.   2. Survival after airplane accidents, shipwrecks, etc.   I. Title.
  G525.F36   1995
  363.12'3'0916448 — dc20   95-34720
                                                                    CIP
Questions regarding the content of this book should be addressed to:
International Marine, P.O. Box 220, Camden, ME 04843, 207-236-4837

Questions regarding the ordering of this book should be addressed to:
The McGraw-Hill Companies, Customer Service Department, P.O. Box 547, Blacklick, OH 43004; retail customers: 1-800-262-4729; bookstores: 1-800-722-4726

McGraw-Hill Book Company New Zealand Limited, P.O. Box 97082, SAMC, Manukau City, Auckland, New Zealand; Tel.: 64-9-262-2537; Fax: 64-9-262-2540

McGraw-Hill Book Company Australia Pty. Ltd., 4 Barcoo Street, Roseville, NSW 2069, Australia; Tel.: 61-2-417-4288; Fax: 61-2-417-8872

Text design by Ann Aspell
Production by Janet Robbins
Page layout by Publisher's Design and Production Services, Inc.
Edited by John J. Kettlewell, John Vigor, Pamela Benner, and Jonathan Eaton

To my crew:
Esmae, Harvey, and Justine,
for encouraging the dreams.

CONTENTS

≋≋≋

FOREWORD

"THE SEAS ARE MOUNTAINOUS." THIS IS THE FIRST MESSAGE FROM one of the sailboats hit by the infamous four-day, hurricane-strength 1994 South Pacific storm, the worst to hit a fleet of yachts in years and—as you soon will see—the occasion not only for some remarkable feats of courage and seamanship but for deep reflection by all sailors about the boats and gear and hopes they sail with. "Mountainous" was close to it. An experienced merchant captain estimated that some waves were 100 feet high. Winds were clocked at near 90 knots, and still many yachts survived.

Here we learn how. Based on extensive interviews with survivors as well as on tapes of radio broadcasts, this is the story of the June 1994 "Queen's Birthday" storm that swept the Pacific north of New Zealand. This storm has been nicknamed "the Pacific Fastnet" because of its similarities to the 1979 Fastnet Race storm in England, the watershed event in recent yachting and boating disasters. In some ways the Pacific storm was worse. The 1979 Fastnet storm blew barely 60 knots, kicked up 50-foot seas, and lasted less than a day. If it killed 15 sailors and sank five boats, far more than the Pacific storm, that was because a fleet of 303 yachts lay in its path, not the 60 sailing north of New Zealand in 1994. But in two ways the pair of storms are remarkably similar: each produced extraordinary adventures for the sailors unlucky enough to have been trapped by them; and each has produced some important, if painful, lessons about taking a boat out into the ocean. *Rescue in the Pacific* is a near-encyclopedia of offshore boating safety information.

Tony Farrington tells his remarkable story through the eyes of three groups of people. First come two dozen sailors in 10 yachts, a mixed band of experienced and inexperienced men and women, caught in the web of this tragedy that they endure, usually with amazing courage. Second are the helpers ashore, especially the knowledgeable rescue coordinators and the devoted operators of Kerikeri Radio, Jon and Maureen Cullen, who, from their radio shack in a pretty village in northern New Zealand, provide a crucial, nonstop communications net for victims and rescuers alike. And third are the disciplined, focused rescuers who saved 21 people from seven yachts—military personnel and mariners in airplanes and ships, performing their searches and rescues almost in defiance of the conditions.

Not all the sailors were thoroughly prepared for the storm. Motivated by the dream of long, hassle-free voyages to distant islands, some had not acknowledged that the sea can be a nightmare. Story after story reveals their shock at how quickly a seemingly safe situation can be unraveled by one big, breaking wave. Waves are like snowflakes: as regular and orderly as they may appear from afar, up close they are strikingly different. Except that unlike snowflakes, and more like apples, one rogue wave can spoil the entire lot. Experts tell us that one wave out of 20, on average, is a rogue running at a sharply different angle from the other 19. Come that rogue in a gale or storm, and the ocean becomes a maelstrom. Over and over it happened: A boat was running relatively peacefully, perhaps dragging an improvised drogue to slow her down, when—without warning—she was tipped upside down as crew, gear, and rigs were thrown everywhere, usually resulting in severe damage. Hatches and ports that had seemed rigid were smashed to bits. Masts that had appeared sturdy were fractured like matchsticks. Decks were stripped of all their gear. Rudders crumbled or jammed into the hull. Crewmembers whose courage and leadership had been unquestioned retreated into panic or passivity. Almost every boat in this narrative was transformed within one or two minutes from a proud yacht into a hopeless wreck.

The lessons here for people headed offshore are legion. Some concern the boat's own self-sufficiency. Nothing points out a boat's weaknesses as effectively as a rollover, and many boats were left unable to be steered, much less sailed, and with broken or clogged pumps and leaking hatches and cockpits. Other lessons here concern possible rescue. When Jon Cullen learned that yet another white boat was invisible in the foamy sea, he thought, "Would it be any other color? They're all white hulls." And of the 406 MHz Emergency Position Indicating Radio Beacons that attracted rescuers like a magnet pulls steel filings, a pilot of a search plane said, "Those beacons are lifesavers. No one should be allowed out without them."

But as important as that equipment is, this book (like my narrative of the 1979 Fastnet Race catastrophe) makes clear that the most crucial safety tool is the crew. If the sailors are not resiliently committed to the idea of self-preservation, they will die. One skipper, caught in the worst of the gale in a cove and unable to anchor, survived by motoring back and forth along a tiny course between two Global Positioning System waypoints. Another, who was just as unwilling to go down without a fight, shouted, "How dare water enter this boat?"

To survive we need gumption, a purpose, and a goal, but what we need first is hope. Hope cannot always be self-generated. Over and over, crews' spirits were raised from desolation by a single act, such as the appearance overhead of a search-and-rescue airplane or the sound over the radio of the voice of one of the Cullens, who relayed messages, dispensed advice on storm tactics, and provided a sympathetic ear. "We're just hanging on, Jon. Just hanging on," says an exhausted skipper.

Besides the Cullens, the coolest heads out there were the skippers of the small commercial and naval vessels that plucked sailors, some badly injured, off their half-sunk or wrecked yachts. It is a lesson in the arts of firm command and sound seamanship to read in chapter 14 how Captain Bruce White maneuvered his fishing vessel alongside the distressed catamaran *Heart Light*.

Heart Light herself is an example of another type of morale-building. While it did not fit the usual pattern of good seamanship, I believe it saved lives. The inexperienced, unskilled crew of this

American catamaran probably should not have been out there. They were propelled into the South Pacific by the dreams of the captain's wife, a clairvoyant who envisioned a venture toward spiritual enlightenment. When the storm hit and the automatic pilot on which they had depended could not keep up with the vessel's wild yawing, the skipper, Darryl Wheeler, steered for almost two days while his wife, Diviana, alternately massaged his aching back and engaged in long bouts of deep meditation. Her mystical purpose took a strange turn (she anticipated a meeting with space aliens), yet her certainty calmed and focused the crew on their survival until they were rescued by Captain White.

The human spirit, no matter how it is manifested, is the best survival tool there is. That is but one of the lessons of this valuable, enthralling book.

JOHN ROUSMANIERE

John Rousmaniere has written a dozen instructional and historical books on sailing. They include *"Fastnet, Force 10,"* about the stormy 1979 Fastnet Race, and *The Annapolis Book of Seamanship,* the standard sailing instructional manual. He is also the host of *The Annapolis Book of Seamanship Video Series.* Rousmaniere lives in Stamford, Connecticut, and has sailed more than 30,000 miles offshore. He has moderated or spoken at 30 Safety-at-Sea Seminars throughout the United States.

PREFACE

≋≋≋

OCCASIONALLY AN EVENT OCCURS THAT IS MORE RIVETING THAN fiction and that, if it were written as such, would be dismissed as the product of an overly fertile imagination. Such an event unfolded in the South Pacific during the first week of June 1994.

At that time I was aboard my yacht, securely berthed in Gulf Harbour, Auckland, New Zealand. I was listening to a high-frequency radio, following the progress of a fleet of small yachts sailing in a regatta to Tonga, 1,000 miles away, and at first I was envious. My plan had been to accompany the fleet, but business demands had kept me firmly anchored in New Zealand.

But as the weekend progressed, I became more and more grateful that I was not out there. The radio crackled with the voices of people in distress. The crews of boats with names familiar to me reported with trepidation their battles in increasingly dangerous conditions. They had sailed into a storm worse than any we had imagined likely at that time of year.

While those at sea fought for their lives, we in port forwent sleep, glued to the radio throughout the days and nights of their ordeal. We followed the fortunes of those we knew and tracked the progress of those we did not. How were they coping? Were their boats and their seamanship equal to it? Would they pull through?

These were hours of high drama. For more than 72 hours, daring rescues were performed by the Royal New Zealand Navy, the Royal New Zealand Air Force, the French Navy, a fishing boat, and two freighters. Despite limited resources and the vast distances involved, 21 people were rescued. Scores of others battled their way through the rogue storm successfully, while three people aboard one boat were lost to the sea.

It was the biggest search-and-rescue operation of modern times in the South Pacific. So vile were the conditions, those who weren't there find it difficult to believe the accounts of rescuers and survivors. In yachting circles, particularly in North America, the storm's intensity has been much debated. The very fact that rescuers managed to save so many lives may have fueled skepticism about the severity of the weather.

It is widely accepted that people on small yachts tend, through no fault of their own, to exaggerate wave heights encountered. The violent accelerations of a vessel in heaving seas play tricks on our eyes and our sense of balance. So how accurate are accounts of this storm, which sprang from nowhere in the South Pacific? Given its distance from weather recording stations, how do we determine its true strength?

There is abundant evidence that a severe depression forming near Fiji exploded upon the yachts as a weather "bomb," producing hurricane-force winds. A freighter involved in the rescues, the *Tui Cakau III*, made a barograph record (see the illustration in Appendix I) of the pressure drop that occurred near the storm's center. It shows the atmospheric pressure plummeting approximately 20 millibars (mb) during a 24-hour period. This is about double the threshold for establishing a weather bomb in that area. The severity of the conditions and the unusual length of time the yachts were forced to endure them combined to wreak the havoc of gear failure, exhaustion, and despair that led to the loss of vessels and lives.

The accompanying map of the storm area, taken from New Zealand Meteorological Service material, shows its vast proportions. The storm's core, harboring winds of more than 50 knots, passed over 234,000 square miles. Gales affected more than 1.25 million square miles of ocean.

The map does not answer the critical question: What was the intensity of the wind at the core? But it does explain why some yachts claiming to be victims of the storm recorded only gale-force

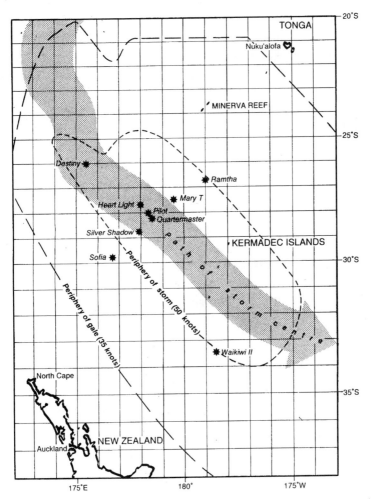

Approximate positions of Destiny, Sofia, Silver Shadow, Heart
Light, Pilot, Ramtha, *and* Waikiwi II *when rescued. Position of*
Mary T *upon issuing Pan call. Last known position of* Quartermaster. *(Courtesy of Graeme Cooper, Consultus NZ Ltd., based
on New Zealand Meteorological Service information)*

winds, and others only Force 10 (winds of 48 to 55 knots). Despite the severe conditions they endured, they were not actually within the storm at all, but only on its periphery. It was the yachts in the vortex that reported winds of more than 64 knots, which is Force 12.

Destiny was the first to be hit by the weather bomb. She was closer to Fiji than the others, and it is likely that the bomb building above the South Pacific actually exploded around her. Her skipper reported his electronic anemometer as showing a consistent 75 to 80 knots of wind from astern. Taking boat speed into consideration, the constant true wind speed must have been near 80 to 90 knots, gusting higher. The skippers of other yachts, all interviewed independently and without an opportunity for collusion, reported reading Force 12 on their anemometers.

Jim Hebden, the captain of the freighter *Tui Cakau III*, is an experienced officer not given to exaggeration. On his way to attempt a rescue of *Destiny*'s crew, he recorded in his log that the storm was Force 10. He admits he was deliberately conservative, however, and he accepts *Destiny*'s record; he was guessing the wind speed because his ship did not carry an anemometer. He also estimates that at times the seas were more than 80 feet high, another indication of hurricane conditions.

K. Adlard Coles states a number of times in his book *Heavy Weather Sailing* that he is prepared to accept anemometer records as accurate, but he questions a person's ability to gauge wind velocity accurately without instruments.

New Zealand Air Force personnel reported the surface wind at 70 to 80 knots. Their aircraft flew as low as 200 feet above the sea, and they recorded waves 100 feet high.

The New Zealand MetService's Chief Meteorologist, August Auer, is satisfied that the yachts were caught in a Force 12 storm. Formerly Professor of Atmospheric Science at the University of Wyoming, Auer said the Orion P3 aircraft in the area were fitted with equipment that could accurately measure surface conditions. Based on their reports that winds reached 70 knots, he would expect gusts to have been in the vicinity of 100 knots. On the Beaufort

Beaufort Scale of Wind Forces (cont.)

Beaufort Number	Wind Speed (Knots)	Description	Effects
0	under 1	Calm	Sea like a mirror
1	1 to 3	Light air	Slight ripples; sailboat just has steerage way
2	4 to 6	Light breeze	Small wavelets; wind just keeps sails filled
3	7 to 10	Gentle breeze	Large wavelets; sailboats begin to heel
4	11 to 16	Moderate breeze	Small waves; sailboats dip gunwales under water
5	17 to 21	Fresh breeze	Moderate waves, many whitecaps; time to reef
6	22 to 27	Strong breeze	Double-reefed mainsails; waves 8 to 12 feet (2.5 to 4 meters)
7	28 to 33	Near gale	Waves 12 to 20 feet (4 to 6 meters); foam starts blowing streaks
8	34 to 40	Gale	Waves 12 to 20 feet (4 to 6 meters), but longer, with spindrift
9	41 to 47	Strong gale	High waves; spray starts to reduce visibility
10	48 to 55	Storm	Waves to 30 feet (6 to 9 meters) with overhanging crests

Beaufort Scale of Wind Forces (cont.)

Beaufort Number	Wind Speed (Knots)	Description	Effects
11	56 to 63	Violent storm	Waves to 45 feet (9 to 14 meters); white foam patches cover sea
12	64 and over	Hurricane	Foam fills air; sea all white; waves over 45 feet (14 meters)

Modified from The Practical Mariner's Book of Knowledge, *by John Vigor (International Marine, 1994). (Courtesy John Vigor)*

Scale, the international nautical scale of wind velocities, a wind speed greater than 64 knots is officially designated Force 12, or hurricane force. Auer says that because of its nature, the storm had a very tight core in which hurricane-force conditions existed.

To those who were "out there," the strength of the storm is of little more than academic interest. Whether Force 10 or Force 12, the sea conditions were such that they had to muster every ounce of psychological and physical reserves to survive.

I have always regarded those who venture to sea in boats as special. I have now also learned great respect for the skill, courage, and tenacity of those who patrol our seas, skies, and radio waves.

This book is an account of an astonishing weekend a few hundred miles off the shores of New Zealand. The background for the story is based on my own knowledge and experience of the sea, but the facts are based on interviews with survivors of the storm and with their rescuers. Throughout, I have endeavored to portray events strictly as described by those involved. To do otherwise would be to debase their achievements.

ACKNOWLEDGMENTS

≋≋≋

Scores of people were involved in rescues during the storm, and it was neither possible nor necessary to interview everyone. The account that follows was given to me by those listed below. I am immensely appreciative of their frankness, courage, and generosity in sharing delicate and intimate information in the hope that their experiences may, one day, help others caught in heavy weather. Dialogue attributed to them during their battles for survival and during rescues has been taken from their recollections soon after the event. All the radio excerpts are authentic, although edited in some instances.

The story was told to me by Dana and Paula Dinius from *Destiny*; Darryl and Diviana Wheeler, *Heart Light*; Sigmund, Carol, and Anna Baardsen, *Mary T*; Greg Forbes and Barbara Parks, *Pilot*; Bill and Robyn Forbes, *Ramtha*; Bill and Linda Christieson, *Windora*; Peter and Murray O'Neil, John McSherry, and Richard Jackson, *Silver Shadow*; Keith Levy and Uschi Schmidt, *Sofia*; John Hilhorst and Cath Gilmour, *Waikiwi II*; Capt. Jim Hebden, *Tui Cakau III*; Jon and Maureen Cullen, Kerikeri Radio; Cmdr. Larry Robbins and Leading Seaman Abraham Whata, HMNZS *Monowai*; Bob McDavitt, MetService New Zealand; Flt. Lt. Bruce Craies, Flt. Lt. Dianna Hales, Wing Commander Craig Inch, Sqd. Ldr. Peter Mount, Sqd. Ldr. Dave Powell, and Sqd. Ldr. Mike Yardley, Royal New Zealand Air Force (RNZAF); Lt. Cmdr. Saint-Martin and officers, *Jacques Cartier*; Don Mundell, organizer of the Tonga Regatta; Inspector John Meads, NZ Police; Jim McLean and Bill Sommer, NZ National Rescue Coordination Centre (NRCC);

Capt. Bruce White, *San Te Maru 18*; Lt. (jg) Erin MacDonald, U.S. Coast Guard, Long Beach, California; Don Hall, Alden Electronics, Boston, Massachusetts.

STATEMENT BY U.S. SENATOR WILLIAM S. COHEN, MAINE:

Each year, hundreds of United States citizens visit the waters of New Zealand by yacht to escape the cyclone season in the South Pacific region. In return, the people of New Zealand generously extend their protection and watchful eye to voyagers of all nations . . . I would like to pay tribute to these heroic men and women . . . and offer my deepest appreciation for their commitment to others.
— From the U.S. *Congressional Record*, July 21, 1994

CHAPTER 1

SOMEONE'S IN TROUBLE
OUT THERE

≋≋≋

On Saturday morning, June 4, 1994, a satellite glided with silent efficiency in polar orbit over the South Pacific. It passed over Fiji, heading toward New Zealand, searching the earth's atmosphere for signs of changing weather. There had been little of note in the region, certainly nothing to indicate the presence of an out-of-season cyclone. But 400 miles south of Fiji, electronic sensors on the satellite were triggered by the glare of an intense light from below. It was sunlight bouncing off a sinister mountain of clouds whose tops swirled 50,000 feet above the ocean.

The instruments worked their routines as the tiny probe sped through space far above the turbulent sea, assembling pictures of the weather system below. The storm embryo it had spied two days earlier was cohering into the beautiful shape of a tropical cyclone, a sprawling reversed comma. The pictures and data were beamed back to the National Oceanic and Atmospheric Administration (NOAA) in America. Speeding on over the ocean, recording and photographing, the satellite continued to transmit routine weather information that NOAA would process and distribute to weather stations all around the world. Forecasters would study this information and predict a modest gale for the area.

The satellite knew or cared nothing of the flotilla of little boats entering the region below. But suddenly another sensor came alive, an ignited plea for help. A pulse, a heartbeat, an electronic buzz that lasted only a fraction of a second. A few seconds later it repeated itself, then again and again until the satellite was too far away to capture the bursts of electronic sound within its antennae.

1

Processors on the satellite immediately transmitted the SOS to a receiving station in Hawaii, which in turn automatically relayed it to the United States search-and-rescue mission control center at Suitland, Maryland. An American yacht was in distress, a microscopic speck in the vast ocean 500 miles below.

Lt. (jg) Erin MacDonald reacted immediately when the message bleeped onto her computer screen in the U.S. Coast Guard command center at Long Beach, California. The local time was 1422 on June 3, 1994.

District 11 Coast Guard Control Center monitors all search-and-rescue activities in an area stretching from the California-Oregon border to the Mexico-Guatemala border and halfway to Hawaii. About 15,000 times a year, the center is summoned to assist vessels and aircraft in distress. Five thousand of those calls result in full search-and-rescue missions in which lives are at risk.

Lt. MacDonald studied the message. The satellite gave two possible locations for the distressed yacht and the probability of each, based on the spacecraft's position at the time: 26° 04.55'S, 175° 48.05'E; or 20° 31.30'S, 151° 05.90'E. The odds favored the first pair of coordinates 53 percent to 47 percent, but both locations were at least 6,500 miles from Long Beach, on the other side of the international date line. There was not the remotest chance Lt. MacDonald would be required to send aircraft or ships to assist the yacht the satellite identified as *Destiny*.

According to the computer, *Destiny* was registered there in Long Beach. Lt. MacDonald telephoned the listed contact, Paul Norman, father-in-law of the boat's skipper, Dana Dinius. Norman confirmed that his daughter Paula and her husband had sailed for the South Pacific four years previously and had intended to depart Auckland, New Zealand, for Fiji on May 30.

Norman outlined all relevant details of the Diniuses' sailing experience and other helpful information about their extensive inventory of equipment, which included a sextant, a life raft, and a Global

Positioning System (GPS). The crew were in their early 40s—skilled, experienced sailors.

Lt. MacDonald passed the information onto U.S. Coast Guard District 14 in Hawaii. But, in fact, the stricken yacht was too far from Hawaii for them to help, either.

SATURDAY, JUNE 4

Thirty-five thousand feet above the ocean, the cockpit of an Air Pacific Boeing 737 was filled with the sound of a whooping siren triggered by an EPIRB in action. The plane was flying from Nadi, Fiji, to Auckland, New Zealand. During the next hour, three Air New Zealand planes confirmed the beacon's location.

Bill Sommer had just returned from a morning jog when the telephone rang at his home near New Zealand's capital city, Wellington.

"Bill, an Air Pacific flight has picked up a locater beacon," the Auckland air traffic controller told him. "We've had it confirmed by three Air New Zealand flights. Someone's in trouble out there."

As coordinator of the country's National Rescue Coordination Centre (NRCC or RCC), Bill Sommer was on 24-hour standby. His job was to bring together all the services involved in searches for ships or aircraft in distress.

He immediately began assembling the search-and-rescue crews. Methodically, he worked through his list, calling in the Royal New Zealand Air Force, the Royal New Zealand Navy, the police, and Maritime Safety.

"It'll be a doddle," he told the team gathering at the rescue center. "The beacon is loud and clear and, according to the Met office, the weather's not too bad. We'll be out of here in a few hours and enjoying the rest of the weekend."

He asked the Air Force's Number 5 Squadron to place an Orion P3 aircraft on standby.

Earlier that morning, at the tip of North Island, 570 miles from Wellington, in the quaint little town of Kerikeri, a woman's voice had interrupted a conversation between Kerikeri Radio operator Jon Cullen and another boat:

Voice: Pan Pan Pan. Vessel *Destiny.*

Jon: Destiny. Kerikeri. Go ahead with your Pan Pan. Over.

Destiny: We are 26° 04'S, 175° 46'E. The seas are mountainous. [Her words were punctuated by pants and gasps.]

Jon: Roger. I copy, *Destiny.* Are you okay? Over.

Destiny: Well, we're still upright. We've got a drogue out.

Jon: Roger, well okay, we'll stay on standby. Ah, just give us a call if you've got any problems. Over.

Destiny: Well, I'm going back out. [She still sounded breathless.] We're going to be out topside anyway, I'll be back if I, if I . . .

Jon: Roger. Okay. You make sure you've got those harnesses on. Over.

Destiny: Roger. Roger.

Jon: Okay. Good Luck.

During the next three hours, from the ham station in a room underneath his house, Jon continued to contact the flotilla of yachts cruising the South Pacific, many of which were being buffeted by a storm that appeared to be gaining force. He was in contact with at least 60 boats between New Zealand and Fiji, each as insignificant as a grain of sand in the Sahara—little boats dotted over 600,000 square miles of ocean.

Each year, usually before November, scores of yachts from America, Germany, Australia, and other countries scurry to New

Zealand to shelter from the Pacific cyclones spinning over the area during the southern summer, from October to March. They sail away again in May and June, joining hundreds of New Zealand yachts in search of the zephyrs that will blow them to the romantic isles of Tonga, Fiji, and Vanuatu—confident that the cyclone season is over. From these stopovers, it is a comparatively easy passage to the Indian Ocean and away to the Mediterranean, or through the Panama Canal to the Atlantic. Among the 60 boats out there on June 4, 34 were participating in an informal regatta sailing from New Zealand to the kingdom of Tonga. Others Jon talked to were heading across the Pacific from Australia, or working their way from island to island, chasing dreams of paradise formed in America, Europe, and South Africa.

Jon Cullen's passion for helping those who venture to sea had consumed him for 11 years. He and his wife, Maureen, were legends to yachting folk around the world. They all seemed to contact the Cullens as soon as their boats sailed within range of Kerikeri Radio. Twenty-four hours a day, seven days a week, the Cullens were on call for any vessel between the equator and Antarctica that required assistance. Working from a bedroom they'd converted into a radio shack beneath their two-story house, they responded to any lonely seafarer who needed a friend, a word of comfort, a weather report, or advice ranging from clearing New Zealand Customs and Immigration to reviving an engine or surviving a storm.

By Saturday night, Jon was deeply worried. Uneasiness had first set in 48 hours earlier when he'd studied the isobars on the weatherfaxes received from meteorological offices in New Zealand and Australia. A massive high-pressure system was hovering over the South Pacific, stretching from the subantarctic regions south of New Zealand to the subtropics. Its progress across the vast ocean had been unimpeded until it had met two low-pressure systems, a mature one to the east of the country and a smaller one forming near Fiji. Caught in the pincers of the two lows, the anticyclone had developed a kink that, to Jon's trained eye, indicated a funnel of extra breeze—perhaps another 10 to 15 knots, enough to threaten a gale. There was also a cold front on the way, but he felt it wouldn't amount to much.

The anticyclone hovering over New Zealand was responsible for the winds rattling his house windows and for the cold air that was spoiling people's holiday plans. It showed a central pressure of 1,034 millibars (mb), which he considered too high for safety. Winds spiraled outward from the center in a counterclockwise direction. Trapped between the two low-pressure systems, the anticyclone's energy was squeezing into a narrow band of intensity. These were the ingredients that could cause a weather bomb to explode over the ocean.

For two days, Jon had studied the weather maps and listened to reports from boats. Most had reveled in the conditions, reporting weather they had dreamed about through months or years of preparation: blue skies, a gentle breeze, and balmy temperatures. The easy conditions made some sailors complacent. They overlooked the subtle changes occurring around them. They piled on canvas to capture the breeze, or turned on their motors, frustrated with the lack of wind. Others lazed about on deck, reading, drinking, eating, and swapping yarns. A few lay in their bunks fighting seasickness as their bodies adjusted to the ocean roll. Many missed the early signs that the weather was changing its character.

As the yachts traveled farther north, Jon's intuition began to tell him the boats should run off to the west toward Australia, or seek shelter. Although the local weather office reported nothing unusual, Jon didn't feel comfortable with the reports coming in from the sailors. In his bones, he felt something was wrong. But he couldn't be certain, and there was nothing in any official weather data to warrant his unease.

Destiny

During the early days of their cruise, Paula and Dana Dinius, aboard *Destiny*, had delighted in the breeze that pushed them from

Auckland toward the warmer air in the subtropical latitudes at 25° south. As they made northing, they congratulated themselves on not having encountered a single cold front, an unusual luxury when sailing from New Zealand.

"We've done pretty well," Dana said to his wife. "Getting this far without a storm is damn good. We should be picking up the trades soon."

Although they had spent winters working at Mammoth Mountain ski resort in the Sierra Nevada, their California bones hadn't adapted to the cold New Zealand winter. As much as they enjoyed New Zealand, they were pleased to be escaping it.

They'd been in New Zealand since 1991, after spending two seasons sailing in Mexico and then cruising to the Marquesas, Tahiti, American Samoa, and Tonga. In 1992 they'd sailed to Tonga and then spent most of the season in Fiji before returning to New Zealand. Now they were on their way to Fiji again, then New Caledonia, and Australia, where they intended to shelter during the next cyclone season.

For the past couple of years they had used New Zealand as a cruising base for the South Pacific, returning to explore the country's beauty in the cyclone season or to lay up for repairs and maintenance. It was cheap there, the security was reliable, the people honest, and the standard of workmanship high.

On Thursday, June 2, Dana noticed that an isobar on the weatherfax had a kink in it slightly west of Fiji. He thought it would not amount to much. He filed it away in his mind when he heard Jon Cullen report on the nightly call from Kerikeri Radio that a shallow low-pressure area appeared to be developing off Fiji.

"It's not sinister," he assured Paula after checking with Kerikeri Radio, "although there could be winds of 30 knots. It can't be too bad. After all, we're well above the 27th parallel and the trades should fill in soon."

The next morning they were both tired, so they hove-to, simply drifting slowly with the wind just off the bow while they rested and tidied the boat. After four days at sea, she was a little cluttered. Experienced sailors, they often hove-to this way when they were tired or caught in rough weather.

The weather forecasts continued to perturb them, however. Later in the morning they received a weatherfax showing a weak low forming between Fiji and Vanuatu, the birthplace of many cyclones. Dana was concerned about the close-spaced isobars on the map. They indicated 35 knots of southeasterly wind on the southern side of the depression.

The low-pressure area forming ahead of them was confirmed in another facsimile. They prepared the boat for bad weather, checked their harnesses, and set a reefed mainsail and a small jib in 25 knots of wind.

In his next conversation with Kerikeri Radio, Dana learned that the gale was intensifying and might reach 40 knots or more. Jon Cullen suggested Dana should slow *Destiny* to 4 knots or heave-to.

"Nothing sinister," Jon said. "It should pass in the night." It was June 3.

Mary T

Farther south, another California family, Sigmund and Carol Baardsen, were sailing north with their 16-year-old daughter, Anna, and a family friend, Lianne Audette, from Connecticut. The Baardsens had spent an uncomfortable 18 months living aboard their boat, *Mary T*, in New Zealand's northernmost city, Whangarei. There they had undertaken a substantial refit of the 23-year-old boat, including extensive fiberglassing to cure leaks that had developed en route from Mexico to New Zealand in 1992.

The rigors of living aboard a 40-foot yawl while refitting in a shed had taken a toll on the family. They had lived with dust, shavings, and pungent epoxy resin fumes for months. Now, at last, they were free from the grime and the cramped living conditions. And now that she was back in the water, *Mary T* was spirited again. Her living space seemed to have expanded, her decks seemed broader. The sea air was fresh and clean. Carol was exhilarated as the yacht forged through the hissing water in sunny skies and a 15-knot breeze.

Before they left, there'd been much discussion about whether they should embark on this voyage. Sigmund was of a mind to sell the boat and return home to San Pedro, California; he'd had enough of dust and boatyards. He wanted to get a job again, earn a few dollars, and stay ashore. Anna wanted to stay at school with her New Zealand friends; the cruising life can be lonely and boring for a teenager. But for Carol it was different. The sea was calling her and she had to obey. After lengthy discussion, they decided to sail to Vanuatu, after which they would decide their future.

With the exception of Anna, who became seasick, they all enjoyed being back at sea. Sigmund was particularly glad to have Lianne aboard because she was a strong crewmember, used to racing. She was good at working on the foredeck and changing sails.

Sofia and Pilot

At about the same time, two 32-foot double-enders, a William Atkin–designed wooden cutter called *Sofia* and a cutter-rigged Westsail 32, *Pilot*, sailed out of Auckland harbor bound for Tonga.

For New Zealander Keith Levy and his girlfriend Ursula ("Uschi") Schmidt, *Sofia* was a magic carpet that would take them to the jewels of the South Pacific and beyond. Keith and Uschi had met in Tonga the previous year when she was backpacking and he was cruising. Uschi, from Kleinandelfingen, Switzerland, had never sailed before. The only water near her village, 30 miles from Zurich, was in the river that meandered near her home. She was thoroughly enjoying her first cruising experience. It was an adventure other 25-year-olds could only dream about.

She seemed at home on the sea. Under Keith's instruction she was mastering seamanship skills. He showed her how to tie a bowline once, and suddenly the knot was popping up all over the boat. She was also a natural at steering the boat, instinctively knowing how best to handle *Sofia*.

Keith and Uschi had met their American friends, Barbara Parks and Greg Forbes, when they sailed *Pilot* to New Zealand from Fiji in December. They had all worked long and hard preparing their yachts for this cruise. In their free time, Greg had taught Keith and Uschi the art of "dumpster diving." The four of them would dig around in the marina dumpsters, huge trash bins filled with a treasure trove of yacht parts and equipment discarded by less frugal sailors. Greg had his friends foraging for pumps, tools, and all manner of useful bits and pieces that, with a little patience and know-how, could be repaired to serve for several thousand more miles at sea. They always enjoyed considerable success. They still reminisced fondly about their most successful find, a toilet so new that Greg swapped it for three cans of expensive antifouling paint.

Uschi kept them amused during their excursions. Despite her 25 years, she looked only 16. Her small, slight frame would disappear right down into the dumpsters and they would have to pull her out, giggling, by the legs.

Keith admired Greg's resourcefulness and the seamanship he'd acquired in 22 years of sailing. Greg was so confident and inventive he did not consider it necessary to carry a life raft aboard *Pilot*, nor even any parachute flares. This worried Keith and, before leaving Auckland, he presented Greg with a set of old parachute flares. He was convinced they'd still work, even though the expiration date had passed.

The two boats had cruised together up the east coast of New Zealand's North Island, remaining in sight of one another until *Pilot* found better wind and current, and opened a large lead.

Ramtha and *Windora*

Not far away, the 38-foot catamaran *Ramtha* was having problems. Australians Bill and Robyn Forbes had sailed *Ramtha*, a Roger Simpson design, from Auckland with 30 other boats heading for Vava'u, the island Tongans call the crown jewel in their cluster of 170 magnificent atolls.

Ramtha had set out on the heels of a gale, but the wind and seas had quickly moderated into the pleasant conditions the rest of the fleet was experiencing.

But now, on the second day out, the boat was not holding a course. The wheel would not turn. Robyn fiddled with the autopilot. She suspected the rudders had jammed.

"Bill, something's up here," she called to her husband.

Bill was fairly certain the problem was a repeat of one they'd experienced before they left Auckland. He set a parachute sea anchor off the bow to stabilize the boat, and went below to investigate. His hunch was correct; a cable had fallen off the steering quadrant again.

Although the weather was pleasant, the sea was confused, throwing *Ramtha* about as it slopped between her hulls. Bill felt queasy as he crammed himself into the confined space of the engine compartment and struggled to get the cable back on the quadrant. He had no luck.

Robyn urged him to seek advice on the radio about how to fix the problem. Their call was answered by a 50-foot motorsailer, *Windora*, which was 15 miles away. *Windora*'s owners, a young New Zealand couple, Bill and Linda Christieson, had never made a deep-sea passage before. They were on their way to Tonga with the rest of the fleet. With typical New Zealand friendliness, they offered to sail over to assist *Ramtha*. Robyn could hardly believe her eyes when, three hours later, the *Windora* caught up with them and a crewmember rowed across the running 9-foot sea to help them.

By this time, Bill Forbes had almost repaired the steering himself, using Aussie ingenuity and old rope. But he had dropped the master link from the chain, and it was irretrievably lost somewhere in the bilge. Patiently, he made an aluminum link, but when he tested it, the steering still didn't work. The link stretched, allowing the rudder to turn at a different angle from that of its mate.

Windora's crewman, David Reid, surveyed the situation, then rowed back to the motorsailer, where Bill, a mechanical engineer, made a link. Dave rowed back again and installed it.

"How about that?" Robyn said when the job was done. "I mean, in the middle of the ocean, we need a fitter and turner—and we get one right here. The service isn't even that good on *land.*"

They invited Dave to stay for a drink. He told them Bill and Linda had sold their house to buy *Windora.* They had been building a beachhouse when they learned about the motorsailer being on the market. They bought her on a whim, sold their land, and set about preparing her for the trip to Tonga. The only boating experience Bill and Linda had prior to setting sail was in runabouts. Dave admitted to having a little windsurfing experience.

After they had swapped stories about their present trips, Dave finished his drink and jumped into his dinghy to row back to *Windora.* Bill and Robyn waved good-bye, still marveling at their luck. But the repairs had sapped Bill's energy. He had spent the last few hours hunched over the engine, and he still felt slightly seasick, so they decided to leave the sea anchor deployed for the night.

Silver Shadow

Far to the south, down near the foot of New Zealand's North Island, the four men aboard the 42-foot sloop *Silver Shadow* were reveling in splendid sailing conditions, reaching up the coast on the tail of a low with a 20-knot northwesterly pushing them eastward. It was the boat's second voyage to Tonga, and she was well equipped for three months of sailing, diving, and relaxing.

The crew, led by skipper Peter O'Neil, was one of the most experienced in the fleet sailing to Tonga. They had raced sailboats for years, mostly across Cook Strait, a 14-mile stretch of water separating North and South Islands. The strait is notorious for the unpredictability of its gales and currents, and locals believe if they can sail there, they can sail anywhere. This crew had also crossed the Tasman Sea, 1,300 miles of stormy ocean separating Australia and New Zealand.

Experience had taught them that thorough preparation is crucial for safe voyaging. Preparations on their boat went well beyond the stringent requirements of New Zealand's ocean sailing rules. They carried gear for rigging repairs, stainless steel equipment for repairing a broken mast, spare aluminum, substantial supplies of stainless steel fittings, fastenings, blocks, spare halyards, plywood, and numerous other bits and pieces, including a large manual bilge pump that they stored below decks "just in case."

Waikiwi II

The southernmost yacht heading toward Tonga was the 44-foot wooden sloop *Waikiwi II*, which had a crew of five aboard—three New Zealanders and two Britons. The owners, Cath Gilmour and her husband, John Hilhorst, had bought the boat 18 months earlier specifically to undertake a circumnavigation of the world. Tonga was to be their first port of call, mainly because they believed it was safer to make their maiden offshore passage in the company of other boats in the regatta.

The obsession to sail the world had started two years earlier when they'd discussed the possibility with Geoff Spearpoint, a friend with whom John had spent much of his leisure time tramping New Zealand's mountains and valleys. What had started as a plan hatched over a cup of tea was now reality. Geoff was with them, chasing their dream.

The Britons, Shirley and Merve Bigden, had arrived in New Zealand in 1989 after traveling extensively around the world. They were working their passage home to Britain, where they would decide whether or not to return and settle in New Zealand permanently.

The crew had spent only one weekend together aboard *Waikiwi II* before waving farewell to friends and families at South Island's largest port, Lyttelton. They had set off under motor for a couple of hours before finding a good breeze in which to hoist sail and head for Tonga.

They had three crew aboard because of Cath's weak arms. Three years earlier, repetitive strain injury (RSI) had crippled her so badly that she was unable to undertake physical chores. At that stage, she had barely been able to move without suffering excruciating pain. But from the time they bought the yacht, her condition had improved greatly. They hoped the warmer climate and gentler life in the trade winds would help her to recuperate.

They sailed up South Island's east coast, accompanied by dolphins and seals, until they encountered the low black clouds of a cold front in Cook Strait. They dropped the mainsail and genoa, replacing them with a storm jib. John spent almost all of the next 24 hours at the helm. The wind was too strong for Cath's arms, and none of the others felt able to cope with the conditions, although Geoff occasionally relieved John. In rain and lightning, their speed increased to 9 knots as they ran with the wind on the starboard quarter.

The seas built to 50 feet. It was bitterly cold, and they wrapped themselves in balaclavas, scarves, and gloves. Dousing the storm jib, they tied a car tire to a warp to make a drogue, which they cast astern to slow the yacht's progress. The boat felt more comfortable during the night, although she wallowed in the steep seas under bare poles. The next morning they retrieved their drogue, hoisted the storm jib again, and continued sailing up the island in 40 knots of wind. The gale took three days to blow itself out, and then they enjoyed the same light breezes and calm seas as the rest of the fleet.

Heart Light

There had been considerable disagreement about the departure date before the 41-foot catamaran *Heart Light* set sail for Fiji. But eventually Darryl Wheeler had his way. *Heart Light* sailed from

Auckland on Tuesday, May 31, 1994, with Darryl; his wife, Diviana; their son, Shane; and their daughter-in-law, Stephanie. Shane and Stephanie were gaining their first cruising experience.

The Wheelers had bought the Catalac catamaran in Florida in 1987. Diviana, a clairvoyant, had received a message that they should buy her, change her name to *Pleiades Child* (they later changed it back to *Heart Light*), and leave the United States. Neither of them had sailed before, but they were not concerned about their lack of experience. Diviana had been assured that the art of sailing would be demonstrated to them. They left America and, sure enough, learned to sail as they cruised down the coast, across the Pacific to the Marquesas and Tahiti, then onto New Zealand, where they arrived in November 1989.

Since then, Darryl had worked as a marketing consultant in New Zealand. They had visited the United States a few times but had rejoined their boat to explore more of the South Pacific.

Now they had arrived at a crossroads in their lives. Diviana had been offered an opportunity to host a radio talk show in Australia, but had turned it down. She wanted instead to pursue a course of personal enlightenment. This, she reasoned, could be better accomplished at sea.

Diviana was concerned that Darryl was becoming ensnared by what she regarded as materialism, as his talents were increasingly in demand. They discussed their feelings and desires at length. Diviana feared that their present path, tending away from the sea, would not allow her to focus on the state of consciousness she desired. At sea they would be close to nature, going to bed with the moon and rising with the sun. No need for watches, clocks, radios, or television. No pollution. No Bosnia. No Rwanda. No anger or stress to inhibit the pursuit of higher levels of consciousness. To her, their yacht was a guru, teaching them about themselves: who they were, what they were, their faith, their purpose.

Diviana had considered returning to the United States briefly to attend to some personal matters while *Heart Light* sailed to Fiji. But she changed her mind after receiving a message that she should accompany them on the voyage, although she was perturbed by a warning that they would encounter a storm if they followed Darryl's planned schedule.

Over the years, Darryl had learned to trust his wife's intuition; it had proved accurate many times. This time, however, he considered it illogical. The weather maps held no hint of storms. On the contrary, the area was basking in one of the largest high-pressure systems since summer. He considered the conditions ideal. There wasn't much wind, but he preferred to motor all the way to Fiji rather than battle 30-knot westerlies under sail. Such westerlies were common off the New Zealand coast at that time of year. He explained this to Diviana, but she insisted a storm would approach. She was adamant they should wait.

Darryl was so impatient to get away, they compromised. They would sail to Great Barrier Island, about 40 miles east of Auckland, and anchor there while they reassessed the situation. If the weather did deteriorate, they would wait there for it to blow over. At least they would be on their way.

Although they were late leaving Auckland, they were optimistic they would make Fitzroy Bay, at the northwestern tip of the island, before dark. As Darryl had predicted, the weather was friendly all the way across the Hauraki Gulf, the fine cruising ground that separates the mainland from the island. He had no doubt they would make their landfall without incident.

They were almost there when a 40-knot gale unexpectedly howled out of the blue sky. The boat jibed, and the mainsail backed because the preventer held the boom in place. Working with his son, Darryl managed to get the jib down, but he couldn't head the boat into the wind to drop the backed mainsail.

"Ease the rope on the preventer," he yelled at Shane, confident that the boat would turn into the wind when the tension was taken off the boom. But Shane, inexperienced and unaware of the tremendous forces involved, uncleated the preventer instead of easing it. The line ripped through his hands, and the gale slammed the mainsail over with such force that rivets popped and part of the sail track ripped out of the mast.

Shane had not sailed on a small boat before, and Diviana could see that he was badly shaken. The boat crashed and pitched, and the boom swung dangerously above the deck. They fought for control as wind and waves grew. Darkness overtook them as a squall swept through the gulf. Rain lashed them and lightning flashes froze the clouds. Amid the chaos they heard a crack. It could have been another clap of thunder, but it sounded metallic. Then they saw it. The gale had snapped the pole holding the wind generator.

Darryl and Diviana had sailed 16,000 sea miles and never experienced anything like the sudden fury, the violence of the wind, the roaring in the rigging, the flogging mainsail, and then the rain and lightning.

"Are we having fun yet?" Diviana shouted, feeling angry at being caught in this situation.

But no matter how they tried, they couldn't control the boat. *Heart Light* seemed to have a mind of her own. Finally, they decided that even under motor it would be too dangerous to attempt to enter the small rocky bay. So they turned away from Great Barrier Island and motored on. They were relieved when the wind eased to a manageable 25 knots.

Darryl believed they had now weathered the storm Diviana had foreseen, and that the worst was past; however, Diviana was not convinced. One hundred miles out from Great Barrier Island, the wind continued to blow from the south-southwest at about 25 knots. It blew a choppy breath across a 6- to 7-foot swell that slammed under *Heart Light*'s hulls. The catamaran lifted and shook and shuddered as she crashed in and out of the turbulence. The stress on the boat worried Diviana. The fiberglass hulls creaked and protested. As her concerns grew, Diviana knew she must consult her oracle, the *I Ching*, the wisdom of which, she believed, had proven itself over 6,000 years.

The warning was unequivocal: They would go to the edge of peril.

CHAPTER 2

MAYDAY! MAYDAY!

≋≋≋

SATURDAY, JUNE 4, AT 1145 (NEW ZEALAND TIME)

As Lt. Erin MacDonald outlined the rescue procedures to Paul Norman in Long Beach, California, a Royal New Zealand Air Force Orion P3 aircraft searched for *Destiny*. The Orion's crew were themselves being buffeted by the gale. Some suffered from motion sickness. The plane's commander, Flt. Lt. Bruce Craies, a yachtsman himself, was concerned by what he saw. He had brought the aircraft down to 5,000 feet and slowed to 120 mph as they started their search for the yacht. He followed a search pattern that would enable him to pick up the bearing of *Destiny*'s EPIRB. He was all the way down to 1,000 feet when they finally found her.

The atrocious conditions alarmed him. The ocean below resembled surf crashing on a gently sloping beach. Huge curling rollers broke in smothers of foam as far as they could see, which was only a mile or so. It was certainly not the weather the meteorological office had told them they would find.

When they'd left their Auckland base 80 minutes previously, they'd expected to be in the area only five or six hours. They'd been briefed that the Royal New Zealand Navy survey vessel, the *Monowai*, was only a few hours away from *Destiny*. A later message had revealed, however, that somehow the wrong coordinates had been transmitted. The *Monowai* was near 175° west, not 175° east as originally indicated. As he studied the conditions below, Flt. Lt. Craies had a feeling it was going to be a trying, tiring day.

Down below, *Destiny* struggled to survive. Streamers of spume tore away from breaking crests, whipped by 80-knot winds. The 45-foot cutter leaped upward, crashed forward, and slewed sideways. She was already badly damaged. Her broken and twisted mast lay precariously across the cabintop, one end angling under the hull to starboard. Waves rushed over the deck and coursed through the tangle of rigging, stanchions, and lifelines. A brilliant red life raft, fully inflated, jerked viciously at its painter on the port quarter.

"*Destiny. Destiny.*" Paula Dinius heard the words filling the boat's interior. "*Destiny. Destiny.* This is Kiwi Three One Five. Do you copy? Over." For a moment the voice confused her. She had just finished struggling to settle Dana, who was racked with pain from broken bones. Then she realized the voice was coming from the VHF radio.

Dana, lying immobile in his bunk in the aft cabin, was surprised that the radio was working, as the masthead antenna was now under water. Paula grabbed the microphone.

Orion aircraft: *Destiny.* Kiwi Three One Five.

Paula: Kiwi Three, yes. [Contact was lost temporarily as the aircraft flew out of range. It returned and circled over the boat again.]

Orion: *Destiny*, do you copy me now? Over.

Paula: Yes, I do, thank you.

Orion: Okay, Paula, I have a doctor on board my aircraft. Do you need advice from him? Over.

Paula: Well, I've got Dana down inside because he was going into shock. I gave him Tylenol Three. I gave him one-and-a-half of those for the pain. He seems to be lucid and adequate, I guess. Is there anything I should do for him?

Orion: This is the doctor. What time did the injury occur? [Before Paula could answer, *Destiny* was hit by a large wave. The broken mast, dangling underneath, hammered a spreader against the hull as if it were a pickaxe.]

Paula: Oh! Oh! [The air crew could hear the fear in her voice.] Maybe . . . maybe three hours ago.

Three hours ago? What did it matter? They were still alive and now there was a voice, a link with civilization, with safety. A strong, confident voice, full of hope and promise and advice.

Thinking back, Paula still could not accept their situation. After spending the morning of June 3 lying hove-to, they had shortened sail in 25 knots of wind. Although Jon had warned over Kerikeri Radio that they could expect a gale of about 40 knots, they were still confident. Such conditions were not new to them.

Gradually, the seas had built to about 18 feet and were breaking, making *Destiny* yaw from side to side. Dana was unhappy with her behavior. She was running too fast. He decided to run under bare poles using his Sea Squid drogue, which was designed to slow the boat down and bring her under control. As it towed behind on 15 feet of ⅜-inch chain and 200 feet of warp, openings in the cone-shaped plastic body of the drogue created turbulence and the necessary drag.

It was the first time Dana had used this device, even though he had lugged it all around the world and frequently cursed it because it was difficult to stow. Now that it was finally being put to the test, he was pleased with the braking effect it had on the yacht. It certainly lived up to the promises made in the promotional brochures, slowing and steadying the boat in the building sea.

When night fell they settled in, confident in the boat as she forged downwind at 3 to 4 knots and confident of their ability to handle the conditions that, although boisterous, were no worse than some they'd experienced on other cruises.

But they got little sleep that night. The ferocity of the wind and sea grew as each hour passed. Its fury built from 30 knots to 40 knots, then 50, 60, 70, until, from their observations, it peaked at 80 knots.

"When you figure in our boat speed, it's about 90 knots. The gusts must be over 100 knots," Dana said incredulously.

Destiny was now surging ahead at speeds of 7 to 8 knots on the faces of the waves, but they still felt the situation was under control. During the night the dodger flogged relentlessly in the gale until the material shredded. The crashing seas bent its stainless steel frame, and then the lee cloths went, too.

Huddling in the cockpit, they realized this was unlike other storms. The night was the blackest they had experienced; it was so intense they could barely see each other in the cockpit. Strobing lightning cut jagged rips in the sky. Thunder rumbled ominously through the night.

With bolts cracking down all around, they began to wonder if they could survive this onslaught. As the sky lit up white and green, they snatched glimpses of the crests of waves being blown away. They struggled to keep *Destiny* end-on to the waves, but each time the sea lifted her, the wind caught her stern and tried to slew her sideways down the mountainside. Dana fought for control. He steered by sheer instinct and the dim glow of the compass.

Paula felt the yacht's lurches in her aching bones and muscles. "She's going to port," she yelled.

Dana made the correction.

"She's still heading up. Correct harder," Paula screamed.

Dana spun the helm and held it hard over for what seemed an eternity. Slowly, *Destiny* responded. It was a pattern he would repeat time and time again through the night. With the drogue working hard to slow her down, *Destiny* ran at 4 knots through the troughs, 7 knots down the slopes. They felt the drogue was keeping the ride as smooth as could be expected in the conditions.

They estimated they were in a trough 50 feet deep, with the wind dial recording 78 knots. "It's like being on a ski slope," Dana said. They had to look up to the tops of the waves, both ahead and behind.

They glimpsed the seascape revealed by the lightning in astonishment. Never before had they witnessed anything like it, and they both sensed a malevolence that they could not explain. This was so powerful, they were consumed by fear for the first time. All around them, in the cockpit, in front of them, port, starboard and aft, they felt engulfed by evil. The noise was unlike anything they had heard before—seas roaring and crashing around and over them, *Destiny* shuddering and cracking as she absorbed the full force of tons of water trying to stop her in her tracks.

Three times that night, Dana thought they would not survive. Each time, he looked at Paula and said simply, "I love you."

She glanced back, silently willing him not to give up, to keep fighting the exhaustion. *Keep turning the helm,* her eyes said. *Don't let the sea win.*

But seas rushing over the stern flooded the cockpit, leaving the yacht even more vulnerable as the drains slowly carried the water away. The anemometer recorded 90 knots.

They now accepted that they could die, but they no longer experienced fear. By the time dawn approached, fear had been replaced by a burning determination to survive. They were attuned to the conditions. They felt no fatigue, even though they had worked the boat through the night without sleep.

Shortly before daylight on June 4, the wind began to abate. It dropped to 47 knots, with gusts up to 55 knots.

"We made it, we're out of it!" Dana exclaimed. But it wasn't over yet.

Daylight revealed the stark reality of their predicament: a bleak world of violence, a colorless, hazy desert of gray and white. It was almost impossible to discern the sea from the sky. Islands of foam, as tall and as wide as houses, blew off the tops of waves. Their mast was 65 feet tall and, from the troughs, the peaks of the waves seemed far above it. Dana knew how difficult it was to estimate wave heights at sea, even in good conditions, but to him at that time it looked as though they were well over 70 feet, perhaps 100 feet, high. They were avalanches that collapsed under the tons of water at their crests, crushing and drenching them, filling the cockpit.

"It's like being in the Sierras," Dana said as he took in the panorama of the seascape. "The breaking crests look like snow on the peaks. It's incredible."

The seas changed their character at dawn. Even as the wind speed dropped, the waves piled up closer together, becoming steeper and breaking more violently. But the calmer wind was only a temporary phenomenon. The storm wasn't finished with them yet. Dana and Paula watched with dismay as the anemometer climbed again to more than 60 knots.

Dana still felt confident they could weather the conditions. The boat was behaving reasonably. And after what they had been through during the night, the worst must surely have passed. While it was impossible to keep *Destiny* on a constant heading, he'd been deliberately working his way out of the storm, keeping the wind on his port side to move out of the dangerous quadrant.

Despite his confidence, Dana thought it would be wise for Paula to contact Kerikeri Radio. She could inform the Cullens of their difficulties but confirm that they were not yet in a life-threatening situation.

Paula was glad for the break. She'd been sitting in the cockpit for hours, encouraging Dana to concentrate on steering. She'd had a bilge-pump handle between her legs, and she'd pumped vigorously every time she'd heard the bilge alarm sound inside the boat. She was wet through, and stiff.

She contacted Kerikeri Radio, prefacing her call with the "Pan Pan" alert that, by international agreement, indicates a need for assistance, but without the extreme urgency of a Mayday distress call. Then she returned to the cockpit to keep Dana company. She fastened her safety harness to the boat with a short tether to keep her from being swept overboard by a wave.

Hour after hour, *Destiny* was lifted up, engulfed in raging foam, knocked down by fists of water, and sent down the mountain again.

Shake, rattle, and roll. Up and at 'em. Up again, hold on for the surf. Here we go again. Then one time it is different. The 50-foot waves seem to stack one on top of another. *Destiny* is knocked by the wind, engulfed by the raging white crest, but she is not going down. For a split second she hovers, suspended above a vertical waterfall that plummets straight down more than 70 feet.

"This feels different, Paula! Something's different!" Dana screamed as the bow dropped and he saw nothing but air ahead of him. There was no water rushing over the bow and along the decks.

"Oh my God!" he screamed as they were catapulted out of the water, briefly suspended in midair until gravity pulled *Destiny* back toward her angry environment. Dana stood frozen to the helm. Break right? Break left? It did not make any difference. Suddenly, 37,000 pounds of yacht headed nose-first into the valley below. "Oh my God!"

"We're going!"

Dana clung to the wheel, weightless, as the boat, almost in slow motion, fell through space and plunged into the water. Her bow dug deep into the sea, and the huge swirling waves slapped the exposed keel as *Destiny* pitchpoled end over end. Dana realized he was under water.

This is nice, he thought. *It's warm and peaceful here.*

His surfing experience returned to him and he patiently waited to come out of the water. The boat ended her somersault and rolled back upright. Suddenly there was air. He breathed again. He saw water. He felt, heard water rushing away. He looked for Paula.

Is she all right? Yes, I can see her. She's on the boat. Thank God! I'm still here, too. Are we afloat? Yes, we're upright. The questions flashed through his mind in the split second the boat righted herself. Their eyes met to say they were alive. He moved toward her.

Searing pain exploded through him. He discovered he was wrapped around the buckled steering wheel. He tried to untangle himself. The mast had come down and was lying, broken and twisted, across the deck. He found to his horror that he was trapped under the boom and rigging. Excruciating pain stabbed at him as he tried to drag himself through the mess of rigging to Paula. She was wedged under the dodger frame at the other end of the cockpit. Despite his efforts, despite the pain, he couldn't move. A thighbone was smashed, exploded as if hit by a grenade.

Paula managed to free herself from the tangle of metal that pinned her down in the cockpit. She crawled to Dana and tried to pull him from under the boom. He screamed with pain as Paula propped him up in a corner of the port side of the cockpit.

"I'm too broken to move or help," he gasped.

"What do you want me to do?" she asked.

"We've got to cut the rigging. Rig an antenna. Check the boat to see how much water we've taken on." Years of emergency planning made the list almost automatic.

But the severity of their situation suddenly struck him. He had never planned for this; he couldn't move. Never had he envisaged circumstances in which he would be completely incapacitated. He had always imagined he would be able to crawl along the deck to free rigging. He had mentally pumped bilges, rigged emergency antennae, made a jury rig, gotten into a life raft. But now, when the time to act had arrived, he couldn't move.

Paula would have to do everything on her own. This wasn't part of the plan. She didn't have the strength, the experience, or the knowledge.

She could navigate *Destiny* anywhere in the world. She understood sail trim, sail balance, and ham radio. She was competent at radar and could read weatherfaxes. She was his chief medical officer. But she wasn't equipped for what she had to do now.

Should they escape in the life raft? Was it still attached? Yes. Its canister was jammed in the broken rigging. No. Stay with *Destiny* unless she was sinking. That was the rule. She was a strong boat. A flimsy life raft might not survive these conditions.

"The rig has to be cut away," he repeated.

"Which part first?"

They thought of the hacksaws with the carbide replacement

blades they carried for such an emergency. Paula went below to fetch them. Conditions down there horrified her. Water splashed over the floorboards as the boat rolled and pitched. Bunk and settee cushions were turned over. Floorboards had fallen out. Closet and cabin doors had been torn from their hinges, and well-stowed gear lay scattered throughout the boat. Smashed crockery littered the floor. Her old teddy bear floated bedraggled in sloshing water. Fortunately, the batteries were still working. They'd been strapped down. She turned on the electric bilge pumps.

Each time the boat lurched, the broken mast grated and hammered against the port side of the hull. Dana felt a surge of irrational anger. That mast was scratching the beautiful paint finish they'd sweated over before setting sail.

Their concerns went beyond mere cosmetics. The aluminum mast had obviously wrapped itself around the bottom of the boat. It went off to starboard, under the boat, and came back up on the port side. It was the point of a spreader that now hammered so relentlessly against the fiberglass hull.

As Paula waited for the water level to drop, she surveyed the rest of the damage. Up forward, the anchor chain had exploded out of its locker. It was all over the V-berth. The force of the chain hurtling through the air had blown the door to the forward cabin right off the bulkhead. The top of the refrigerator had flown to the opposite side of the boat, and the contents of the freezer were strewn throughout the cabin. Dirt from her potted plants littered the interior.

The good news was that they were not taking on any more water. Paula returned to the cockpit and turned on the EPIRB. It was the latest model, designed to contact passing satellites on a radio frequency of 406 MHz. As she switched it on, its strobe light began flashing. She hoped that meant it was working. Their radio antenna had gone down with the rig, and at least for now, the beacon was their only means of calling for help.

She thought about her mother and the anxiety she would suffer when the U.S. Coast Guard contacted her. The strobing EPIRB was now as important to Paula as breath itself, the only thing in the world between life and death.

"Please God," she said, "please God make it work."

She wedged Dana back into the corner from which a wave had dislodged him while she'd been below. Then she crawled along the deck on her stomach to try to release some of the tangled rigging. She had to free the mast, to get it away from the hull it was trying so hard to rip open.

With the hacksaw tied to her arm, she inched her way along the port side. The lifelines, hanging limply from bent stanchions, were of no use. She could barely hold on. The boat was rolling excessively. The thought flashed into her mind that there was not another boat for hundreds of miles. It was such a long way from America. *Oh, for the Coast Guard.*

Paula was angry that she could not stand upright on the deck, that she was reduced to slithering on her belly. She was angry that she could only inch forward, bit by bit, as waves raced down the deck and crashed over her.

She started to cut through a shroud. The boat rolled, and she heard the mast spreader bang against the hull below her.

It's scratching my paint, she thought.

But the task was hopeless. She couldn't cut through the rigging and hang onto the boat at the same time. The motion was too extreme. Time after time, she lay face-down with water rushing over her, waiting for *Destiny* to lie steady so she could try to saw again. Then, for a few seconds, she could scrape the little hacksaw back and forth against the stainless steel shroud wire. But then the waves would crash again, as *Destiny* lay broadside in the troughs, and Paula would have to give up sawing to hold on.

With her energy sapping fast, she slowly inched backward to the safety of the cockpit. She looked helplessly at the mast, now lying impotent across the cabintop, and she was consumed with despair.

"I can't get it off, Dana. I've done as much as I can," she said.

Then she forced herself into action again. She went below to listen to the mast drilling the hull and decided it was not hitting hard enough to penetrate.

When she got back to the cockpit, Dana had been hurled out of his corner again. This time he was sprawled along the limp lifelines, and he was in considerable pain. She carefully pulled him back into the safety of the cockpit.

Dana was obviously in shock. He was deathly white. His lips were two thin blue lines. He trembled and muttered incoherently, apparently trying to tell her to rig an emergency antenna so they could send a Mayday by radio.

Paula wanted to get Dana down below. But once he was below, she wouldn't be able to carry him up on deck again if they had to abandon the boat. Yet she knew he couldn't survive long in the cockpit in these conditions.

"I've got to get you below before you get tangled in the rigging again and it pulls you overboard," she told him.

"An antenna," he insisted. "You've got to rig an antenna." He explained what she had to do. He told her to cut the backstay. She balked. Not again. She'd already tried cutting the rigging. It was impossible in these conditions.

Dana insisted she do it, so she cautiously made her way to the stern. In fact, when she got into position, she felt more secure than she had felt on the exposed deck. She found she was able to saw through the backstay after all. She freed the antenna for the single-sideband (SSB) radio, then rerigged it as high as she could on the bent stainless steel antenna tower.

Back in the cockpit, she found Dana dizzy, nauseous, and trembling even more violently. Paula decided not to wait any longer. He had to get below, and quickly. No argument.

Racked by pain, Dana forced himself toward the companionway, using the strength in his arms to lift his 200 pounds. He faltered, the pain so intense that he didn't believe he could manage it.

Paula insisted. He had to get warm if he were to survive. But how to get him below? She tried to make a stretcher out of a cabin door, only to discover it wouldn't fit through the opening. She tried to drag Dana inside, but he was too heavy, and he bellowed in pain. She was terrified by the thought that he might die because she was powerless to help him. She urged him to force himself below, regardless of the pain.

Eventually, bracing himself for the inevitable, he swung through the entrance. Paula moved backward ahead of him, supporting the bottom part of his body. He hung in the hatchway, spinning on the brink of unconsciousness. His hands gripped the top of the companionway as the boat lurched and rolled. His damaged leg dangled and swung limply with the motion of the yacht. He freed his good leg from Paula's grasp and used it as a prop as he reached the floor at the bottom of the companionway. Paula guided him back and he flopped onto the aft bunk, which was almost adjacent to the entrance. There she propped cushions around him, wedging his broken body against the port side of the cabin.

It had taken an hour to move Dana the few feet from the cockpit to the cabin.

Paula cleaned up the boat as best she could, putting floorboards back in place and scooping up frozen chickens and other items that could clog the bilge pumps. She had just finished those jobs when another big wave hit *Destiny* broadside on, rolling the boat through 120 degrees, and dumping back on the floor much of the mess Paula had cleaned up.

She called for help on the long-range SSB radio, but there was no response. She hoped the EPIRB was working, but there was no way to confirm it.

The sea continued to pound the helpless, drifting boat. With frightening regularity, *Destiny* would rise and shudder as an enormous wave smashed into her. A period of weightlessness would follow the deafening explosion, and then she'd roll over on her side, knocked down by tons of water. Each time, Dana was thrown out of his bunk and slammed against the ceiling, then the starboard side of the cabin. He seemed to stay there, suspended, for a long time before falling to the bunk as the boat swung upright again. *Destiny* was knocked down at least six times by giant waves. Near-knockdowns were too frequent to count. Despite everything, Paula continued to clear debris that could obstruct the bilge pumps.

Dana experienced severe pain every time he braced himself against the boat's roll. He had never been so badly injured. He felt exhausted and useless. Yet, despite his own problems, he was concerned for Paula. When she was not tidying the boat, she sat before him like a zombie, staring ahead, not responding to the violent movement of the boat. She, too, was exhausted and in shock. She was frightened, and he could offer nothing to lift her spirits. They were entombed in the boat, each suffering a private pain, neither daring to speak, their innermost thoughts too grim to share.

Paula sat on the floor listening to the mast hammering the hull. It seemed determined to penetrate the boat and sink them. There was nothing they could do except wait and listen. She hadn't the strength to go outside again in those conditions. Every time *Destiny* was knocked down, the mast spreader made a different scraping and banging sound on the hull. The noise gradually changed from a hard bang to a mushy squelching. Had it penetrated the hull's core? Was it chipping away at the inner layer of the fiberglass sandwich?

It was while she was wondering how she would get Dana on deck again if the boat started to sink that the small miracle occurred. The cabin was filled with the sound of a human voice. A man's voice. A voice with a New Zealand accent.

"*Destiny, Destiny,* this is Kiwi Three One Five. Do you copy? Over."

Incredibly, the VHF radio was working. Its antenna was at the head of the fallen mast, which was dipping in and out of the water. Paula seized the mike. She discovered to her joy that the voice came from a Royal New Zealand Air Force plane circling overhead on a search-and-rescue mission. And there was a doctor on the plane.

Conversation was difficult. They kept losing radio contact when the Orion P3 flew more than a mile and a half away, or when the yacht rolled to port and the antenna was submerged. Bit by bit, she described Dana's condition, his pain, the difficulty he had breathing. She thought his ribs were broken, as well as his thigh. The Orion crew were concerned he could puncture a lung if he was thrown about on his bunk.

As they talked to Paula on the radio, they could hear the mast banging against the hull. Bruce Craies was concerned at the danger it presented. He needed to get a better look at *Destiny*'s predicament. True to the nickname "Crazy" Craies he'd earned when flying with the RNZAF aerobatic team, the Red Checkers, he took the plane down to 200 feet, almost skimming the sea in driving rain and bad visibility. He reduced power as much as he could and surveyed the situation as he went overhead.

Paula was still talking to the doctor about Dana's condition as the Orion flew by. "Oh," she exclaimed, "I hear your plane. God, I wish you could lift me off."

It was a pathetic, forlorn cry that affected the airmen, filling them with compassion for the desperate woman who they only knew by voice. The low-level flight confirmed the seriousness of *Destiny*'s situation. She was severely crippled. The Orion crew feared she would not survive the pounding she was taking. The conditions were so abominable that there was, in reality, little the crew could do except maintain watch and try to keep up the Americans' spirits.

Farther back in the aircraft's fuselage, the officer responsible for tactics, Sqd. Ldr. Mike Yardley, sat before the bank of screens and electronics the Orion normally used for locating submarines or drug-running ships. While Craies concentrated on flying, Yardley maintained radio contact with the National Rescue Coordination Centre, rescue vessels, headquarters, and the vessels in distress. His job also included navigation and monitoring fuel levels. His was one of the voices from which Paula drew her strength.

He was grateful to be flying this mission with Craies. "Crazy" Craies was an amateur sailor, and was able to build a special rapport with Paula Dinius. He offered advice Yardley would never have thought about, such as getting more drogues out to steady and slow the boat.

"The 406 EPIRB has got something to say for itself, doesn't it?" he said, referring to the emergency beacon that had alerted the world to *Destiny's* predicament.

"Yeah, shit yeah," Craies responded, looking down at the bleak ocean below. It was full of ugly, breaking, rolling waves, crashing about, confused, moving in all directions. Long tracks of spume blew above the ocean as far as he could see. A white yacht might look good in port, but here, at sea, it was almost impossible to find a white boat. Half the ocean was the same color. "There's no way anyone would have found her otherwise."

While the Orion was in the air, the rescue center at Wellington combed their logs for vessels in the area that might assist *Destiny*. They thought the 7,246-ton container ship *Tui Cakau III* would be the best bet.

The Orion raised her on Channel 16. Her skipper, Capt. Jim Hebden, said they were battling a gale and huge seas. He was only 30 miles away, but in a Force 10 gale gusting to Force 12, who knew how long it would take to reach *Destiny*?

Craies didn't think *Destiny* would survive the night. His view of the boat from 200 feet up confirmed that the mast was wrapped completely under the vessel. The spreader would probably penetrate if the pounding continued. There was no sign the weather would abate.

Furthermore, *Destiny's* crew was in a bad state. Paula sounded exhausted and distressed. Her husband was immobile, life possibly ebbing from him because of complications from his injuries and perhaps punctured lungs. There was little the aircraft could do except circle overhead while the air crew kept talking to them.

Craies arranged to contact Paula every half-hour and painted a brighter picture of their chances of rescue than he really believed possible. He was not even confident that the yacht's battery power would last much longer. After that, radio contact would be lost. He arranged to keep in touch with the *Tui Cakau* every hour on a different frequency so that Paula wouldn't hear Capt. Hebden's reports. The only positive aspect of their predicament was that it was Jim Hebden who was battling his way through the storm to rescue them. They had high regard for his determination and seamanship.

Orion: Paula, this is the doctor.

Paula: Yes, I'm here.

Orion: One more question. How old is Dana?

Paula: Dana is 42. Do you copy?

Orion: Copy. Forty-two. You've done everything you can and help's on its way. I'm sure he'll be fine.

Paula: I'm sure he will too. I'm real worried about this massive bashing of the hull, though . . . [the communications began to break up as the plane flew out of range] . . . I don't know if I'll get Dana out.

"Fuck it!" someone exclaimed on the aircraft, annoyed at losing communication.

"If they don't get that stick out, it will definitely knock a hole in the boat," Craies said. "It's definitely going to do it within eight hours."

Paula briefly came back on the radio. "Can you please stay in contact with me . . . ?" It died again.

Orion: Paula, this is Mike on the aircraft. We will be staying overhead your position and attempting to talk to you all the time. Over.

Paula: I see, and will you be circling or something? You're coming in loud and clear at this point.

Orion: Paula, we're just coming past your boat at this time and we'll be staying right overhead your position. We can stay here and still talk and see this other vessel on our radar.

Paula: Okay. So you think it'll be eight hours. That will be at night. What is the procedure?

Orion: I think we'll worry about that when it gets a little closer. I'll have to talk to the captain of the *Tui Cakau* himself. Over.

Paula: I understand that. Okay. Well, I'm not sure if I should go outside and try to get that mast off. There's really nothing to hold onto. A lot of the stanchions have blown off and the boat is rocking over so far that I just, ah, [she paused and braced herself while the boat rolled] and if I go out, Dana . . . he can't, he can't move. Ah, I don't know what to do.

Orion: Yeah. G'day Paula, this is Bruce. What I'm going to do, I'm going to come down and make a low-level pass along the side of your boat again and I'll see what I can see with regard to your mast, and I'll give you some advice from there. Over.

Paula: I see that it's still connected somewhat at the base. [Her transmission started to break up as the Orion passed out of range.]

Orion: Okay. Just stand by and I'll fly past you very soon.

He made another low pass and discussed the possibility of Paula's getting outside and cutting free the shrouds. But after her previous experience, she was too afraid and too tired. Craies also believed it would be too dangerous because she could be swept off the boat. If that happened, there would be nobody to haul her back on board. They would have to take their chances with the *Tui Cakau*.

Meanwhile, he suggested, Paula should throw more lines over the stern in an attempt to make the boat lie end-on to the waves, rather than broadside to them as she was now. If this tactic was successful, they would be safer and more comfortable, he said. Dana would be thrown around less, too. Craies did not disclose his true motive for sending her outside again. He was concerned that the boat might roll over completely if she continued to lie beam to the weather.

For the second time, and with just as much trepidation, Paula cautiously ventured to the stern, taking slight comfort from seeing the life raft. It had deployed itself during one of the many knock-downs but was still attached to the boat. The wind and waves lifted it like a balloon as it strained at its painter. She did not relish having to set off in such a flimsy vessel in these conditions and doubted whether it was sturdy enough to protect its occupants. She and Dana had discussed the possibility of evacuation. His plan was to get on deck as best he could, stand on the gunwale near the life raft, and then simply fall overboard into the sea. Paula could then attempt to drag him into the raft. Looking at it now, she knew it was a futile plan.

She hauled a couple of 300-foot warps to the stern. Working slowly with one hand, using the other to hang onto the yacht, she secured a warp, uncoiled it, and then threw a few feet into the gale. It blew back at her. She tried again and began laughing in despair as it boomeranged a second time. After several more attempts, she eventually succeeded in setting both warps, but, despite all her effort, they did not turn *Destiny* end-on to the waves.

Down below again, she and Dana found their morale ebbing with their energy. The din and violent motion of the storm denied them the rest they so desperately needed to recuperate.

The Orion's crew knew that Paula and Dana were under severe stress. Over the radio, they heard them scream and shout when waves knocked the boat down. Each time the air crew waited anxiously for confirmation that the couple below was still alive. Dana and Paula were gradually becoming more than a routine assignment. They were becoming friends. Friends in need.

The Orion made another pass above them. Craies could not see the life raft. It was gone. He did not tell Paula. No point in adding to her ordeal. Later, however, Paula went on deck and discovered the truth herself.

"Oh my God, the life raft has gone," she blurted over the radio. "We'll die if the boat sinks."

The air crew tried to calm her fears. They had two life rafts that they would drop to *Destiny* if necessary. If they dropped the life rafts to windward, they would drift down to the yacht.

She appreciated their intentions, but Paula knew better than to pin her life on that probability.

The Orion crew were actually confident about their ability to provide *Destiny* with life rafts. They were not giving her information they considered infeasible. If *Destiny* was eventually mortally holed, they would fly low over the boat and bomb it with a life raft. Rope tentacles, 1,500 feet long, would be secured to the life raft. Craies believed that with a bit of luck the tentacles would wrap themselves around the boat, enabling Paula to haul the raft alongside for her and Dana to clamber into.

Night fell, taking with it the air crew's morale. The Orion flew low over *Destiny* again and dropped a sonar locater beacon usually used when pursuing submarines, the crew's regular activity. They dropped it as a safeguard against the boat's EPIRB failing during the night.

Sqd. Ldr. Yardley felt so depressed he could not bring himself to continue radio contact with Paula. He had talked to her all day and now there was nothing left to say. As tactical officer, he also knew the Orion could not stay there all night. They would have to return to base for fuel and rest.

During the day, Craies had shut down two engines and feathered their propellers to enable the aircraft to extend its watch over *Destiny*. He hoped the *Tui Cakau* would make it in time, but high seas had forced Capt. Hebden to slow down and alter course slightly away from *Destiny*. His estimated time of arrival was further delayed.

CHAPTER 3

WE'RE TAKING ON WATER . . .

≣≣≣

Jon Cullen was discussing the plight of *Destiny* with the Orion crew when he was interrupted by another urgent call. It was the 45-foot New Zealand sloop *Quartermaster*, whose crew of husband, wife, and son had earlier reported being pounded by the storm.

Quartermaster: Kerikeri, do you read? Over.

Jon: Roger. Yeah. I was just dealing with the Orion that's on its way out to assist. Go ahead, over.

Quartermaster: Yeah. We've just intercepted a call from *Mary T* at 27° 02'S, 179° 47'E. They're taking on water and they're not quite keeping up with it, so they've put out a Pan call.

Jon: Roger. Okay. Just stand by. I've got to get my log book in front of me. I had everything away from me just as you gave me that info. Now that's the *Mary T*?

Quartermaster: That's correct, Jon.

Jon: Roger. Okay. Do they have any idea of where it might be coming from at this stage? Over.

The voice from *Quartermaster* said he would call *Mary T* to establish the cause of the problem. Faintly, through the static, Jon heard a woman's voice responding to the questions from *Quartermaster*. It had an accent that was common at this time of the year: American.

Jon: Roger. I can just copy the *Mary T*. I can just copy. Can you copy me? Over.

Mary T: Yes. I can just hear through the static.

Jon: Roger, *Mary T*. I've got you there, strength two now. Have you got any idea where the water is coming in? Over.

Mary T: No, that's our problem. We can't stop it. [The woman's voice was urgent. It kept breaking up, drowned by the static.] We're just bare-poled at the moment. We're trying to get away from it. We're taking so much water on board that . . . [she faded out again] . . . so we're going to try to run away from it. Do you have any advice on the weather? Over.

Jon: Roger. Okay, well going westerly is, in fact, going to help a little bit. But it's minimal, I'm afraid, especially at 179°. We've just had the latest weather map and the low-pressure center is predicted to be, for noon tomorrow, in a position of 28° south at longitude 180°, so it is moving in a south-southeasterly direction. Over.

The *Mary T*'s transmission was lost in the static again, and Jon called *Quartermaster*. He told Bob Rimmer, *Quartermaster*'s skipper, there were serious problems aboard the *Mary T* and asked him to stand by to act as a relay station. Bob agreed and reported he, too, was running at 6 knots with bare poles, streaming two drogues. They seemed to be handling it all right. Bob sounded confident of meeting the demands of the 50-knot southeasterly conditions.

Mary T came back on air and made contact again with *Quartermaster*. She, too, reported 50 knots of wind.

Quartermaster: Could you let us know how many you have on board and size of boat, et cetera?

Mary T: We're a 40-foot yawl. We're also running under bare poles. There are four people on board. Myself, one crew, and my husband and 16-year-old daughter.

Quartermaster: Okay, I've got that. Four people on board. Yes. I'll relay this through to Kerikeri. Just hang on a moment.

Mary T: Standing by.

Jon: I copied. I copied all. Over.

Quartermaster: Did you get the lot?

Jon: Roger. I copied. I need the color of the vessel and details. Over.

Quartermaster: I'll get the color now. *Quartermaster* to *Mary T.* Do you read? Over.

Mary T: Copy. Copy. We are not in any immediate danger, although we are taking on water. Over.

Quartermaster: I missed the first part of the color of your boat. Could you try that again please?

Mary T: White hull. White hull. Over.

Quartermaster: White hull and gray dodger. Okay Jon, did you get that one? White hull with gray dodger.

Would it be any other color? Jon wondered. *They're all white hulls.*

Jon: White hull and gray dodger. Are there any identifiable features we should know about it? We just need it in case something happens. Over.

Quartermaster: I'll try and find that out. *Mary T,* he'd like to know if you have anything that makes you recognizable. Do you have an orange rescue chute [a flag that could be draped over the deck] with a sail number that you could display?

Mary T: Ah, negative. We do not have that.

Quartermaster: Okay. Jon, they have not got any distinguishable feature other than they're a yawl rig.

Jon: Roger. Roger. All copied. All copied. Understood. We'll stand by all day. Over.

Quartermaster: Okay. We'll stand by all day, too, *Mary T*, so if you wish to relay anything we'll be waiting for you.

Mary T: Thank you. Thank you very much. Perhaps if you have anything that Jon has to say about the low I gather they are having. Is that correct? Over.

Bob repeated the weather prognosis Jon had given earlier.

Mary T: Okay. We're hoping the wind will go around. Over.

Quartermaster: I know . . . I wish . . . we're moving away across to the west as we can.

Mary T: We've had varying reports of this low. This morning someone told us it was moving south-southwest and last night someone told us it was moving southeast. Where does Jon get this information? Is he fairly confident about it? Over.

Quartermaster: Yes, well, he gets all the latest weatherfaxes from the New Zealand meteorology service and I would say he is the best weather forecaster for the South Pacific.

Mary T: Roger. Well, I'm delighted to hear that. So you are moving west, and hope that if you keep moving west you'll avoid it also? Over.

Quartermaster: I don't think we're going to avoid it, but at least we'll try and decrease the wind speed that we get.

Mary T: Roger. Well, okay. We will try and keep in touch and we will try and make contact again in about two hours. Over.

Jon: Roger. I copied thanks, Bob. Their next call 1430. That's what we needed. We need an update on it, if they've activated a Pan call. We will be on standby. Over.

Quartermaster: We're on listening watch here. *Quartermaster* over and out.

Jon: Bob, make sure your VHFs are on. There is an Orion flying the area, so make sure your VHFs are on. Over.

Quartermaster: Okay I'll advise that. *Mary T, Mary T.* Could you please keep your VHF on [Channel] 16? There's a New Zealand Orion out searching for a boat called *Destiny*.

Mary T: Oh that's good. [She sounded relieved that there was a searching aircraft nearby.] Okay. Well, I don't think they'll end up looking for either of us, so thank you. We'll keep our VHF on, and if we see anything of a vessel called *Destiny* we'll report in.

Quartermaster: Okay, we'll keep on standby for you. *Quartermaster* out.

Jon: Kerikeri Radio standing by.

Mary T

Carol Baardsen had made the Pan call to Kerikeri Radio when they discovered *Mary T* was leaking faster than they could pump her out. They had searched the boat for the source of leaks as the water rose above the floorboards.

Anna pumped below. Carol and Sigmund took turns on deck while Lianne stayed at the helm trying to control the yawl as she slid down huge waves that came at them from all directions. A wave would pick *Mary T* up, swirl in white fury about her, and propel her down its face at 8 knots.

She would slew sideways, exposing her quarter to the threatening waves, which would then cascade down the side decks and into the cockpit where the drains couldn't cope with the flow.

Sigmund searched for the leak. He found small problems: water was being forced into the bilge through the pipe to the electric bilge pump; pinholes in one of the pipes leading off another pump made it next to useless; and water was leaking in through the stern gland around the propeller shaft. However, the source of the main leak eluded him. While the crew pumped toward exhaustion, the water kept rising in the boat. He felt increasingly desperate. Only a few hours ago, things had been so different. . . .

It had been a good sail from New Zealand and, on reaching 30° south, they celebrated the warmer latitudes and the prospect of lounging about in bathing suits, enjoying warm sunshine. They considered heading for Minerva Reef, a treacherous atoll whose coral had grown only slightly above sea level. Behind its protective barrier, the fishing was legendary. Some said lobster could be scooped out of the underwater nooks and crannies at 10 feet.

Carol was on the ham radio when a voice as welcoming to yachting folk as Jon Cullen's interrupted her listening. It was Arnold, the renowned radio operator from Rarotonga. They had relied on his advice on their way to New Zealand, and they were concerned when he told them a low-pressure system had formed off Fiji and was heading directly for them. He suggested they run west as quickly as possible.

From his description, it sounded as if it were going to be severe. Sigmund still vividly remembered the havoc caused by Hurricane Raymond, which they sheltered from in Mexico. As he plotted a course to follow Arnold's advice, his mind filled with all the preparation needed to secure his boat. In his haste, he inadvertently laid a course that took them in the opposite direction to that recommended by Arnold. He was heading into the storm's center. Carol tried to convince him he was going the wrong way, but he would not listen.

They battened down, and closed all the portlights. Carol pondered their predicament as she cooked rice in the pressure cooker so there would be sustenance for them to scoop up in their hands during the blow that Sigmund hoped they would out-run, and which she knew they were heading for.

"Give him time to cool off," she told herself. She knew he was dyslexic when he responded to Arnold's warning. He read the coordinates incorrectly, and had the *Mary T* heading into the storm instead of skirting it. Anna knew he was wrong, too, but he would not listen to them. They were both anxious for an opportunity to broach the subject with him.

Eventually, armed with charts, protractor, and dividers, they cornered him. "Listen, Sig, you've got to come and look at the charts," Carol said. "We do not need to go east right now, we need to go west."

They understood the problem, but Sigmund could not see the point the others were making until Carol put it all on a chart. Then he realized his mistake.

Poor Lianne. She was on a strange boat with strange people, sailing into a massive low-pressure system, and here they were, arguing about which way to go. It was not good for her morale or confidence in the crew. As they sailed the new track away from the storm, she took her frustration out on the boat, aggressively tackling headsail changes and any other tasks she was asked to do.

They sailed 86 miles through the night before their scheduled radio call with Arnold the next morning. Arnold apologized and gave them more worrying news. Nadi Radio had misinformed him. The storm was heading just east of south, and they were, unfortunately, actually running directly into its path. Confused, they did not know what to do or believe. To escape, Arnold advised them, they would have to change course and sail hard on the wind, which was blowing at 50 knots. They would have been wise to remain on the track Sigmund had set after all.

They followed Arnold's suggestion. It was a slog, but at least they still moved forward. The sea grew, and they turned on the engine to assist them. As the storm intensified, they cut free five jerry cans of fuel stowed around the pushpit and threw them overboard. Sigmund was afraid the lashings would foul the propeller if they unraveled in the storm.

Sigmund found traveling down the huge waves exhilarating. The water filling the cockpit and cascading over him was warm as it trickled down the neck of the new foul-weather gear and boots he had treated himself to before leaving Whangarei, a reward for the eternity they had spent living in the dust and discomfort of the refit.

They kept hard on the wind under reduced sail. *Mary T* traveled well, but continued scooping water along her decks and into the cockpit. Anna was exhausted. No matter how hard she kept pumping to save the boat, the water level did not seem to fall. Thankfully, it was not rising, either.

The waves crashed over little *Mary T*, and she shook and shuddered and tried to continue her forward drive. Increasing quantities of water washed into the boat until it was dangerous to continue sailing, even under storm jib. They would be unable to avoid this storm, so they decided to run before it.

They lunged forward under bare poles. Five knots. Seven. Nine. Ten knots. Far too fast. The seething white crests of enormous waves attacked them from several directions, roaring and whooshing so loudly the couple on deck could not hear each other even when they shouted. Nor could they hear their engine revving as the boat slewed one way, then the other, throwing the crew off their feet. Each time, Sigmund and Lianne picked themselves up and continued to pump and steer. Despite the violence of the sea, *Mary T* would not give in. Even with her bilge full of slopping water, she declined to broach.

The wheel was hard to hold. Lianne tried determinedly to keep *Mary T*'s bow pointing in the right direction as they surfed and slid down each precipice. Amid the commotion surrounding her, she thought she heard, or perhaps felt, a small "clunk" from the helm. Then, next thing, the steering was gone.

Mary T took control as she hurtled down the waves. They wrestled 300-foot warps into the cockpit and made a huge bight in one end. They secured the other end to a winch and cast the warp into the sea. It worked. Gradually their speed slowed to 6 knots, still far too fast in these conditions. They needed even more drag.

Sigmund attached an old mizzen sail and a dinghy anchor to a sheet and tossed it over the side. It pulled *Mary T* back half a knot. He pulled out an old mainsail, attached it to 60 feet of anchor chain, tied it to 300 feet of 1-inch nylon warp, and let it stream aft. *Mary T* slowed to a more sensible 3 knots.

Unimpeded, she was a bucking bronco. Now she was bridled, and she did not relish being restrained by the lunging rein streaming behind. She brooded by keeping her beam to the waves. She still had a mind of her own and would not be tamed in these inhospitable conditions. The drogues ran off at 90 degrees to the wind and fell, at 45 degrees, toward the bottom of the ocean.

Sigmund knew it would be safer if *Mary T* lay with her bow to the waves, rather than lying beam-on, as she appeared to prefer. He crawled along the deck on all fours to the bow and tried to reposition the drogues so they would act as sea anchors and keep her head into the weather. But the sea beat him. He couldn't do it. He gave up and returned to the comparative safety of the cockpit.

So much for the textbooks, he thought. *We're doing everything the way they say, and it's not working. The boat's not lying right.*

It was time for the scheduled call to Kerikeri Radio. Carol found reception better than it had been when she made the Pan call. She could hear other skippers talking to Jon.

Quartermaster: Quartermaster to *Mary T.* I'm receiving you. Over.

Carol: Quartermaster, I can hear Kerikeri Radio loud and clear. I don't know if he copies me. Over.

Jon: Roger. I copy. I copy strength two to three. Go ahead. Over.

Carol: Oh, thank you, Jon. I'd like to report we are in slightly better circumstances. We are towing a heavy rope with a weight on the end of it. We are trying to run off. The wind, unfortunately, is on the beam but we are riding fairly comfortably, compared relatively to what we were. We were heading west, but unfortunately the boat has jibed and we're heading south and we're going to try to rectify that. We've got the water out, and as long as we don't take any waves in the cockpit we think we should be all okay for a while. Over.

Jon: Roger. Okay. So you've got her head to the water. [Jon had apparently misunderstood. *Mary T* was mostly lying broadside to the waves.] Have you found the leak? Do you know where it's coming from? Over.

Carol: It's leaking in the cockpit itself, unfortunately. There might be some ahead [on the foredeck] and we've taken plenty of water on that, but we are also fairly open and we take some waves in the cockpit too. Over.

Jon: Roger. I understand. Can you report again in an hour or two hours' time, and let us know as soon as possible when you've found the problem and if all is well? Over.

Carol: Okay. Okay. At this time we are not working heavily on that because we really are somewhat ahead of the water and we just have one person on standby to . . . they are not really assisting. Over.

Jon: Yeah, I understand, you can only do one thing at a time. Thanks for the report. Can we make another time? In one hour's time? Over.

Carol: Thank you very much. And thanks for being there. It just makes it that much easier if you can talk to somebody. I hope you realize that. Kerikeri Radio, we'll be standing by. This is *Mary T* and we'll call you back in an hour.

Jon: Kerikeri standing by. Good luck.

It was her birthday. She suddenly remembered as she switched off the radio. In their struggle to survive, they'd all forgotten. Carol jokingly reminded them and, as the boat slowly rose up another swell, the crew of the *Mary T* sang with gusto, competing with the crescendo engulfing them: ". . . happy birthday, dear Car-ol, happy birthday to you." It was an odd way to celebrate, in the middle of the ocean, in a leaky boat in an unexpected storm they might not survive. The only birthday present she wanted was for the storm to abate.

A birthday card from her mother had conveyed an ironic message: "May the winds of life blow you to wherever your heart desires." At that moment, her heart desired a warm bed, dry clothes, and hot sunny skies.

With the steering gone, and the boat lying beam to the surf, *Mary T*'s engine began to misbehave. Without the motor they would lose their electricity supply and the vital radio links they had established with the Orion and the Royal New Zealand Navy's hydrographic survey vessel *Monowai*, which was on its way to assist them.

The *Monowai* had left the weather station on Raoul Island, 600 miles northeast of New Zealand. After unloading provisions, she had set course for Tonga to the north. Just after noon the following day, while they were steaming well east of a low-pressure system forming off Fiji, they were asked to go to the assistance of *Destiny*.

The request puzzled the *Monowai*'s captain, Cmdr. Larry Robbins. After all, the stricken yacht was 420 miles southwest of him. He turned the survey ship in the direction of *Destiny*, however, while he gathered more information, only to discover to his embarrassment that the *Monowai* had transmitted incorrect coordinates indicating she was only 75 miles from the vessel in distress. The RCC had her position as being west of the date line, when she was actually east. Once the true position was established, they diverted the *Monowai* toward the *Mary T* instead.

As the storm continued to intensify throughout Saturday, the RCC and Kerikeri Radio were overwhelmed by calls from yachts struggling to cope with the conditions. It was obvious to everyone that the weather was changing rapidly and that a number of the boats traveling north were directly in the path of a major storm. *Destiny*'s troubles were, in fact, a precursor of worse to come.

The search-and-rescue crews had given the Baardsens great comfort. They had discussed a checklist to help find the leak that continued to fill the bilge. Sigmund had already checked most of the areas they'd suggested without discovering it.

Anna was badly seasick. But she battled away, nevertheless. She pumped and vomited, and pumped and vomited. She ate a little rice and some cracker biscuits, but could keep nothing down.

Jon: Mary T, Mary T. Kerikeri Radio calling. Do you copy? Over.

Carol: Kerikeri Radio. Mary T. [She sounded more confident now.]

Jon: Roger. Got you there loud and clear. How're you going? Over.

Carol: Well, we're now moving one of our better bilge pumps down below decks so we can cope with things if we do get more water inside, but we have not discovered the source of our leak.

Jon: I see. I couldn't copy too well, but do I understand that you've cleaned up most of the water, but haven't found the leak problem? Over.

Carol: Roger.

Jon: All right. And everything is okay with you at the moment? Over.

Carol: Everything is okay at the moment, but we're not thrilled with the prospect of being left to cope with this thing. But there is not really much we, or you, can do about it. Over.

Jon: No, unfortunately we can't. Okay, well, we'll leave it with you then. I'll leave it for you to call us as soon as you're happy with the situation. Over.

Carol: Thank you very much. I don't want to call off that Pan yet. I hope that *Monowai* will be in the vicinity anyway.

Jon: No, that's all right. We don't want to run any risks. Just leave it until you are happy. Over.

Carol: Kerikeri Radio this is *Mary T* clear.

When she wasn't on the radio, Carol pumped. She used the larger pump they'd installed down below, and led its discharge hose up through the companionway into the cockpit, from where the water could drain away. It worked well and reduced the water level to below the cabin floor. She was about to take a break when the boat shuddered and rolled under the weight of a huge wave that cascaded down the companionway into the cabin. She started pumping again. It was heartbreaking. Her arms ached from the tedious work.

At last they solved the riddle of the leak. It wasn't water on deck that caused the problem, but the lockers in the cockpit, the only part of the boat they had not reglassed at Whangarei. They should have thought of that. What a relief. They weren't holed after all.

Lianne and Anna stuffed rags into the gaps along the lips of the lockers. It did the trick. Pumping was reduced to once every three hours. Perhaps they would survive.

Carol: Kerikeri Radio, *Mary T.*

Jon: Mary T, go ahead. Over.

Carol: The station calling *Mary T*, I can barely copy.

Jon: Roger *Mary T*. It's Kerikeri Radio. Go ahead. Over.

Carol: Okay Jon, this'll have to be brief. There is a lot of lightning now. The wind is down to about, oh, maybe 40 [knots], if that. It's changed to a northerly. We are proceeding west with two drogues now, so we're proceeding very, very slowly. . . . We're a little bit less apprehensive than we were. Over.

Jon: Roger. Present position. Over. [Despite having been up most of the night, he was still self-controlled and professional, wanting the vital details before the niceties.]

Carol: Stand by. I have an 0500 [*Ed. note:* GMT; 1700 hours local time] position for you. Hope that will be adequate. At that time we were at 27° 50'S, 179° 32'E and, as I said, heading west, but we're not going anywhere very effectively.

Jon: Roger.

Carol: I would expect we will get back into 50 or 60 [knots of wind] as the low gets closer. What's your assessment? Over.

Jon: Yes. I would expect the wind to pick up in places, and I certainly would expect it to be 50 or 60 still for later on. Over.

Carol: Okay. Well, we're going to continue to drift. What would you expect will be a reasonable time to call you again in the morning? Over.

Jon: What say we do it . . . I guess you want some sleep . . . but, ah, what about giving us an update at 2100 hours or 0900 Zulu [Greenwich Mean Time]? Over.

Carol: I did not copy. Is there anybody that could relay?

Quartermaster: Quartermaster reading you *Mary T.* Could you give them a call at nine o'clock tonight?

Carol: I'm sorry. He wants me to call him at nine o'clock? Over.

Quartermaster: Correct. Kerikeri wants you to call him back at nine o'clock.

Carol: Okay. We'll talk to you again at 0900 [GMT]. We've got intermittent lightning. *Mary T* clear.

Kerikeri: Understood.

Aboard *Mary T* they used earplugs and tried to sleep. But the storm's relentless scream and the unpredictable roller-coaster seas prevented it.

Sigmund lay in the comparative safety of his bunk, confident *Mary T*'s body language would alert him to anything untoward. He couldn't sleep, but at least he was resting, allowing his strength and emotions to recuperate for the storm's next assault. Fearing Anna could be dehydrated, Carol gave her some water from the yacht's tanks. It was revolting. The constant pitching and rolling had stirred sediment off the bottom of the tanks. Brown flakes floated in the water. Anna settled for sucking candy.

Although their next scheduled report to Kerikeri Radio wasn't due until 9 PM, Carol contacted Jon Cullen again:

Carol: Ah, Jon . . . finally everyone else in the crew has stopped working long enough for a crew conference and you had asked earlier about the Pan call. We wouldn't regard it as more serious now, but if it doesn't inconvenience the navy vessel we really would like it to keep heading our way. One of our two manual bilge pumps is only useful when we don't have the seas coming aboard and also we have a steering problem that is pretty much solvable, but we are still working on it. At any rate, we would very much like it if the navy vessel would continue in our direction. The crew, three out of the four are . . . exhausted and we would appreciate it if they would continue in our direction and stand by. Over.

Jon: Okay. That's fine. I'll call the RCC now and confirm that. Okay. We'll leave it with you then until you are happy, and then we can cancel the Pan call. Okay. Good luck. And we'll catch up with you later this evening. Over.

Carol: Please keep them heading in our direction for now. Over.

Jon: Roger. Roger. I understand that. I understand. But I have to give updates. I must give updates, you see, over.

Carol: Roger. I will be back at 0900 [GMT] with an update. Over. [She spoke with considerable urgency, but at the same time the exhaustion in her voice was obvious.]

Jon: Okay. All the best then, and we'll catch up with you later. 'Bye for now.

Carol: Jon. Thanks. We want to confirm that the navy is still on the way. Thanks. We're clear.

Jon: They are still heading your way. Over.

Carol: Very good. Thank you very much. Any idea of his position now? Over.

Jon: No. I haven't got it. I'll see if I can find out what their present position is. Over.

Carol: Roger. Can I get that from you at 0900? Over.

Jon: Yes, it'll take a little while to get it, so I'll have to give it to you at 0900. Over.

Carol: Very good. Thanks very much. We'll copy you at 0900. *Mary T* clear.

What Jon didn't have the heart to tell them was that the *Monowai* was about 200 miles distant. She was still too far away to be able to offer assistance if the leaks worsened and they needed immediate help. In the conditions she was experiencing, the *Monowai* was making slow progress.

When the Orion flew over *Mary T*, Carol learned in a radio chat with them that the *Monowai* was being diverted away from them to assist another yacht in distress, *Ramtha*.

Shortly after nine o'clock that evening, Carol made her scheduled call to Kerikeri Radio:

Carol: Just a few minutes ago we were at 27° 54'S, 179° 36'E, so we haven't moved really very much since our last report. Over.

Jon: Roger. Okay. Thank you for that. Now, do you have an EPIRB on your vessel?

Carol: Yes we do. It's the old-fashioned kind, so it's not the registered sort. Over.

Jon: Roger. Just stand by one minute will you? We've got to contact RCC.

Carol: Roger. Standing by. [The radio was unusually quiet while Jon gave the information about *Mary T* to the rescue center.]

Jon: How old would you say that EPIRB is? Over.

Carol: The beacon could be quite old. The battery is only a year old. Over.

Jon: I missed that with the static. Could you say again? Over.

Carol: The beacon is old. The battery is only one year old. Over.

Jon: I see. Just stand by . . . is there any chance of looking at that EPIRB of yours? What frequency does it transmit on, do you know? Over.

Carol: Yes. It doesn't say on the outside. It just says it's a Class B EPIRB and it's an ACR. Over.

Jon: Roger. Class B. Okay that's fine. Can you give us a rundown on the wind and sea conditions that you've got there? Over.

Carol: We have less wind than we've had before. The anemometer is really hard to read at night. It looks like it is 45 [knots] to me, although a little while ago we did have up to 60. Every time I say it is less, it blows up again. We've had quite a bit of rainfall and we have lightning and thunder around us. The seas are quite confused. Breaking tops. We haven't, luckily, had any water in the cockpit for a little while, but we do tend to get the seas on the stern all the time, from different directions, so we're rolling quite a bit. Over.

Jon: Okay. I understand. How are you getting on with the water situation? Have you got that under control? Over.

Carol: Well, we have it under control in that we haven't had any seas in the cockpit yet. We have some pretty bad leaks in the cockpit. As long as the seas hold down like this we're fine. If conditions worsen, I expect as the front gets closer, then we could be in trouble. Over.

Jon: Okay. That system is coming down over the top of you in your present locality. Yeah, it's going to be coming over you during the night. Over.

Carol: Roger. [She laughed nervously.] That's not what we wanted to hear, but what we expected. Over.

Jon: Roger. Well, just stand by. I'll see if there's anything further that the RCC needs to know. Over.

Carol: Standing by.

Jon: Do you have a GPS and can we let the family know? Over.

Carol: Ah, we do have a GPS and don't let the family know. It is only my mother, who is 76 and up in California, and I don't see any reason to bother her. Over. [Her tone was emphatic.]

Jon: No. Well, okay. Just stand by one.

Carol: Standing by.

Jon: Okay. You'd better give us your mother's phone number. It's got into the press and it's been on TV, so we'd better let her know first, so we can tell her what's happening and make sure she's assured that you're all well. Over.

Carol: Okay. Oh dear. Oh well, I hope it hasn't hit the press in California. [She gave him a telephone number for America.]

Carol: My husband has some technical questions . . . stand by . . . okay. Here's Sigmund, Jon. I'm handing over to Sigmund.

Jon: Roger.

Sigmund: Good evening, Jon. Can we chat about strategy?

Jon: Roger. [He could not suppress a laugh.] Okay. I don't know if we can help you much with the weather. But ask your question. Over.

Sigmund: Okay. *Mary T* is a 40-foot Offshore yawl and we have some particular problems. Being a yawl, we have a lot of windage aft. I've been trying drogues and she lies beam-to. I've shifted the drogues forward, she lies beam-to. She doesn't want to run off with the windage in the mizzen. Also, I'm wondering what sort of speeds we should be doing. I'm wondering if my drogues are too big. What we are trying to do is avoid filling the vulnerable cockpit. Every time we fill the cockpit, the water goes into the boat.

Jon: Roger. Well, if you've got that as a problem, have you tried to heave-to with head into the wind with sails up? Over.

Sigmund: Ah, with four reefs in the main and full diesel power, it can't be done. Over. [His response sounded slow and pensive.]

Jon: Oh, I see. Okay. At the present moment, then, you're just towing drogues with bare poles? Over.

Sigmund: Ah, bare poles and drogues. I have an anchor warp out with an old main on it and I have a second anchor warp out with an old mizzen on it, and that has us going in the calmest of winds at 2½ knots and maybe 1 knot. So, we're moving very slowly and I'm a little concerned if we see more big seas. Over.

Jon: Roger. And getting pooped. Okay. Just stand by one. Let's see if there's anybody out there who's been involved with a yawl who can offer some helpful suggestions. Is there anybody there who could offer some suggestions for heaving-to in a yawl, and that matter only? Go ahead. Over.

Unidentified voice: Try to heave-to with just the mizzen up.

Jon: Suggestion is to heave-to with just the mizzen? Over.

Voice: I'm aboard a ketch and that's my plan.

Jon: Mary T, have you tried that combination? Over.

Sigmund: We lie with the bow maybe 5 or 10 degrees above perpendicular. Over.

Sigmund was aware that during the previous season, three boats had rolled over because they lay with the seas abeam. He was concerned *Mary T* would do the same if the waves increased, and it seemed certain they would. It was already blowing 60 knots, and boats nearer the vortex had reported much stronger winds. His fears increased later as he sat in the cockpit drinking coffee. A loud sloshing sound warned him it was coming. *Mary T* was engulfed in foaming water. He lost his balance and spilled his coffee. The yacht rolled steeply, knocked down by the solid wall of water.

After she'd righted herself, Sigmund studied the mizzenmast. Perhaps he could remove it, tie warps to it, and let it float overboard to slow him down. That would be a better use of it than hoisting a sail in these conditions, as suggested by the unidentified voice on the ketch.

He and Carol had often discussed the expense involved in having a mizzen that provided only 88 square feet of sail for a lot of extra rigging. Now would be as good a time as any to change the configuration, he thought.

Meanwhile, back in Kerikeri, Jon Cullen felt impotent. He knew that the most valuable role he could play for the *Mary T* and other boats caught in the storm was to offer encouragement while letting them make their own decisions. All he could give *Mary T* were words of support and hope. He could only trust that good seamanship and a degree of luck would get them through their ordeals. Neither the *Monowai* nor any other rescue vessel would be able to offer immediate help.

CHAPTER 4

HELP'S ON THE WAY

SATURDAY, JUNE 4, AT 1300

Captain Jim Hebden was uneasy about the weather reports he received as the 7,246 ton roll-on, roll-off container ship *Tui Cakau III* sailed from Fiji toward Auckland. The weather had been idyllic when they departed the port of Lautoka on June 2, but as the ship steamed farther into the South Pacific, Hebden became increasingly concerned. Instincts acquired during 18 years of sailing the Pacific warned him that all was not right.

He studied the barometer and noted in the log that it was still plummeting. It had fallen from a pressure of 1,000 mb at midnight to 985.5 mb at noon. The rapid drop was alarming, an indication that they were in for trouble from the weather.

"There are no old, bold sailors," he would often remind his Fijian crew, most of whom had sailed with him for more than a decade. It was a simple philosophy. It meant he was not one to take unnecessary risks. He ordered the crew to tighten the cargo lashings and to check them every two hours. They were on a cyclone watch.

He had encountered his share of storms and cyclones in the South Pacific. One storm had thrown him out of his seat on the bridge. Another had ripped out a seat bolted down to the deck of the bridge. He'd seen lockers hurled across the deck, and cargoes slip their lashings. Experience had taught him to prepare well in advance. You could never be sure that even the combined technology of the meteorological offices in Fiji, Australia, and New Zealand was sophisticated enough to spot in advance the often beautiful, spiraling wisps of cyclone, hurricane, or storm formations.

To the west of the *Tui Cakau*, a larger cargo ship traveling from Suva to Sydney reported it was battling a 60-knot storm that had ripped out a radar mast. The ship was taking on water.

Given a choice in threatening conditions, and had he been forewarned, Jim Hebden would have elected to stay in port or run from the storm. Now, however, it was too late to take evasive action. His only comfort was that the *Tui Cakau* appeared to be on the fringe of the storm. As long as she remained there, she would avoid the worst of the weather.

Two hours later, the rain squalls stopped and the sea fought with itself, confused that the wind had suddenly dropped. Capt. Hebden spotted birds flying in the distance. Blue sky broke through the clouds. To a less-experienced sailor, it could appear the worst had passed. But Jim Hebden suspected he had, in fact, reached the outer edge of the vortex itself.

His suspicion was confirmed when the wind and waves rose once more. The *Tui Cakau* was lifted and shaken and dropped again and again by seas attacking from all angles. He checked the barograph. It had fallen another three points.

He reread the weatherfaxes. The high-pressure zone over the South Pacific was trapped between two depressions in a pincer movement, as if locked in combat. Three giant forces were contesting their strength; cold polar air reaped by the southern low in Antarctica was spinning against warm air the northern low had harvested in the tropics. This clash of invisible gladiators intensified as they moved closer, locking horns to form a swirling, roaring demon that raged across more than 20,000 square miles of Pacific Ocean. It was a rogue "bomb" storm, one that should not have been awaked at this time of the year.

"Bombs" in the subtropics may deepen faster than a weather map can reasonably show. The resulting weather may change from fair to foul faster than a boat can travel. North Atlantic bombs are well known by English sailors (for example, the Fastnet storm of

August 1979). The frequency of such storms in the South Pacific has not been determined exactly but is roughly two to four times a year. In June 1983, one such bomb destroyed the *Lionheart*, and seven crew were lost as they tried to enter Whangaroa Harbour in eastern Northland (New Zealand). In June 1989, another bomb capsized the trimaran *Rose Noelle*, and her crew of four drifted at sea for five months.

Now the *Tui Cakau III*, 450 feet long and 60 feet wide, was trapped in the storm area with 60 yachts, few of which were more than 50 feet in length. In the center of the storm lay the yacht *Destiny*, tiny, vulnerable, disabled, and alone. She was the first yacht the storm had attacked.

The air force had raised the *Tui Cakau* on Channel 16, and he had immediately offered assistance. He was now unsure about the wisdom of his decision, but he would never have refused to aid another vessel in distress unless the rescue attempt clearly jeopardized his own vessel and its crew. With only 1,000 tons of cargo aboard, the ship was light. The reduced weight affected the ability of its catamaran hulls to handle the enormous seas. He was constantly forced to head off the waves. As the weather worsened, Capt. Hebden reduced speed to 3.5 knots, and he became increasingly concerned about the ship's ability to continue toward the yacht. The Orion's air crew kept regular radio contact with him, and he listened anxiously as they talked to the woman on *Destiny* every half-hour.

He couldn't pick up *Destiny*'s weak radio signal, but he knew from the one-sided conversation of the air crew that their plight was desperate. The strong, confident voice of Flt. Lt. Bruce Craies continued to offer advice and reassurance, and belied his true feelings about the odds of a successful rescue.

"Paula, are you there?" he heard Craies call. Again he could not hear the response.

He heard a voice from the plane: "Paula, this is the doctor . . . one more question, how old is Dana?"

"Copy. Forty-two. You've done everything you can, and help's on its way. I'm sure he'll be fine."

Jim Hebden was not as confident as the doctor sounded. He estimated the wind at Force 10 (up to 55 knots) and heard from the Orion crew that around *Destiny* it was blowing at more than 80 knots.

"We're still 50 miles away. At this rate it'll be two o'clock in the morning before we get to her," he told his officers.

The sea swirled under the gap between the *Tui Cakau*'s twin hulls as it raised her on each crest, rolling her precariously. Tumultuous waves attacked her sides. With each roll, the crew grabbed at handholds and steadied themselves. An officer, clutching a VHF microphone, was hurled across the bridge. Water cascaded over the bow and onto the bridge four decks above the weather deck, itself four decks above the sea.

Capt. Hebden was awed by the forces at work. Even as he stood on the bridge, almost 50 feet above water level, he still had to look *up* to the crest of a wave curling ahead of the ship. He studied the sea's fury. A series of waves about 40 feet high, then a monster towering over the bridge itself, possibly 100 feet high, crashed over them. The pattern was irregular but repeating. They curled up over him, their white crests blocking the sky.

"Jesus, there's another one!" he exclaimed, when yet another gigantic wave reared over the ship.

They held him fascinated. The troughs were as long as the *Tui Cakau* herself, the faces of the tumbling seas were near-vertical.

Jim Hebden and his officers had their hands full. They used all their skills to keep control of the ship. Each time they recognized an attack, they reduced power a little. The *Tui Cakau* sat there, momentarily waiting for the ocean's punch, and then, just as it hit, they gunned her forward to hold her course.

Despite their ability, they did not always win. She was frequently caught off-guard. On one occasion, two large waves wrestled each other and tumbled ahead of her. They lifted her up and rolled her over 40 degrees. The *Tui Cakau* shuddered as the cargo of wood stacked in the hold was strewn about like discarded matches. A Fijian crewmember was tossed into the air as if a carpet had been pulled from under him. The chief officer was lifted out of his chair and hurled through the air. He crashed to the floor, breaking a leg.

It was obvious now that the Orion's crew feared *Destiny* would break up. They called the *Tui Cakau* for confirmation that she could still reach the yacht. The woman on *Destiny* had reported that the sound of the mast smashing against the boat had changed. It was now less brittle, more spongy, indicating that the spreader tip may have reached the core of the fiberglass sandwich that comprised the hull.

Jim Hebden radioed back to confirm he was still trying to achieve his mission. He estimated his time of arrival at 2 AM. But he wondered if he'd be able to find *Destiny* in the dark, storm-tossed seas. Chances were he would steam right by her or, even worse, accidentally collide with her. Even with radar he wouldn't be able to detect *Destiny* because of the screen clutter caused by the rain and spray.

The crew of the Orion reported their concerns about the increasingly low morale aboard the yacht. As the limping *Destiny* endured more pounding from the waves, screams echoed over the radio. They knew Dana was in considerable pain and immobile. The doctor aboard the Orion indicated the man could have broken a rib, and that it may have punctured a lung. He also suspected he had a broken femur.

Capt. Hebden took instructions from the doctor on how to treat Dana if he were successfully lifted aboard the *Tui Cakau*. As they battled their way toward the yacht, a sick bay was set up to accommodate *Destiny*'s crew. An oxygen bottle was taken from an oxy-acetylene set, and a hose and primitive face mask were attached to supply oxygen should they need it. Capt. Hebden considered it fortunate he had, himself, been hospitalized recently and remembered how a saline drip had been attached to his arm. He checked again to make sure the *Tui Cakau*'s course would place them just north of the stricken yacht.

In the early hours of Sunday, June 5, the Orion's crew radioed that they were running low on fuel, and were heading for Nadi, Fiji.

They had been airborne for 13 hours. It was tedious work. The Orion was a proven aircraft, 27 years old, a survivor of the Cold War when New Zealand, Australia, and the United States patrolled the Pacific, hunting for Soviet submarines. Its interior was sparse, and few comforts were available to the 11 crewmembers.

"This is the worst weather I've experienced in the couple of thousands of hours I've had up here," Flt. Lt. Craies told his copilot. "I've never seen it like this before."

Sqd. Ldr. Yardley agreed. He admitted to feeling queasy. Motion sickness plagued all the crew. The Orion had bucked and bounced for hours. To have to sit at the back of the aircraft, strapped into their seats, was a particularly unpleasant endurance test for the crew who worked at the bank of instruments along the side of the plane. The spotters, peering out of the bubble windows at the sea below for hours on end, also had a hard ride.

All day, Yardley had maintained radio communications with the RCC, *Destiny*, and the *Tui Cakau*, plotting the Orion's course and assessing its range and fuel reserves. To extend their flying time they had climbed to 8,000 feet, where conditions were surprisingly better than at lower altitudes. There, cruising with two of the four engines shut down to conserve fuel, they found blue skies, smooth air, and only 8 knots of wind.

Before shutting down two engines, Craies assessed the risks. The plane could not fly on a single engine. On one engine the plane would descend toward the ocean at about 500 feet a minute, giving him about 16 minutes to restart one of the others. Moisture could enter the shut-down engines, where it might turn to ice, preventing ignition or possibly damaging the engines.

The bond that the Orion's crew had developed with the American woman they had never seen made them reluctant to leave *Destiny* in the perilous conditions she still faced. It was a curiously intimate relationship, nurtured by hours of conversation across radio waves. The crew felt pity for her. She sounded strong, yet gentle; frightened but determined. They shared her terror, her hope, her desperation, her tenderness, her faith, and her frustration. To Paula, they were angels out of the blue, her only hope for survival. They flew so low, so close, they were almost beside her, at times only a couple of hundred feet away. Yet they were incapable of holding out a hand she could grasp, to pluck her out of the maelstrom. It was cruel to be so close and yet so helpless. This was the ultimate frustration.

They would never forget her pitiful cry as once more they flew low over *Destiny:* "I hear your plane. God, I wish you could lift me off."

Paula's psychological state worried Dr. Powell. She would need great physical and mental strength if things got worse. It was vital she maintain her judgment and energy to assist with the rescue. He suggested that the crew aboard the Orion try to improve her morale by keeping her constantly busy. They did so by prompting her to check batteries, tidy the boat, and watch over Dana.

As the day progressed, Dr. Powell was impressed with the impact Craies and Yardley had on her spirits. Their reassuring manner gave her hope that she would, indeed, survive this ordeal. He fed them ideas continuously on how to maintain the conversation.

Nevertheless, the incessant pounding took its toll on Paula. "Oh God!" they heard her scream with despair as the boat rolled again and again. "Oh God!"

The slight improvement in her spirits evaporated at nightfall, and she questioned whether they would be able to continue the battle for survival.

"I don't know if I can cope with this," Dr. Powell heard her confide at one stage. "Did you say the boat would be here in the morning? I'm not sure we'll last that long."

Yardley was so depressed by the remark that he could no longer talk to her, despite Dr. Powell's urgings. Craies kept up the banter in an attempt to lift her spirits.

It appeared to work when, at about 2100, she was back on the air saying: "Dana says he wants a can of Fiji Bitter. It would be good."

During previous search-and-rescue operations, Sqd. Ldr. Yardley had never closely identified with people in distress. He had always tried to remain detached, but for the past 10 hours he had been consoling, encouraging, and advising Paula, participating in her ordeal. There had been long periods of anguish that seemed to last an eternity. They had heard the hapless couple praying for survival, and pitied them as the radio caught them screaming, terrified, when the boat rolled.

Just trying to keep the plane aloft was a stressful occupation. The concentration required for the task was accentuated when they dropped a sonar locater beacon beside *Destiny* to keep track of her during the night, insurance against losing her if either the EPIRB or the boat's batteries failed. Activating the beacon should have been a simple, routine task, one that Craies had performed scores of times previously. They simply flew over the sonar beacon and pressed a button in the cockpit to start it working.

Now, flying conditions were so bad that even the simplest of jobs was difficult, and Craies found he couldn't press the button. He jokingly cursed his slow reflexes and apologized to Yardley, who peered at his screen, waiting for the electronic signal to respond. But his crew knew that all Craies's attention was needed to keep the plane on course as it bounced about, only a few hundred feet over the ocean. It was not until the third pass that he finally managed to press the button at the right time.

It was like flying in mountains, precision flying that demanded exhausting concentration and skill. It was not as if they were dealing with a stationary target. *Destiny* drifted at about 2 knots. Even with their sophisticated electronic equipment, the Orion's crew often had difficulty locating her. They could keep track of her only within a two-mile radius. With the plane slowed to its minimum flying speed of 120 mph, there was still very little time to make contact with the yacht. When they dropped down low to search for *Destiny* they could see little, even in daylight. Driving rain and sleet hit the cockpit windows, and the sky and sea merged in a gray shroud that kept visibility to a minimum.

When their fuel ran low, they radioed the RCC:

Kiwi 315: Suggest Kiwi 315 be replaced by an aircraft.

RCC: Kiwi 315, understood . . . at present investigating opportunity for Australian or American assistance. Will have to confirm. HQ are looking at getting aircraft airborne to meet your PLE [position of last exit]. Over.

Kiwi 315: RCC. Copy. Obviously aircraft must stay with *Destiny* as it may be holed at any time and has no life raft.

RCC: Copied. *Destiny* no life raft. We agree it must be continuous on-top coverage. Over.

Kiwi 315: Don't be surprised by [wind] velocity in excess of 70 knots. Sea state nine. Over.

RCC: Copied. Information we have is vessel has a life raft. Can you confirm it is either damaged or washed overboard? Over.

Kiwi 315: Life raft has come adrift from vessel and has now floated away. Over.

RCC: Will discuss possible requirement to drop life raft to vessel before last light so that it could be retired prior to, or in case, the vessel is holed in the night. Over.

Kiwi 315: I will take up that suggestion on board but believe that will be impossible because the one person who can walk does not want to get outside the vessel due to the conditions. Over.

RCC: Understood. Have nothing more for you. Will be transmitting to you updated weather information when it comes to hand from the Met. office. Over.

Kiwi 315: Standing by. Out.

At the rescue coordination center, Bill Sommer was trying to find a plane and crew to replace the departing Orion P3. The air force had another plane on standby, but finding off-duty airmen was difficult on a holiday weekend.

He knew how important it was to have another Orion in the rescue vicinity during the night to keep morale high and to guide the *Tui Cakau III* to the area.

He contacted Hawaii and Australia to ascertain whether any U.S. Coast Guard or naval ships or aircraft were in the area, or if the Australians had any craft at Fiji or Norfolk Island that could lend assistance. But the U.S. Navy no longer cruised the region, and the Australians had nothing stationed on the islands.

Finally, the New Zealand Air Force managed to scramble together another crew, and another Orion set off to replace Kiwi 315.

En route to Fiji, Kiwi 315 briefed the relieving aircraft about *Destiny's* background, the psychological condition of her crew, Dana's suspected injuries, and the sea and wind conditions. Dr. Powell was not optimistic. He doubted Dana would remain well enough to be rescued, nor did he believe Paula could keep her spirits up through the longest, blackest, and coldest period of darkness. The possibility of the boat's breaking up was foremost in their minds.

Kiwi 315's flight to Fiji was tense. Low on fuel and with no reserves for a diversion, they were concerned with their own survival. The plane's three officers and crew were tired and grim as they finally flew over the lights of Nadi and put the Orion on the tarmac with only 1,000 pounds of fuel left in the tanks.

On the way to Fiji, Kerikeri Radio had informed them of the plight of another yacht, the *Mary T*, which was taking on water 200 miles away from *Destiny*. It sounded like another job for this weary crew.

But the aircraft's engineers, meticulously inspecting the Orion's engines as they cooled down after its stressful patrol, found oil leaking from the Number 2 engine. It was a substantial leak and would need to be repaired before they could take off again. The crew volunteered to start repairs immediately, but Flt. Lt. Craies discouraged them. After all, it was after 2 AM. Fifteen hours in the air had taken its toll on these men. They all needed to snatch a few hours' sleep before setting off later in the morning, probably at around 1000 on Sunday, June 5.

Meanwhile, aboard *Destiny*, Paula and Dana could not fathom how they would be rescued. Dana, lying helpless in his wet foul-weather gear, wondered if he would be able to get out of the cabin and on deck without passing out. Paula wasn't strong enough to carry him. The cold had tightened the muscles in his legs and hips, adding to the torture from his broken bones.

As they worried and wondered, a new voice came over the VHF radio. It, too, had a New Zealand accent that could be difficult to understand occasionally. The relief Orion had arrived. It would guide their rescue ship to them. However they were going to be rescued, they were on the last lap now. Tired as they were, a mixture of fear, excitement, and anticipation robbed them of any desire to sleep.

CHAPTER 5

WE'VE JUST BEEN ROLLED!

AS HE WORKED THROUGH THE ROLL CALL ON THE NIGHT OF Saturday, June 4, Jon Cullen received continuous reports about the worsening conditions. They suggested the storm was much more severe than the Meteorological Office had predicted. Bob Rimmer, captain of *Quartermaster*, had exuded confidence over the airwaves only a few hours earlier when he'd acted as relay for the *Mary T.* He'd said he was running off while streaming warps in 60-knot winds. He now sounded exhausted and a little uncertain:

Jon: Quartermaster. Copy Bob?

Bob: Yeah . . . boy, we've just had a real bouncer. Our position is 28° 25'S, 178° 24'E. [He was a little breathless.] Winds are still excessive. Sixties. There's major seas out there. We're running under bare poles at about 4 knots. Winds are from the easterly direction.

Jon: Roger.

Bob: Ah, we're all a little frightened out here, but we're all well.

Jon: Okay. Yep. Okay. Well, you'll be right there. East-northeasterlies, it shows, tending to become easterly quarter and what you've got, unfortunately, is going to continue. You're right in the path of the system and there's little you can do about it. So good luck with it there, Bob. We'll be thinking of you. We will be on air all night if there's any problems.

Bob: Thank you, Jon.

Jon: Okay. Take care all of you, then. Good night for now.

Jon felt there was no point in deluding them about the storm's ferocity, or the horrible night they were in for. Better that they should be prepared for what lay ahead. Allowing them to cling to a false hope might encourage them to risk their safety. Now and then, however, he wanted to soften the brutal truth, especially for crews cringing in their bunks, listening to the violence, their boats twisting and slewing down phenomenal waves.

Predicting the path of a storm is extremely difficult. Studying the weatherfaxes, Jon could not determine which way it would go. There were at least 60 boats out there, all desperate for his wisdom, all longing to hear that they would be bypassed by the worst of the blow. Watching the storm evolve from nothing, he had followed its track through the South Pacific during the past 48 hours, its center passing directly over the weather station at Raoul Island. There the storm's full fury spun from its core, out across the ocean, cutting a swath of fierce intensity across an area 900 miles long by 270 miles wide. The gales that spun from its center almost reached the shores of Fiji, New Zealand, and Tonga, each more than a thousand miles away from the others. Its destructive advance would take it down the east coast of New Zealand, directly over stragglers in the fleet heading for Tonga.

A number of yachts taking part in the regatta to Tonga had sought shelter inside Minerva Reef, a beautiful but treacherous outcrop of coral. About 13 boats lay at anchor there, but this low atoll offered scant shelter in a gale. Jon joked over the radio about the "Minerva Reef Yacht Club," but at least there was comfort in numbers. One boat that dragged anchor was blown onto the reef itself. Its crew was fortunate to have experienced help nearby to free the boat from the jagged coral lances.

Yachts in the lagoon reported the storm increasing to 70 knots. They watched in awe as huge seas exploded like geysers against the low coral reef that was their only protection from the ocean. The usually tranquil waters of the lagoon were lashed into choppy 4-foot waves.

By the time the storm reached Raoul Island, about 500 miles

south of Minerva Reef, two boats had sought shelter there. One of them was *Windora*. That night was the longest of Linda Christieson's life. Earlier in the day she'd visited a German catamaran called *Fallado*, their companion in the tiny anchorage. When the storm struck, she was trapped. She couldn't return to her husband and two young children on *Windora*.

Windora, meanwhile, was motoring up and down constricted Boat Cove because the bay was too small to hold two boats anchored at full scope in the 70-knot winds. While *Fallado* lay to her anchor, Bill Christieson spent the entire night powering between waypoints he'd set on the GPS.

Linda worried that she might never see her children again. The night was pitch-black, so dark it was impossible to distinguish between land and sea. There were no navigation lights in the uninhabited bay. *Windora* had no radar, and Linda was scared the yacht would hit the rocks that showed plainly on *Fallado*'s radar display.

Somehow, miraculously, *Windora* came through it without a scratch. As dawn's light filtered through the cloud cover above them, Bill could not believe how they had managed to keep *Windora* from going aground, so close were the rocks they motored between.

Back at Kerikeri Radio, so many boats called in for advice and assistance that the roll call took Jon three hours. It was exhausting work, reading down the list of boats he'd contacted over past days, recording their positions and telling them what weather they could expect. He'd worked worse cyclones than this, but they'd seldom occurred when there were so many boats at sea.

As he called boat after boat, he became concerned that many seemed to be reacting wrongly to the conditions. Some ignored his advice to sail west, others appeared ignorant about how to heave-to, and many reported taking waves beam-on. The storm had trapped at least six boats in its grip. He knew good seamanship was vital for survival in those conditions.

So many unforeseen things could go wrong. Warps streaming aft could tangle around propellers. A leaking hatch could admit enough water to sink a boat in a knockdown. Smashed ports could let a boat fill with water if they weren't protected by storm covers. Bilge pumps could seize if they hadn't been checked and serviced. Batteries might be flung out of their stowage compartments if they weren't secured firmly. Stoves could jump their gimbals and maim crewmembers in a rolling, rocking boat. The sea could force its way into a boat through engine exhaust pipes, or seacocks that were not shut. Scores of other unforeseen problems were likely to surface in a storm. Preparation before leaving port was vital for survival in these conditions. But, once out at sea, each sailor was in charge of his or her own destiny. A well-found boat is likely to survive the most violent of storms, provided it has a strong, rested crew with the knowledge and experience to handle the vessel. But ocean cruisers, like most of the fleet out there on that night of fury, were mostly short-handed, often just one man and one woman.

Jon thought about all these things as he took the reports from the yachts. *Destiny* had alerted him to the intensity of the storm. Now there were many other boats in trouble. They were all scheduled to call him hourly, so he could learn how they were coping.

He regretted that the crew of *Mary T* had been led to believe their rescue ship, the *Monowai*, was only 50 miles away. They'd been so relieved. He couldn't yet bring himself to tell them the *Monowai* was actually a couple of hundred miles distant. He felt he was justified in not disillusioning them. Although their plight was serious, it was not as perilous as that of some others, and they appeared to be coping reasonably well.

Jon went off to catch some sleep after being on duty for almost 24 hours. Maureen took over at Kerikeri Radio and was soon in the center of the action. A distress call came in from Bob Rimmer:

Bob: Mayday! Mayday! Mayday! Can you hear? *Quartermaster* calling!

Maureen: Ah, *Quartermaster*. Kerikeri. I copy. What's the problem? Over. [A hollow silence followed. *Quartermaster* failed to respond.]

Maureen: Ah, *Quartermaster,* Kerikeri. I copy. I copy. [Maureen sounded as if she were willing them to come alive, giving verbal mouth-to-mouth resuscitation. Again, nothing.] *Quartermaster, Quartermaster,* Kerikeri Radio copies. [Maureen trilled the words, as if to entice a response through tenderness. It worked.]

Bob: Yeah. This is *Quartermaster.* We've just been rolled. Umm . . . [His fear transmitted itself through the radio and he sounded on the verge of tears.] . . . and we're just checking everything now. Windows are all still in . . . [He breathed heavily, perhaps bracing himself as the boat lurched sideways and pitched and slammed into the waves again.] We'll come back to you in a couple of minutes.

Maureen: Roger. Roger.

Bob: I'll give you our position: 28° 24'S, 178° 32'E.

Maureen: Roger. How's everybody on board?

Bob: Oh, we're okay here. [His voice blended despair with exhaustion.] We had an earlier accident where Marie [his wife] got a big cut over her eye that we didn't report.

Maureen: Roger. Well, you check everything and come back. We'll be standing by here.

Bob: Okay. [After a couple of minutes' silence, *Quartermaster* returned.] Kerikeri. Do you read? Over.

Maureen: Roger. Go ahead. How's things?

Bob: We're all intact here. It was just a knockdown, not a rollover, but boy, oh boy, it's a good . . . I don't know how many knots of wind we've got. We'll just have to tidy up here at the moment. It's just a mess everywhere. [The combination of tiredness and fear slowed his speech, and he was breathing very heavily beneath the static and warbling on the radio. He sounded disoriented.]

Maureen: Roger. Okay. That's good to know, it's not as bad after all. This accident of Marie's. What is the problem? How bad is the cut? Over.

Bob: She's got a cut that is around about, oh, an inch-and-a-half long over her, ah, left eye. It's a split. It'll need stitches later on.

Maureen: Roger. Okay. Can you pull it close together and plaster it up? Over.

Bob: Yes, we have done that.

Maureen: That's good. Okay, then. Well, take care out there. We're standing by here. We're actually sitting by the radio. We're taking turns about. So take care out there.

Bob: Okay, thank you very much.

Maureen was concerned about *Quartermaster*. They were in serious trouble. You could hear it in their voices. Of those aboard, only the skipper, Bob Rimmer, had any real sailing experience, and he did not sound as if he were coping very well. Neither his wife, Marie, nor his 23-year old stepson, Jim Anderson, had much practical bluewater knowledge.

It was bad luck they now found themselves in the middle of the storm. They should have been well away from their present position, but they'd departed Auckland three days later than they'd planned. They were delayed when *Quartermaster*'s propeller shaft dropped out of the transmission coupling. Had it not been for that, they would have been more than 200 miles to the north, closer to Tonga and certainly sailing in more manageable conditions.

Forces beyond one's control—whether luck, providence, or fate—often play a critical role at sea. Most of the stragglers participating in the Tonga regatta were caught by the storm, but through good fortune, those who set sail at the official start time and stuck to their course escaped the brunt of the fury.

When Jon came back on duty at Kerikeri Radio, the reports were worrisome. Five yachts near Raoul Island were struggling. Three more yachts near *Destiny* were being severely battered. Jon tried to keep their spirits up by reporting the progress of the Whitbread Round-the-World Race. The boats skippered by New Zealanders,

Tokyo, Yamaha, and *New Zealand Endeavour,* led the way as they raced along the south coast of England, over part of the course for the notorious Fastnet Race.

Fastnet! There was a name to strike fear into a yachtsman's heart. In 1979, a Force 10 storm struck 303 fully crewed racing yachts participating in the classic 605-mile ocean race. Fifteen people died in that treacherous storm with winds of 60 to 70 knots. Five boats were sunk.

The Fastnet victims were well served by search-and-rescue craft. A British Royal Air Force Nimrod and a French Atlantique patrolled above the foundering yachts to coordinate rescue activity. RAF Whirlwind, Sea King, and Lynx helicopters, with supporting aircraft from the Royal Navy, hovered over the waves, plucking people off their boats and from the sea. Eight military ships, five merchant vessels, and 13 lifeboats also took part in rescue operations. Despite all these resources, more than 15 lives were lost, and the 1979 Fastnet Race is remembered as one of the worst yachting disasters of all time.

By comparison, the resources available for the 1994 storm off New Zealand were minimal. The situation was further complicated by the national holiday in New Zealand, which meant crews could not be easily located to staff aircraft. In addition, rescuers had to travel much greater distances to reach the victims than was the case in the Irish Sea.

Jon broadcast the bad news about the complex weather system during the roll call. He read the message slowly, pausing as he went, so the navigators on scores of boats could trace the weather patterns on their charts and in their minds.

He'd hardly finished when the yachts started calling in. Swiss, Germans, Britons, Australians, New Zealanders, and more Americans required help. He took time to talk with each one, recording their positions and weather conditions. Without a doubt, most of them were experiencing conditions worse than the forecasts.

A New Zealand charter yacht on a delivery voyage from Auckland to Fiji, the *Irresistible,* reported she was taking a pasting. The crew were seasick and their motor would not start after a knock-down. There was something extraordinarily forlorn about the way the skipper described the darkness out there in the middle of the ocean.

The *Obsession*'s radio operator reported in a broad South African accent that they were hove-to in winds reaching 60 knots and seas of more than 20 feet. Their barometer had dropped to 993 mb.

Jon told them the low-pressure system had probably passed straight over the top of them.

"That's what we think," replied the South African.

"Well, that's strange," Jon mused, "you've still got northerlies. Someone else had that happen to them too. By all accounts, you should really have westerly quarter winds, or southwesterly quarter winds, coming off the back of that system in your locality. So, I'm not sure what's happening there. There could be two centers to it, because you shouldn't really have had a lull as yet, and then have northerly."

As he called the boats, Jon offered them advice. Go west, he told some. He warned others that it was too late to do anything: They were trapped in the storm's path.

One skipper wanted to know how to find the center of the storm. Jon told him if he went outside and faced the wind, the center would be on his left-hand side.

Then *Quartermaster* was on the air again:

Bob: Quartermaster to Kerikeri. Can you read? Over.

Jon: Roger. You're loud and clear. Go ahead.

Bob: We've just had a second knockdown, Jon. I don't know what to do. [His desperation was obvious from the inflection in his voice.]

Jon: No. There's not much you can do. Are you head into it? Over.

Bob: I've got the autopilot trying to keep us with the seas now on the back quarter. We're steering course 266 [degrees].

Jon: Roger. Gotcha there. Your heading is 266 at roughly what speed? Over.

Bob: That's got me worried. It's showing naught. Oh! Help! [A long tense pause followed. None of the other boats waiting to talk dared break in.] It's just showing us at naught knots.

Jon: Yeah, that just doesn't seem to quite tally. Okay, so you've had your second knockdown. How's everybody on board? Is anybody hurt, at all? Over.

Bob: No. We're just hanging on, Jon. Just hanging on.

Jon: Okay Bob, well good luck there. I think you should check in . . . let's check in regularly. Let's check in at hour intervals if that's okay with you. Can we do that? Over.

Bob: Yeah we can do that. We'll check in at hourly intervals. Over and out. [The confidence he'd displayed while relaying messages for *Mary T* seemed to have evaporated. Jon's voice, too, sounded almost as desperate as he tried futilely to offer comfort and assistance.]

Jon: Yeah, okay. You can do it less if you want to. We're standing by anyhow, but we'll look for you every hour and, if we don't hear from you, then we'll have to get things under way. Over.

Bob: Okay. Thank you Jon.

Jon: Okay. Good luck there.

As they finished their conversation, pandemonium broke out on the radio. Another boat cut in and tried to call *Quartermaster* just as a third cut over him with a Pan call.

"Pan, Pan, Pan. This is the yacht *Tranquillity*," an American voice called.

He reported he had a torn mainsail that was flogging in a 50-knot wind. He was about to go on deck to try to secure it.

"We thought we'd better let somebody know where we were and the situation," he said.

No skipper likes to make a Pan call, or even to admit to being unable to cope with the circumstances testing him or her. He gave his position as 24° 33.7'S, 179° 23'W.

"We have loose gear on deck. We're taking a little bit of water," he said.

For Jon and Maureen Cullen, it was almost as exhausting as it was for the yacht crews on the ocean. Jon was snatching some sleep when *Quartermaster* came through again:

SUNDAY, JUNE 5, AT 0035

Bob: Quartermaster to Kerikeri. Do you read? Over.

Maureen: Ah, *Quartermaster*, yes, good morning. How are you going out there?

Bob: Well, it's a little better. We've got the autopilot and the engine going, keeping batteries and things going and we're trying to get the seas to come in over the back quarter. It seems to be working. We've had one hard knockdown since, but otherwise we're surviving here. The inside of the boat's a complete shambles.

Maureen: Roger, yes. Not very pleasant conditions at all. How's everybody inside. How are they coping?

Bob: Sorry, I didn't hear that last message. [The tiredness in his voice was stark.]

Maureen: How is everybody coping inside? Over.

Bob: Oh, we're just lying down where we can. Um, by the way, our GPS is frozen as hell, so I think that it's not working.

Maureen: What has frozen itself?

Bob: The GPS is not shifting from our original knockdown position.

Maureen: Oh, Roger, okay, the GPS. Oh, that's a shame. Okay then. The main thing is just to try to keep yourself comfort . . . well, in a place where you can be thrown around as little as possible until the morning, and have a look then to see how things are. Getting through the worst of the night now, it's getting closer to daylight as the time goes by. Not very pleasant conditions, I'm sure. Over.

Bob: Yeah. Well, we'll keep in contact with you every hour or so.

Maureen: Roger. Roger. Yep. We don't mind, we're just sitting here waiting for the calls and thinking about you all out there.

Bob: Thank you very, very much. [He sounded exhausted. Even speaking seemed to be an effort, and he slurred his words.]

Maureen: You're welcome. Keep your chin up; it's going to improve.

Maureen felt completely inadequate. She wondered whether she had offered the wretched crew aboard *Quartermaster* enough succor. Was there more she could have said? Was there, perhaps, something she could have suggested that would have helped them survive? *Oh for more wisdom. Please God, make them be all right.*

The Cullens worked on through the night, talking to boats and keeping the RCC informed about the conditions, which continued to deteriorate. Other boats were also in trouble. *Sofia, Heart Light, Silver Shadow,* and *Waikiwi II* were all struggling to survive. Some were in desperate situations.

Mary T

Aboard the *Mary T,* Sigmund peered though the darkness at the barometer. What he saw scared him. He had last seen the instrument behaving in such a bizarre way when they were holed up in Mexico, waiting for Hurricane Raymond to pass. The barometer was pumping. Its erratic movement suggested to him that they were in the eye of a cyclone. He considered their plight desperate. They would be lucky to survive.

Carol called Kerikeri Radio, but her transmission could hardly be heard. An unidentified boat cut in to act as a relay station. Carol told them about the barometer.

> Maureen: Roger. I got the barometer. Let's see if we got it right: [Position] 28° 03'S, 179° 26'E. The winds are from the north, 40 knots. The seas are larger than before. Barometer 29.2 [inches]. Is that a Roger, Mary?

> Relay: Roger. [Maureen made another comment about the barometer.]

> Relay: Two nine decimal two, and pumping. Over.

> Maureen: Oh, the barometer is dropping. The barometer is dropping. And how are things on board? Over.

> Relay: They have somebody up on deck. Everything's okay on deck.

> Maureen: Okay. Well that's good news to hear that part. Not so good to hear about that barograph dropping. Okay, well take care out there . . . hang on in there Mary, it won't be long to daylight.

Early Sunday morning, Alex Gibb, the Search and Rescue Coordinator for the Maritime Safety Authority, telephoned Kerikeri Radio with the news that they believed *Quartermaster* was in serious trouble because her EPIRB had been activated. Jon recounted the conversations he and Maureen had had with *Quartermaster*'s skipper, Bob Rimmer. He mentioned that Bob had not sounded in control of the situation.

"The Orion at the *Destiny* doesn't want to leave until daylight when the Hercules relieves them," Alex said. "He's going to stay there because they [the crew of the *Destiny*] don't seem too good. The Herc's going to do a dogleg to investigate *Sofia*, and they'll see if they can find *Quartermaster* as well."

Meanwhile, the *Monowai* had reported slow progress. The seas had forced her to reduce speed and head farther west, Alex said. She was doing only about 4 knots in a 40-knot northerly gusting to 60 knots.

The next time Alex telephoned from the rescue center, he found Jon concerned about *Heart Light*. She had not checked in on schedule.

"They're in the same bloody locality as the *Quartermaster*." He sighed deeply, obviously worried. "They haven't come up, and I've been calling and calling them. They've been bloody reliable up till now. They're on the hour every hour, so it's 20 minutes overdue on their time."

"Okay, well . . ." Alex said.

"Their last position reported was 28° 07'S, 177° 58'E."

"And what time was that?" Alex inquired.

"That was 0325, and they had drogues and everything out. They're a multihull, goddamn it, heading at 315 [degrees] magnetic. Oh, hang on, I've got a more updated one than that. Sorry."

Alex waited patiently for the most recent information.

"Four twenty-eight, 0428, was their last check-in. They were then at 28° 03'S, 177° 56.42'E. Their heading at that stage was 320 [degrees] and they couldn't slow the boat down less than 7 to 8 knots, and they were in south-southwesterlies of 60-plus. And that was from wind equipment they have on board."

"Okay. We'll get the aircraft to have a look for them as well," Alex said.

"Yeah, I think it would be worth it."

"How are you getting on? I'm starting to get bloody tired now."

"Well, Maureen has just showed her face here, so I'm going to go and put my feet up for a couple of hours," said Jon. "I'm getting a bit stuffed, actually."

"Is there anybody that can take over from you?"

"Not easily. No. No. We'll be okay."

"You take care," said Alex.

At the RCC, the list of storm casualties was growing. *Quartermaster*'s EPIRB was sending a desperate call for help and her crew could not be raised on the radio. Nor could the crew of *Sofia*, whose beacon was also transmitting. *Heart Light* was probably in trouble and the *Monowai*, on its way to *Mary T*, which could well be sinking, had spotted a distress flare from an unknown vessel. And then there was *Destiny*, slowly breaking up in the darkness.

CHAPTER 6

I'M HERE TO SAVE YOU

≋≋≋

As Kiwi 315 touched down at Fiji, the *Tui Cakau III* arrived in the vicinity of the stricken yacht *Destiny*. It was one of the Pacific's darkest nights. The *Tui Cakau* rolled and heaved, her engines straining as the stern lifted out of the water.

Capt. Jim Hebden stood alone on the wing of the bridge, peering into the blackness but seeing nothing, as rain and spray stung his face.

There was no doubt they were close. The Orion that had relieved Kiwi 315 was keeping them informed and, when they heard them talking to Paula on the VHF, the air crew were encouraging her and Dana by telling them it would not be long before the rescue ship arrived. The airmen sounded confident that once the freighter arrived, rescue would be a simple formality.

Jim Hebden knew better. The rescue attempt could place the American couple in even greater peril. The ship might accidentally steam right over them in this bad visibility.

The sea conditions were so atrocious that he didn't dare to launch a tender. Holding a 7,000-ton ship alongside a 45-foot yacht in calm conditions was difficult enough. In this storm it might prove impossible, particularly as the *Tui Cakau* had a 6-foot lip protruding from her hull at water level. That lip could crush *Destiny* in an instant if she drifted underneath.

He would not normally even attempt to enter a port or go alongside a wharf in a wind blowing as hard as this, so laying the *Tui*

Cakau alongside a tiny yacht was a daunting prospect. It would take only one misjudgment, or one lapse of concentration, to destroy *Destiny* completely.

When he'd received the call for assistance from Kiwi 315 15 hours earlier, the swell had been so bad that he couldn't head directly toward the yacht. Instead, he'd plotted a course that would take him north of the yacht. The new course was easier on the ship and her crew.

Had it not been for the distress call, Capt. Hebden probably would have chosen to heave-to and ride out the storm, particularly since one of his officers had broken a leg. Even on this easier course, they could make only 3 knots instead of their normal 11. Getting this far had been a long, hard, uncomfortable slog.

There was still no sign of *Destiny*. Nothing. Even the radar screen was a senseless profusion of glowing dots depicting rain, spray, and myriad huge seas.

"Can you mark her for me?" Capt. Hebden asked the Orion pilot on the VHF. "I can't see a damn thing. The sea clutter is throwing stuff all over the radar screen. Has she, by any chance, got a light?"

The air crew said she did, indeed, have a faint light that he should be able to spot when he was within range. They agreed with Capt. Hebden that it was too dangerous to attempt a rescue in the darkness.

The *Tui Cakau* would stand by for the rest of the night. If the yacht did break up before dawn, Capt. Hebden said, he'd go to their aid immediately, despite the extra complications. But, if it came to the worst, how could they possibly save the couple in the darkness? They'd surely be swept away, lost in the churning white crests of the seething ocean. If *Destiny* didn't hold together until daylight, the chances of her crew's surviving, even with the *Tui Cakau* standing by, were dismal indeed. Sunrise was still four hours away.

The *Tui Cakau*'s crew still talked to the Orion P3 on a radio channel that *Destiny* couldn't hear. Nobody wanted Paula to know the difficulties confronting the rescuers.

Capt. Hebden had heard the American woman begging the

Orion crew to have them rescued as soon as possible. She feared the boat could soon disintegrate. They had no life raft and no way of surviving if *Destiny* sank.

For a long time, Capt. Hebden and his Second Mate discussed the best way to rescue the American couple. Eventually, a simple plan evolved. It was born of pure desperation. Two men would descend the side of the *Tui Cakau* and jump directly aboard the *Destiny*. They would go below and carry the injured man on deck. The woman too, if necessary. It would be extremely dangerous. It was not a task the captain could *order* anyone to carry out.

The officers and crew aboard the *Tui Cakau* were a close-knit community. Some had served with Capt. Hebden the full 18 years he'd been with Sofrana Unilines. The majority had been with him for at least 10 years. They trusted his seamanship and he, in turn, had full confidence in their strength and bravery. Most were good friends, tough men, but blessed with the gentleness and tolerance typical of the Melanesian race.

The thought of endangering any of his crew caused Jim Hebden great concern. But there was no alternative if they were to save the couple aboard *Destiny*.

He had in mind two men. The first, Joeli Susu, had been a soldier in the Fijian Army. He had served with United Nations peace-keeping missions, and his strength and fitness were legendary. He was often seen jogging around the ship's decks, holding two oxy-acetylene bottles above his head. He stood 6 feet 3 inches tall and he weighed about 260 pounds. The second, Seruvuama Valagotavuivui, a mechanic, also was a fitness enthusiast. He was as big as Joeli, and just as brave.

"I'm asking for volunteers," Capt. Hebden told them. "I won't think any less of you if you don't want to do it. It'll be very dangerous. The boat will be rolling and it'll be slippery."

Both men volunteered immediately. Of course they would rescue the Americans.

Capt. Hebden was proud of them. And he knew that, had he asked any of the other men, each would have responded just as selflessly. He had great respect for the integrity and generosity of Fijians, and could imagine no better people to work with, particularly on an assignment like this.

"Oh, by the way," he said, "I think you should go down to the boat in bare feet."

That wasn't a problem for either of them. They were used to going around barefooted. They spent most of their time at home shoeless. And everybody knew that nothing gripped a slippery, wet deck better than bare skin.

After a while, the Orion flew low over the *Tui Cakau*. They all heard it. Then there was an orange glow appearing and disappearing in the sea ahead as the plane dropped the first flare in the darkness. The whole exercise surprised and reassured Capt. Hebden.

He knew there wasn't far to go now. The plane's captain had promised to drop the first flare when they were a couple of miles from *Destiny*.

The *Tui Cakau* rolled heavily as she held a course in the direction of the fading flare. The sea was still very angry. Capt. Hebden kept the ship forging ahead slowly.

Another flare appeared farther away. They were getting closer. The Orion's crew had promised to drop it about 300 yards from the yacht.

He marveled at the skill displayed by the men in the air. They were flying in winds of 80 knots, jolting though the pitch-black night a few hundred feet above the sea, dispatching flares to guide them to the yacht, a pinprick in a vast and hostile ocean. He admired their precision, their bravery.

Excitement gripped the tiny group on the bridge. One of them thought he saw a light. They all peered ahead. Capt. Hebden resumed his post out on the wing of the bridge. Nothing. The boat lumbered over the waves in the darkness. Still not a sign of anything. Somebody called: "There it is again."

This time, the light remained long enough for all to see. This time, there was no mistaking it. Capt. Hebden quickly punched a button on the satellite navigation system to record the ship's position. Now the GPS could guide them back to this spot anytime they wanted.

And now that they'd got this close, Capt. Hebden was determined not to lose the yacht's crew even if *Destiny* broke up before dawn. He suggested a contingency plan. They would fire a line across to her and have the woman haul a life raft aboard the sinking yacht. But, as he discussed it with his officers, it seemed doubtful that the woman would have enough strength; and her husband was incapacitated.

There was, in fact, little else they'd be able to do in the darkness, at least little they could logically plan in advance. If the worst came to the worst, they'd attempt some sort of rescue. No doubt about that. Meanwhile, their earnest hope was that *Destiny* would hold together a few hours longer.

Capt. Hebden encouraged the off-duty crew to snatch some sleep while he circled the *Destiny*, waiting for dawn. It wasn't easy to keep contact with the yacht in that black storm. If Capt. Hebden went outside a two-mile radius, he lost the pinprick of light that marked *Destiny*'s position. When the *Tui Cakau* came stern-on to the wind in her circling, her speed catapulted to 11 knots. When she came beam-on, the seas rolled her 40 degrees. And when she came head-on, she would rear and plunge, and slow to 3 knots.

He used the solitude to plan the rescue. He had to have his ship on a course that would bring her close alongside *Destiny* and enable her to hold her position there. It had to be the track on which the 7,000-tonner would be most stable; if she rolled down on *Destiny*, the little yacht would be crushed to splinters in seconds. Once again, he worried about the projecting 6-foot lip at *Tui Cakau*'s waterline. His main objective was to reduce the freighter's roll as much as possible. It was unfortunate he did not have a full cargo on this trip: The greater weight would have made the ship easier to control during the rescue. In her light condition, her considerable windage pushed her to leeward as soon as she lost way.

The *Tui Cakau*'s bridge and accommodation sections were forward. Containers were lashed to her weather deck amidships. Aft was a large superstructure from which the smokestack protruded. The storm-force wind pressed hard against all this top hamper, complicating the precision piloting necessary for the rescue. On the positive side, the ship had twin, variable-pitch screws, twin rudders, and bow thrusters, all of which added considerable maneuverability.

Capt. Hebden chose an approach heading of 300 degrees. It was the bearing on which the *Tui Cakau* rolled least. Unfortunately, it placed the wind and sea on the starboard quarter, and increased her speed. But he believed he could check her way and hold her against the weather, to leeward of *Destiny*, while the yacht drifted slowly down toward the ship.

Dawn arrived slowly to reveal a tumultuous ocean on which 50-foot waves broke. Islands of foam hurtled past them. At 0600 on Sunday, June 5, he raised the ship's crew; all of them, engineers, cooks, and deckhands. He lined them up on the starboard deck, where he intended lowering the ship's life raft with the two volunteers and a stretcher down the hull side. All hands were needed to lower the raft and haul it back up again with the Americans inside.

He set up a communications relay with handheld radios. It involved cadets, the quartermaster, the radio operator, and the Second Mate keeping in touch not only with each other, but also with the Orion and *Destiny*.

"You stay in the wheelhouse," Capt. Hebden ordered the radio operator. "I don't want anyone to disturb me. Everyone just stay out of my way. And if the lady comes off the boat and wants to talk to me before I get off here, I don't want to see her. Just everybody keep the hell out of my way."

They didn't take offense at their skipper's abruptness. They had not worked together for more than 10 years without understanding why he behaved this way as he stood isolated on the starboard bridge wing. Capt. Hebden needed to be alone. He needed total concentration for the task ahead. From his position, he had a full, unobstructed view of his men on the weather deck, the life raft dangling over the side, and the crippled little *Destiny* herself, now just yards away. His vantage point enabled him to work the ship's engines, rudders, and bow thrusters while keeping an eye on the yacht.

Working in tight situations from the wing, he always felt confident. From here, he had piloted the ship into all sorts of tight corners of the South Pacific. From here, he had an unobstructed view along the starboard side and across the deck. He poised himself over the controls.

Sunday, June 5, at 0630

Aboard *Destiny* they were not so confident. The constant drilling on the hull had continued its soft mushy sound. As the night had progressed, they'd listened to wood splintering. The spreader was inching closer to total penetration. Paula had pleaded for the ship to come alongside in the dark and get them off, or at least cut away their rigging and let their mast sink to get rid of that dangerous spreader. They didn't believe *Destiny* would survive till morning. But Capt. Hebden had been adamant that a night rescue, unless in an absolute emergency, posed unacceptable risks for all involved.

Now, in the pale light after dawn, Paula huddled in *Destiny*'s cockpit. The yacht was a wretched sight, broken and disfigured; disgustingly littered with oil, dirt, food, and trash.

A few hours earlier, she'd glimpsed the *Tui Cakau* through a porthole, steaming past in the darkness. She had disappeared in the swell, then reappeared as the massive waves lifted her. With only her lights visible, she'd looked fairly small: a little ship lost in the vastness of the black ocean.

But when Paula got a look at her in daylight, she was astounded. "Oh my God!" she exclaimed as the *Tui Cakau* loomed out of the grayness. "Oh my God! Dana, get up here! Look at the size of this vessel."

But Dana, of course, couldn't move. He called to her, but she didn't hear him.

She and Dana had not thought much about the vessel that would rescue them. Paula had deluded herself that the rescue would echo scenes from the television program *Bay Watch*; a lifeguard's boat would slide alongside for her to step into. As simple as that. She'd never imagined her rescuer would be a middle-aged British sea captain piloting a ship eight stories high.

Below, Dana lay on his bunk, still tormented by pain. He could hear the *Tui Cakau*'s engines and, although he could not see the ship, he felt her presence on the sea outside. He was gripped by a strong sense of foreboding and fear.

Paula watched the container ship as she wallowed out of the murky seascape. It was still difficult to distinguish the point in the distance where the sky met the sea. The ship appeared to be bearing down on them at a tremendous pace, towering above them larger and larger the closer she got.

Dana heard the throb of the ship's engines through the howling wind. The closer she moved toward them, the louder the noise. The motors now sounded so close, he thought the ship was on top of them. His fear intensified.

Out on the wing, Capt. Hebden was apprehensive. With the wind aft, he was running toward *Destiny* faster than he had anticipated. He saw the solitary figure of the woman in the cockpit, half out of the companionway.

As the ship approached, Paula realized with dread the new problems that now confronted them. The *Tui Cakau* rolled heavily in the opposite direction to *Destiny*'s roll. It seemed impossible that the two vessels could get close enough for them to evacuate. Above her, somber black faces craned over the rails.

As the boat passed her port side, she saw Capt. Hebden far up on the bridge. Their lives were now totally in the hands of this stranger. Only his skill could save them. There were no other rescue vessels within hundreds of miles and there was no sign that the storm would abate. The stranger on the bridge had the power to pluck them from the sea, to rescue them from the hell in which they had cowered for an eternity. Or he could fail—a thought too horrible to contemplate.

Capt. Hebden had been on duty for 24 hours. Strangely, he did not feel tired. He was totally focused on his mission to save lives.

The truth was, it wasn't just his skill that counted. The sum of all the skills of all the crew of the *Tui Cakau* would decide whether the rescue attempt was successful or not. One slip, and the couple would die. One mistake at any time would have them crushed under the freighter's side. *Destiny* would shatter into hundreds of pieces. Her crew would be hurled into the sea, carried away, scuffing and tumbling in the cresting waves.

Capt. Hebden fought with the controls, thrusting them into reverse to slow the ship, using the bow thrusters to keep her nose to weather. But the wind kept pushing her down the swell. He thrust the controls into reverse on full power, with the rudders to starboard, at the same time forcing the bow thrusters on full throttle to port so that the combined force of the power would shove the ship closer to *Destiny*.

Paula stared in horror. The *Tui Cakau*'s stern lifted out of the sea. The big ship was so close, it sprayed water all over Paula. As her propellers spun at the top of a wave, her bow fell down the other side. The engines roared their protest above the shrieking of the wind and the crashing of the sea. The propellers seemed to pull *Destiny* toward the vessel's sheer cliffs of blue steel.

The *Tui Cakau* rolled and pitched and roared as Capt. Hebden fought to control her. He could see now that this approach wasn't going to work. The side of the ship crashed into *Destiny*'s bow, smashing her pulpit. *I've misjudged it*, he thought. *I've got to get out of this.* He'd have to go around and try again. He pushed ahead on full power and burst away from *Destiny*, leaving Paula staring up at the side of the ship, convinced the wake would suck her under the stern.

Well, Capt. Hebden thought as the ship rolled violently, *she's not impressed with that one, is she?* He saw Paula ducking inside the companionway.

Dana lay paralyzed in his bunk below, terrified as the noise and the ship's shadow passed over the portlight in his cabin. Then, as quickly as it appeared, it was gone.

"What happened? What happened?" Dana wanted to know as

Paula appeared below. Her face was drained of color from the shock of the experience above.

"We almost got sucked under the stern and into the propeller," she said. "It was sucking us sideways. I could hear the engine and see the churning water. It, it was just awful. I don't think they can get us off." Hopelessness and fear seeped into her soul. "Maybe we should stay on *Destiny*," she said.

Capt. Hebden had a new plan. "Look," he said to the Second Mate, "I can't hold her with the wind aft. We'll have to attempt a go from directly downwind of the yacht."

On that course, heading straight into the wind and swells toward *Destiny*, the *Tui Cakau* would pitch, raising and dropping her bow and her stern, rather than roll. It would be a much safer motion for the rescue. But, even using the full power of the bow thrusters and the engines, he wouldn't be able to keep her pointed into the wind and alongside *Destiny* for long. And it was still risky.

Nevertheless, he had to try. There wasn't much choice. It was too rough to chance sending his men across in a small boat. The only way to get the Americans off the yacht would be to place his 450-foot-long ship alongside their 45-foot yacht and hold her there long enough for his men to slip down the side, board *Destiny*, and assist her occupants to scramble up the ship's sheer, four-story-high steel hull.

While he held the *Tui Cakau* steady, eight pairs of strong Fijian hands would lower his two volunteers over the side in a life raft. A gangway net and a boarding ladder would be secured on the ship's side, just in case they had to climb up from the boat. It seemed an ambitious strategy in hurricane-force winds, but there was no alternative.

Suddenly, the conditions changed. The wind unexpectedly eased to a mere gale. Capt. Hebden reacted quickly. Here was his chance.

The ship's radio operator told Paula to prepare for another rescue attempt. She reluctantly returned to the cockpit to receive the lines they said they would shoot across to her. Dana, terrified at their prospects for survival after the shock of the first futile attempt, tried to get out of his bunk. But the pain was too much.

The *Tui Cakau* approached *Destiny* a second time, rising and plunging in the swell. Capt. Hebden braced himself against the motion, focused on the job in hand.

They're meant to live, he told himself. *The wind has dropped. They're not meant to die.*

On the weather deck below, men held the lines to the life raft. The two rescuers waited for the order to jump in and be lowered down the ship's side. Other men stood ready with a rocket, to fire a line over *Destiny*. Paula stood by to secure the line. It would hold the yacht alongside the ship long enough for them to escape.

The *Tui Cakau* inched closer. They fired the rocket. The wind caught it and it veered away from its target.

"Why did you shoot so high?" a voice shouted.

Dana heard the noise of the rocket being fired, but he had no idea what was going on outside, only that the ship seemed to be terrifyingly close. It loomed above him like an evil black shadow, darkening the portholes.

Paula braced herself on deck, awed by the huge bow bearing down on her, then sweeping past at what seemed excessive speed. The men above rained lines down on her as the *Tui Cakau* drifted closer to *Destiny*. She grabbed one and made it fast around a winch. A gangway net and a pilot ladder hung enticingly over the side.

As the *Tui Cakau* came alongside, Capt. Hebden again used all his piloting skill. He gunned the bow thruster to port and gave full thrust forward to one engine while he powered the other in reverse. He held the rudders full to starboard. With the wind and the engines working against each other the *Tui Cakau* sat alongside the little boat, acting as a breakwater.

But nothing could prevent the final jarring contact between the two vessels rolling, rising, and falling at different rates in those giant seas. The sickening "crack" of metal splitting fiberglass pierced the storm's crescendo as *Destiny* smashed into the *Tui Cakau*. It was as if she had screamed in pain. Part of the yacht's caprail tore away, and she lurched back, bouncing off the unyielding metal wall. Paula fell backward on the deck. She picked herself up and quickly jumped back into the cockpit, out of the way of the plummeting life raft. Again *Destiny* crashed and lurched sideways as she scraped along the freighter's side.

Below in his bunk, Dana was terrified. He felt like a trapped animal. He listened to the explosive sound of the engines churning the water outside as Capt. Hebden worked the controls in his battle to keep the *Tui Cakau* alongside *Destiny*. The yacht rolled and crashed against the ship, and once again the sound of splintering fiberglass echoed through the cabin.

The two vessels collided time and again, throwing Paula across the deck and jostling Dana in his bunk below. The looming steel wall beside his head terrified him. The recurring, deafening grinding made him fear the ship would crack his cabin open like the shell of an egg.

Either I'm going to stay here and die, or I'm going to stand up and get out of this square I'm in, Dana thought. With that, he lifted himself up. The pain that shot through his limbs was overshadowed by his fear and his determination to save his life.

He grabbed the overhead handholds and pulled himself along, hand over hand, dragging his useless leg through the water that splashed beneath him. Hobbling on his good leg, he pulled himself to the companionway steps. As he hung on with both arms, he wondered how he would swing his damaged limb up and out through the entrance. Then he saw Paula. She was hanging precariously on a gangway net wrapped around the ship's life raft, holding on by her hands, her feet dangling in space as the ship rose upward in the swell, taking Paula with it. His pain was so great, Dana was sure he would pass out.

As the life raft had been lowered toward her, Paula had tried to position herself to jump into it as it landed on the yacht, but she had been forced to lurch toward the companionway to avoid being crushed as it crashed to the deck.

Before she could decide what to do next, a big Fijian, the former soldier Joeli Susu, jumped out and grabbed her, Capt. Hebden's words still ringing in his ears. "Get them off. No arguments. Just get them off. The first thing you do is get the lady and throw her into the life raft. Ignore it if she wants to stay with her husband. Get them out." Susu knew he had to act swiftly to save not only their lives, but his own as well.

"I'm here to save you," he said by way of introduction. Voices from above shouted, urging her to get into the raft.

Paula clung to a bag into which she had packed a few meager possessions—passports, money, and other documents. Susu grabbed the bag and tossed it into the life raft, and before Paula could comprehend what was happening she was hurled toward the rubber craft.

I can't miss it, she thought, but at that moment the boats rolled apart. Paula missed the life raft but managed to grab the net surrounding it, and clung to it desperately. At that moment, the line holding the two vessels snapped.

"Oh no! Oh no!" Paula screamed as her left hand started to lose its grip on the wet net. She looked down at the maelstrom below as it yawned up in one last determined attempt to claim her. Without the tether the boats drifted farther apart.

Dana peered out of the companionway in horror. *She'll be crushed between the boats,* he thought.

Paula heard someone yelling at her: "Get your legs up. You've got to get your legs up the side."

She struggled to comply. Then, suddenly, large hands grabbed her. Valagotavuivui, the second Fijian volunteer, took her by the arms and the seat of her pants, and yanked her up and into the raft, which was quickly hauled up to the deck of the ship.

She staggered when she reached the deck, and they steadied her. She looked over the side for Dana, but she couldn't see him. She wanted desperately to see him. She might never see him again. She wanted to stay, but they led her away to the sick bay. She was too weak to resist.

On the wing of the bridge, Capt. Hebden had his own problems. The Chief Engineer had warned him to cut back on power; the engines were overheating under the stress of jockeying the propellers against the drive of the bow thrusters and the rudders. *Only a few minutes more,* he thought. *That's all we need.*

The crew of the *Tui Cakau* had sent more lines down to Susu to help secure *Destiny* closer to the ship again, and Valagotavuivui descended to join him.

Dana, standing in the yacht's companionway, thought: *I'm going to die here.* He recoiled as the pain stabbed him again. *I'll be killed next time the boats collide. I've got to get out of here.*

Before he could move, the two Fijians descended on him.

"Oh good, you can stand. Good. Come up and get on the ladder," one of them said.

"I can't even move. I've got to have a stretcher."

They yelled to the *Tui Cakau* in a language he did not understand. An old canvas stretcher, a relic from World War II, appeared from nowhere.

In the cabin, Dana hung from overhead handholds while the men secured the stretcher firmly around him. The pain was indescribable, searing through his damaged ribs and his shattered leg. Then they lowered him to a horizontal position and got him to the foot of the companionway steps. There they tilted him upward again and tried to carry him up the steps into the cockpit. It was a difficult task. It took all their strength and agility to haul Dana's 200-pound weight up and through the narrow passageway while the yacht jerked and bumped unpredictably against the ship. There were no secure footholds anywhere. The men fell over him and over themselves as *Destiny* tossed and rolled viciously. Time after time, they picked themselves up and dragged Dana a few feet farther before another wave smashed the two boats together and they were knocked off their feet again.

Finally, they dragged him into the cockpit. There they fastened lifting lines around the stretcher near his feet, his hips, and his head. Pain shot through his body as they tightened the lines around him.

Then the line from the ship to the foot of the stretcher tightened as the vessels rolled apart. Dana was dragged along the deck. Only *Destiny's* port lifelines saved him from falling into the sea still trussed to the stretcher.

The Fijians dashed after him but were knocked down as the ship and the yacht rolled and smashed into each other. The men picked themselves up and pulled him from the side of the yacht before he could slip overboard and be crushed when the ship crashed against *Destiny* again.

Dana looked about him, totally confused and delirious. *Where's the land?* he wondered. The combination of pain, exhaustion, medication, shock, and hypothermia was taking its toll. Off and on, over the hours of his ordeal, he'd imagined he was in a cove surrounded by mountains, not in an angry ocean of enormous waves.

After being hoisted a little way into the air, he slammed hard against the side of the *Tui Cakau*. As the ship rolled, he swung far out and then hurtled back toward the freighter's steel sides again, striking even harder.

The hoisting stopped and he grabbed the lifting line, trying to relieve the pain it caused as it cut into his damaged ribs.

He yelled as, once again, he swung out from the ship's side. "Oh, no!" He knew what would follow. He braced himself. The stretcher rammed into the side of the freighter again. He felt a new pain shoot through his back. The ship rolled to starboard and he plunged down toward *Destiny*.

But suddenly he felt himself being lifted at full speed. He reached the ship's gunwale. People pinned him down. They held him tightly to stop him falling back into the sea that had tried so relentlessly to claim him. Then they gently lowered him onto the *Tui Cakau's* deck as his two rescuers clambered up to the deck and safety. It had all happened with bewildering speed.

Dana looked up at the Fijians' smiling faces. He was safe, but he would never again see *Destiny*, the faithful vessel that had been his home and companion for seven years. He felt he had failed her.

On the bridge, Capt. Hebden was relieved. It was over. He'd managed to hold the ship steady long enough to get the couple off in some of the worst possible conditions for a rescue. Thank God his crew were safe as well. Miraculously, the lethal lip near the ship's waterline had not lifted out of the water above *Destiny*. Had it done so, it would have crushed her and those on board.

Above the *Tui Cakau*, the crew of the circling Orion cheered at the news of the successful rescue. But there was no time for celebration. The plane banked and set off to search for *Quartermaster*. She still had not reported her position. As they flew away, the crew of the Orion told Capt. Hebden that he might be required to assist another yacht, *Sofia*. She was 80 miles to the south.

CHAPTER 7

THEY LOOK LIKE STUNNED MULLETS

≣≣≣

Under the remnants of their spray dodger on board *Ramtha*, Bill and Robyn Forbes hunched over the red glow of the compass light. They had huddled like this for hours while Bill fought to control the helm. It was exhausting. Waves had attacked *Ramtha* relentlessly, slamming against her, pushing her sideways down their steep ridges, trying to lift her hulls high enough for the wind to snatch them and roll them over completely. Torrential rain had drummed on the flimsy, flapping canvas of the dodger. Curling waves had crashed around them like storm-tossed surf pounding on a beach.

But now something had changed. Something was different. At first Robyn had trouble identifying it. Then she realized. They were bathed in light!

She moved out of the shelter of the dodger and stared in awe at a green orb that hovered to port, illuminating the angry world about them. She couldn't believe her eyes.

It was impossible to pinpoint the exact source of the light. It was unlike anything she'd experienced before, certainly completely different from the lightning that had shattered the darkness earlier in the evening.

"Bill, come and look at this," she called.

"What the hell is it?" he asked. He didn't think it was an electrical storm because its light lingered and gradually turned white and then orange, lending an eerie hue to the impenetrable cloud cover.

"It's changed from green to white. Now it's going orange," Robyn said. "It's right above us, right above the mast."

"I've never seen anything like it. What is it? It's massive."

As an aircraft pilot, Bill believed he had seen every type of lightning, but he had never encountered anything like this.

"Maybe it's a fireball. It's not lightning," he mused. "It's just hovering."

"I've never seen a fireball," Robyn said thoughtfully.

The watch officer aboard the New Zealand Navy survey ship *Monowai* also was puzzled by a white light he saw in the distance. He thought it was a flare, and sent a message to the ship's captain, Cmdr. Larry Robbins, who was in his cabin trying to sleep.

"That's a bit of a puzzle," he said as he listened to the officer's description of the sighting. "White is not a sign of distress and we haven't been told there are any vessels on our track."

By the time he arrived on the bridge, the light had disappeared. After a further briefing, he took the VHF microphone and spoke into it, confident that any vessel within 40 miles would hear him: "Would any vessel firing a white flare please report."

Robyn and Bill heard the radio crackle to life, but the voice on the other end broke up and was lost in electronic clutter.

"Do you think they're calling us, or someone else in the area?" Robyn asked. She swung herself through the companionway and reached for the radio to respond. Battling poor reception, the two vessels finally managed to understand each other.

As he listened to Robyn's response, Cmdr. Robbins noticed the log book recorded that the Officer of the Watch had sighted a white "flare" at 0421. He established that *Ramtha* was an Australian catamaran, registered in Brisbane, and she was making good a course of 065 degrees in very unpleasant and difficult conditions.

Robyn told Cmdr. Robbins they had not lit a flare. She described the strange light to him, how it had been green, then changed to white, and then orange. She also outlined the pounding the storm had given them. *Ramtha's* mainsail had blown out and her self-steering was inoperable, she added. But they were coping with the conditions and did not require assistance. Cmdr. Robbins noted the conversation and passed the details onto the RCC in New Zealand.

After *Windora* had assisted them with steering repairs off the New Zealand coast, *Ramtha* had spent the night drifting behind her sea anchor. Bill had been queasy and tired from crouching in the engine room, fixing the steering quadrant. But when they awoke next morning, they found the 300-foot sea-anchor warp was hanging directly below them instead of straining ahead and holding them bows-on to the wind and sea. They tried to trip it, so they could pull it back on board, but the tripping mechanism failed to work. *Ramtha's* winches could not drag the extended sea anchor on board. Reluctantly, Bill capitulated to the sea. He slashed the warp and let the sea anchor sink.

A couple of days of good sailing followed. The southwesterly wind gradually turned to the east, leading them to believe they had at last reached the edge of the southeast trade winds. *Ramtha* was reveling in the conditions, skimming over the 6-foot swell at 15 knots.

But Robyn became apprehensive after hearing a radio call. "They say a low is forming off Fiji," she told Bill.

He allayed her fears. "That's 600 miles away," he said. "We're at 28 degrees south. We'll be okay."

"It'll probably head toward Australia anyway," she said.

"Yeah. We're about halfway to Tonga, soon be crossing the date line, so we'll just keep going."

Having made such good progress on their way to Tonga, they felt they should now contact the radio station at Tonga's Royal Sunset Hotel, rather than Kerikeri Radio. Jon Cullen had enough boats on his schedule, and the regatta organizers had arranged for relays through the local station.

The next evening, Friday, June 3, the radio operator at the Royal Sunset warned *Ramtha*, along with several other yachts in the regatta, that they were in the path of the low-pressure system that had, indeed, formed off Fiji. The broadcast urged skippers at Minerva Reef to flee the area and to take evasive action if at all possible.

"Jeez, six o'clock at night is not the time to be getting out of an atoll," Robyn observed. "It looks like it's going to be another Lady Musgrave," she added, referring to the first significant gale they had experienced in *Ramtha*.

Fifty-knot gales had caught them a couple of times previously, but their first one, the one they experienced off Lady Musgrave Island, was still indelibly etched on their minds. They found comfort in the knowledge that they'd successfully coped with extreme conditions five years previously at the southern extremity of the Great Barrier Reef.

Now, as they headed toward Tonga, they changed to a storm jib and put two reefs in the main to slow the boat down. The wind built from the east, touching 30 knots, then 40. Throughout Friday night they tacked and tried various courses that would take them away from the storm center. But *Ramtha* seemed to be drawn deeper and deeper into the vortex, no matter what they did. By the afternoon of Saturday, June 4, they were in the thick of it. The wind was blowing 50 knots. Then it changed direction to the northeast and dropped to mere gale force. The seas, already large, became increasingly choppy and confused.

"The change may mean it [the storm center] has gone through," Robyn suggested. "We should get some rest."

The clouds lifted, revealing blue sky between their scattering forms, and replacing the piercing rain with shafts of warm sunlight.

They spent the afternoon in exhausted sleep while *Ramtha* looked after herself as best she could in the gale, slopping about on the confused ocean. It was just as well they got some rest. There would be no sleep for them that night as the wind gradually increased until it was back to more than 50 knots.

While Robyn was on watch and Bill was down below, *Ramtha* slid stern-first down a swell at nearly 3 knots. "We're going backward," she screamed. "The rudders are locked. We're going backward."

She realized she didn't have the strength to handle the helm in these conditions. "I don't know that I'll be able to go on much longer," she called down to Bill. "You'd better come out."

The wind played a violent tune of power, and the ocean performed a frenzied dance to this accompaniment. It demanded an audience and *Ramtha* obliged by lurching and lunging to the music in a senseless jig. So erratic was the boat's movement and so deafening was the storm's symphony, it precluded any possibility of further sleep.

Ramtha danced through the night, twisting, turning, sliding, slithering, and shuddering. Bill battled to keep her moving safely. It was exhausting work. The concentration and stress drained his energy.

As Paula had done for Dana aboard *Destiny* a few hours earlier, Robyn remained in the cockpit beside Bill, talking to him, encouraging him, making him focus on the task of keeping the catamaran upright.

Bill realized how much progress he'd made since the Lady Musgrave storm. Then he had been fearful. His imagination had taken control. Adrenaline had dried his mouth. None of those symptoms were present now as he confronted this much bigger and more dangerous challenge. Although he was tired, he was still in command of himself.

After the Lady Musgrave storm, he and Robyn had vigorously sought self-enlightenment. It was a journey of exploration that had worked miracles. Bill had previously suffered asthma so badly that he was rushed to the hospital in an ambulance on one occasion, and arthritis had partially crippled him. His physicians advised him to accept that he would never fully recover. They suggested he should forsake his dreams of sailing the world's oceans.

Then a chance encounter with a chiropractor changed Bill's life. He and Robyn learned about alternative medicine. They learned how to get their bodies balanced. They found out about their energy levels; about channeling; and about many other aspects of self-healing.

They learned to meditate, and purged themselves of stress, anger, fear, resentment, and jealousy. Their new knowledge transformed them physically, emotionally, and spiritually. To their great joy, Bill's chronic asthma and arthritis disappeared.

Now, in the middle of a Pacific storm, Robyn reflected that they were well equipped to cope with any crisis. Before starting the cruise, they had prepared themselves mentally to conquer as many situations as they could imagine. They had pictured their reactions in situations similar to those in which they now found themselves. Robyn had convinced herself that if *Ramtha* rolled over, they would be all right. She had read books about the capsize of the *Rose Noelle* and other multihulls to learn about survival. She had found out what food and equipment shipwrecked sailors needed to sustain life. She, too, had traveled far on her journey of self-knowledge since the Lady Musgrave storm.

Ramtha now sailed with four reefs in the mainsail. The little triangle of cloth clung stiffly to the mast. But not for long. An extra-hard gust ripped the sail and flattened the spray dodger. Robyn reacted quickly. She fetched two jugs and jammed them under the sides of the collapsed dodger. It formed a forlorn tent under which they huddled, their noses pressed to the compass, as they fought to hold *Ramtha's* heading.

When they had her going steady again, Bill groped his way along the deck to the mast. He tried to lower the flaying shreds of mainsail that flogged and cracked loudly in the wind. But the slides were buckled and refused to drop down the track, no matter how he tugged. He crawled back to the cockpit for a knife to cut the sail free.

"It must be pretty bad out here," he said to Robyn. "We've been in 70 knots before and the dodger's never been affected." He edged back under the flattened shelter. "You'd better let someone know how we're doing and put our position out."

Robyn went below to the radio. "All ships, all ships. Is there anyone listening?" she called.

She was relieved when another sailor, identifying himself simply as Duncan, responded to the call. She gave their position and arranged to call him every hour. The next call was scheduled for 0300 on Sunday, June 5.

Keeping the boat on course was now even more difficult. The noise was deafening and, although there was no phosphorescence, the seething tops of the approaching wave crests glowed dimly in the dark as they engulfed the catamaran. She wobbled uncertainly under their churning foam before bursting free and hurtling down their steep faces, the surf angrily roaring around her and exploding against her sides.

Bill spun the wheel to port and to starboard, trying to anticipate the yacht's heavy lurches. Needles of rain and spray stung and bruised them when they dared put their faces outside the dodger.

"Jeez, it's like going down a mountain in a wooden box," Bill commented.

"Nah, it's like a roller-coaster ride that doesn't end. It just goes on and on," Robyn replied.

Robyn had just completed one of her radio calls to Duncan when a monstrous wave slammed against the side of the catamaran with a resounding crack. *Ramtha* lifted high on her starboard hull and hovered precariously as the sea tried to flip her on her side. But it didn't succeed. She fell back heavily. Bill's harness checked his fall, but Robyn, still in the cabin, was untethered. She was flung through the air, and crashed against the side of the boat.

Aboard the *Monowai*, Cmdr. Robbins was in no doubt about the difficulties *Ramtha*'s crew were encountering. He was experiencing similar discomforts on a ship of 4,000 tons. Earlier in the evening they had been pounded by seas so huge the ship had rolled 48 degrees from vertical, throwing the crew about and damaging equipment. Concerned for the safety of ship and crew, Cmdr. Robbins had reluctantly ordered a course alteration of 50 degrees to put them on a northwest track at reduced speed. It had helped a little, taking the wind and sea off the beam, but she still rolled precariously; at least the changed direction made it a little more bearable for all on board.

They recorded winds of 50 knots, gusting much higher, and logged the sea state at over seven on the international scale, indicating very high seas of 20 to 40 feet. They were making only 4 knots through the storm. The plan was to gain ground to the west until the ship could safely turn and approach the stricken *Mary T* from the north.

The sea was nobody's friend that night. It surged along the *Monowai*'s decks, forcing itself through unlatched doors and unblocked cracks.

Lashings worked free on a refrigerated container on the fo'c's'le. Sailors ventured into the night to tighten the cables and heavy chains holding it. Crashing seas had already tried to snatch an inflatable that was rigged as a sea-boat and stowed nearby. The boat's aluminum bottom boards were ripped out from between the side tubes.

The sea's power was awesome. It washed overboard two large, bomb-shaped weights, each weighing 1,100 pounds, that were used to sink sidescan sonar equipment. It snatched them from secure metal straps, leaving nothing but grooves on the wooden quarterdeck.

Throughout the night, seas pummeled the *Monowai*, testing the 34-year-old ship to the limits of her endurance. Water entered cabins and the galley through submerged ventilators. A heavy safe broke loose from a bulkhead to which it had been secured for as long as the crew had been on the ship. Closer inspection revealed a surprise: The safe had never actually been secured at all.

Officers quickly scrambled out of their bunks to assist the duty watch at 0200 when news spread about a near-disaster in their mess. The beer cooler had come away from its bulkhead. The violent movement of the ship hurled a glass at an officer working to reclaim the cooler, slashing his face. He was one of three people injured aboard the ship during the storm.

Down below, engineers kept a watchful eye on the port engine. A faulty saltwater cooling system had blown the relief valves when the ship traveled at speed. They mistrusted its performance in these atrocious conditions.

Throughout the mayhem, the duty watch on the bridge discussed the white flare that had caught the attention of the Officer of the Watch. No vessel had appeared in the green glow of the radar screen. They had called on VHF Channel 16, the international calling and rescue frequency: "Any vessel firing a white flare make contact."

Through the static on the VHF, they'd established that *Ramtha* had not set off a flare and if there was a vessel requiring assistance it was not them.

"Where are you in regard to our position?" Robyn had inquired.

"About 12 miles away. We're going to another boat in distress."

"Okay. Message understood. We are coping with the conditions," she'd replied.

Bill had mused that if the *Monowai* was so close, he wouldn't be averse to abandoning *Ramtha*. His fight with the sea had been exhausting and, despite the mental preparation he'd undertaken, despondency had crept into the recesses of his mind.

"My husband says if you could take him off now he would go," Cmdr. Robbins had heard Robyn say.

The message was ambiguous. Cmdr. Robbins had been unsure how to respond. Was she saying they were having a dreadful time but, despite the discomfort and danger, they would soldier on? Or did they really want assistance? The *Monowai* already was battling toward the *Mary T*, whose crew were pumping water from the bilges to save their lives. *Mary T* had four exhausted people on board and his priority was to reach them before they were lost to the sea. The severity of the storm had forced him to change course away from the yawl, thereby delaying his time of arrival. The *Mary T*'s plight sounded desperate. Cmdr. Robbins did not want to divert from his route again unless the *Ramtha's* crew were experiencing similarly grave circumstances and required immediate assistance. Indications so far were that they were coping with the conditions and that he should continue plugging along toward the *Mary T.*

"I sympathize with your husband's point of view completely," he'd replied diplomatically. "If somebody could take me off here, I wouldn't stay, either."

An hour or so before dawn on Sunday, Robyn made her hourly call to Duncan. This time it was not Duncan himself, but one of his crew who replied. Duncan's boat also was taking a beating. A bond had grown between the two vessels, born of their common enemy, the storm. Robyn was greatly comforted by the other boat's presence.

A particularly large wave slammed against *Ramtha* and lifted her high in the air just as Robyn entered the companionway.

"Hang on!" Bill yelled.

She saw him tumble backward, out from under the dodger and into the cockpit. She, too, was thrown from her feet and slammed into a bulkhead. *Ramtha* shuddered with one hull in the air. After what seemed a very long time, the hull crashed back onto the crest of a wave. *Ramtha* was still upright.

Bill crawled back to the helm. Water had spilled into the cabin, which was now littered with crockery, cutlery, books, and food.

"The rudders have gone. We've lost our steering," he shouted.

Robyn reached for the VHF and called the *Monowai*: "We just about got tipped over that time. We came close to capsizing."

"What do you want me to do?"

Bill grabbed the microphone from her.

"What's the name of it?" he asked her urgently.

"I've been calling her *Monowai* or something," she responded, perturbed at his action.

Without discussing his decision further with her, Bill told

Cmdr. Robbins what had happened. Now he couldn't steer the catamaran. If it was possible, they needed to be taken off their boat.

"I cannot guarantee the safety of life and limb but if you wish to abandon your vessel I will assist you in any way I can," Cmdr. Robbins replied. "I have to ask you: Are you and your wife relatively spry?"

"Why do they ask that?" Robyn asked. "What are we going to have to do?"

"We'll probably have to jump into cargo nets or something," Bill replied.

"Yes," he responded to the ship's captain. "Do you mean to get in the water? What do you require?"

"We'll discuss the actual procedure when we get some light, but it may get to the stage where you have to leap into the sea tonight."

"No problem," said Bill, sounding more confident than he felt.

"Could you also confirm, please, that you have lifejackets."

"Yes, we're wearing lifejackets. Anything else you suggest we should put on or take off?"

"If you have wetsuits we suggest you put those on and put the lifejacket over the wetsuit."

"Okay. I've got one. My wife's got one."

They asked the *Monowai* again how they would be rescued, but nothing had been settled yet. They'd be informed later.

Robyn turned on all *Ramtha*'s lights, including the deck lights, to enable the *Monowai* to see them if she approached in the darkness.

Cmdr. Robbins discussed the options for a rescue with the First Lieutenant. The Wasp helicopter couldn't operate in such a fierce storm. The traditional ploy of dropping scrambling nets over the ship's side would also be too dangerous. The *Monowai* was rolling so badly, he feared *Ramtha* would be crushed alongside.

Furthermore, the *Monowai* was not easily maneuverable. She was a low-powered vessel with small, twin screws tucked closely together in front of the rudder. On top of that, the engineers were worried about the port main engine.

After considering his options, Cmdr. Robbins told the crew of *Ramtha* he couldn't provide assistance in the darkness. They'd have to wait until sunrise, which was a little over an hour away. Bill inquired about the *Mary T*, and sympathized that Cmdr. Robbins's decision was difficult. But Bill was no longer confident about *Ramtha*'s ability to endure the storm's violence without steering. He said again that he would appreciate being rescued. Cmdr. Robbins assured him he had no intention of continuing toward the *Mary T* without first attempting to rescue *Ramtha*'s crew.

Dawn on June 5 revealed a frightening seascape. The wind raged across the ocean at more than 70 knots, creating seething mountains that rose more than 40 feet. Whitewater rapids tumbled along them and plunged into gushing waterfalls. They, in turn, plummeted down steep ravines.

The *Monowai* rolled through the tempest searching for the catamaran. Spotting a cream hull in these conditions was almost impossible. Officers crowded the bridge, grabbing at handholds as the ship lurched from side to side.

Cmdr. Robbins realized it was Sunday. Silently, he prayed for his ship, his crew, and the bedraggled Australians he intended to rescue. They certainly needed God on their side to protect them during their ordeal.

Down below, the sailors and survey crews assembled on the vehicle deck, all 135 of them. The Executive Officer explained the captain's plan. It was too rough to hold the *Monowai* alongside *Ramtha* because the ship could roll over her and sink her, probably before the Australians were evacuated. Nor was it possible to lower a boat to them, or send the Wasp helicopter out in this weather.

Therefore, they would take the *Monowai* as close as possible to *Ramtha*, and fire a line to the catamaran. Two lifting harnesses of the type used for helicopter rescues would be attached to the line. *Ramtha*'s crew would haul the harnesses aboard and get into them. Finally, the Executive Officer said, the Australians would be dragged through the water and hoisted aboard the *Monowai*.

If any of the ship's crew considered it a bad rescue plan, they held their tongues. There were no practical alternatives. Tasks were delegated to the crew. Two able seamen were selected to fire the lines. A team was chosen to work on the fo'c's'le, exposed to the weather and the sea, and haul the Australians hand over hand to the ship. Lookouts were posted to shout warnings about approaching waves that could wash the rescue party overboard. Lifejackets were mandatory, and safety harnesses with tethers were issued so the crew could secure themselves to the deck.

Cmdr. Robbins talked to the Australians about his rescue plan. When they retrieved the helicopter harnesses, they were to get into them immediately. He would give them other instructions nearer the time.

He advised them to remain in their wetsuits and lifejackets, and to bring personal effects such as passports, money, and documents.

He didn't disclose the rest of his plan. He'd calculated that if they lost consciousness because of the water they swallowed while they were dragged through the sea, there would still be enough life left in them when they were hoisted aboard to enable his crew to resuscitate them on the *Monowai*'s deck.

But even with the light of dawn, they couldn't spot *Ramtha* in the heaving, white-crested seas. Distinguishing her from the waves and spume was nearly impossible. They asked Bill to light a flare, and at last they saw the tiny catamaran as she rose on a swell. The rescue was on.

It was soon obvious that the speed of *Ramtha*'s drift was going to be a problem. The *Monowai*'s radio operator asked Bill to deploy a sea anchor to slow her down. Bill had stowed a set of drogues, comprising warps tied to car tires, at the stern when the first signs of foul weather had threatened. He tossed them overboard. But they didn't work to hold her position. They slowed her, as they were intended to, but *Ramtha* was still drifting too fast for the big ship lumbering in the swell. The distance between them continued to grow until they were about a mile apart.

The survey vessel was not behaving much better herself. Cmdr.

Robbins had her moving, beam-on to the seas, in *Ramtha*'s direction, but the yacht was constantly being blown away from her. The *Monowai* could not outmaneuver the storm; she had neither the pitch in the propellers nor the turning circle to cope with these huge seas and winds now gusting to 80 knots. To make matters worse, the port engine began to lose power. The engineroom watch struggled to keep it going.

Bill Forbes started *Ramtha*'s engines and tried to guide the catamaran toward the ship. Gradually, the catamaran turned through the waves, rolling and lurching alarmingly as he brought her around to face the *Monowai*. Slowly he motored toward her, powering the starboard motor, then the port, to steer her.

"*Ramtha*! Drive into me now! Drive into me now!" Cmdr. Robbins demanded over the radio as the catamaran approached. Her hulls lifted high out of the water, almost throwing her bow over stern, as a giant wave forced her back. *Ramtha* slammed down and continued toward the *Monowai*, where seamen huddled on the fo'c's'le, anxious to shoot out a line as soon as the catamaran came within range.

Bill kept jockeying the engines, but she wouldn't change direction. The wind and seas prevented her from pointing directly toward the *Monowai*. The catamaran continued to move ahead of the ship, only a few feet in front of the *Monowai*'s towering bow. Slowly, very slowly, *Ramtha* cleared the ship rolling above her.

The party on the foredeck rushed to the port side, looking for another chance to shoot their line to the Australians. They skidded and slid on the slippery deck, ducking and grabbing cables and bolts for handholds when the lookouts shouted warnings that tons of water were about to crash over them. Each time they changed position, they had to rearrange the coil of line so it could run free if they got a chance to fire it to the catamaran.

It took almost two hours of maneuvering for Bill to position *Ramtha* close enough for the seamen to fire a line to them. They saw the missile coming their way. Bull's-eye! It landed aboard the yacht. Bill shuffled along the deck and secured the line to a winch. Then the boats rolled in opposite directions and the line snapped. The vessels drifted apart. They had to start all over again.

Three more shots were fired. Robyn and Bill watched with disappointment as two of the missiles approached the boat and then curled away again as the wind caught them. Another got tangled in *Ramtha*'s rigging. The ship's crew quickly slashed their end of the line to avoid any damage if the boats rolled away from each other.

The failed attempts were beginning to take their toll. Despite Robyn's resolve not to surrender to her imagination, fear gripped her when she saw a giant wave explode against the *Monowai*. Robyn pictured herself being picked up by a similar wave, and then being hurled against the ship's side. She imagined her body smashed against it, as if she had fallen six stories to a sidewalk below. How could they ever survive the ordeal of being dragged across this horrible, vicious, merciless sea? Then she got a grip on herself. She was disgusted at her weakness; she would not succumb to her imagination and fear.

They were almost close enough for another shot to be fired, but again the wind and sea pushed them away.

"Jeez, Bill," Robyn said, "we have a good boat here, especially after what it's been through. You sure you want to abandon this boat?"

Bill had decided to build his own catamaran nine years earlier. He'd picked up a magazine on a plane he was piloting and read an article that changed his life. They had sold everything—two properties, horses, and cats—to finance their dream of sailing away. They'd worked long hours to put *Ramtha* together. She'd become their life, assuming much of their personalities. They'd learned to sail in her. Now, after all this, they were on the brink of deserting her.

Robyn called Cmdr. Robbins on the radio. "We'll have to abandon this," she said despondently. "It's not going to work." She was very frustrated at the unsuccessful rescue attempts. She also was a little unsure about whether she really wanted to leave *Ramtha*, her home and her friend. "We can't seem to get the nose around toward you when we get near," she added.

"We'll give it one more try," Cmdr. Robbins replied positively.

"We haven't gone to all this trouble for you to change your mind," he mumbled when his thumb was off the microphone button.

The smell of curry wafted from the galley onto the bridge. It made him suddenly feel very hungry. He glanced at his wristwatch. It was 1000. The last thing he'd had was a cup of tea at 0300. He'd been on the bridge ever since.

The fo'c's'le team emerged from shelter once more. A rifleman dropped into position beside the guardrail, lifted his weapon, and fired. Bill held his breath. The missile went over the starboard hull, just forward of the cockpit. It was coming directly at Robyn, who stepped backward to avoid being hit. Bill shuffled along the deck and retrieved a handful of line, pulling it toward him until he had secured the stout rope to which the harnesses were attached. Without a pause, he secured it firmly to a winch.

They could hear Cmdr. Robbins calling instructions on the radio to Robyn. "The strap goes over your shoulders and under both armpits," he said. "The grommet must be pulled right in, otherwise you'll slip out of the straps. You should check your husband's, and vice versa."

The harnesses resembled horse collars. "Are you sure you want to get into that?" Robyn asked. Bill ignored the question.

The boat lurched again and Robyn fell awkwardly to the deck. Silently, Bill helped her into the harness, then finished securing his own. Both of them were filled with a sense of foreboding.

The arrangement was that the Australians would give a thumbs-up sign to indicate they were ready to evacuate *Ramtha*. Next, the *Monowai*'s siren would signal them to jump into the water. Then the ship's crew would haul them to safety.

As they struggled with the harnesses, another curling breaker exploded against the *Monowai*'s side, rolling her to starboard, away from *Ramtha*. At the same time, a wave struck the catamaran's beam, shoving her in the opposite direction. Without warning, Bill and Robyn were wrenched off the side of their boat and into the water, a stanchion bruising Robyn's ribs as she fell.

This isn't the plan. We haven't signaled. The ship's siren hasn't sounded, she thought as she fell into the sea.

As the ship righted herself, the *Monowai*'s crew tensed, realizing what had happened. They sped into action, pulling the 660-foot line in hand over hand, determined to get the couple aboard before they drowned.

The line went taut, and Robyn and Bill felt themselves being pulled through the water like hooked fish. The whole incident occurred so quickly they had not had time to check each others' harnesses. Robyn's was loose. She twisted around and was dragged backward, totally submerged in the sea.

On the bridge, Cmdr. Robbins had the emergency stops ready. He was concerned that the unpredictable seas could inadvertently carry the *Monowai* over the warp to which the Australians were attached. If the ship's propellers chewed through the line, there would be no hope of saving the couple. They would be whisked away by the wind, and disappear forever.

Robbins had seen Bill helping Robyn into her harness, but they disappeared as he grabbed a handhold when the ship rolled. As the *Monowai* righted herself, he saw them bounce along *Ramtha*'s deck and into the water.

"Did the line get free or was it caught on a lifeline?" he queried his crew, momentarily alarmed.

"They're okay. They're free of *Ramtha*," he was assured.

"I told them to wait for the horn," Cmdr. Robbins said lightly, relieving the tension on the bridge.

"The headline in the newspaper will be: 'Navy Jerks Off Yachties,'" someone quipped.

Bill resurfaced, gasping for air, and glanced around to find Robyn. She was still under water, struggling to turn herself to face the right direction.

She's not going to make it. She'll drown, he thought in panic. The line pulled him, and he went under water again, dragged helplessly through the mountainous sea.

"Get your breath!" Bill called weakly to Robyn when they both surfaced again. Robyn kicked herself around in the harness to face the right way. Suddenly, the line went taut and they were submerged again.

Just relax. The lifejacket will bring you to the surface, so don't worry about it, Robyn calmed herself as she sped through the water. *I'm not going to drown. I'm not going to drown now. If I take in water, they'll be able to pump it out.*

Her eyes were open! She was underneath the surface of the Pacific Ocean, being pulled along like a gamefish on the end of a trolling line; the water was rushing past her and she had her eyes open. She marveled that she could actually see.

Suddenly they were in the air, dangling on the end of a white torpedo davit that leaned out above them.

Oh, I'm okay. We've made it, Robyn thought. She could feel Bill beside her. *I haven't taken in any water. I'm all right.*

"Are you all right?" Bill called to her. He swung his legs toward the hands trying to grab him.

"He's on!" A cry went out on the bridge as they hit the deck.

"You guys are great," Bill said to their rescuers.

"They look like stunned mullets," someone on the bridge commented.

A spontaneous cheer went up from the ship's crew. They applauded the Australians, their captain, the officers, themselves, and the *Monowai*. Nobody doubted they had been part of a remarkable rescue.

"How unusual," Cmdr. Robbins observed about the spontaneous jubilation. New Zealanders were usually so restrained, a relic of their British origins.

Down to leeward, *Ramtha* drifted aimlessly away from them in the distance, her motors still idling and her companionway door open, vulnerable to the violent sea in which she had struggled so valiantly to survive.

"Well done, sir."

Cmdr. Robbins turned to acknowledge the compliment. He recognized the sailor and felt buoyed by the sight. Before him stood a man he had severely disciplined a few days earlier.

"Thank you," he said, concealing his delight that the seaman now felt so much a part of the team that he was moved to congratulate his captain. For Cmdr. Robbins, it was one of the happiest consequences of the rescue.

Destiny *after being pitchpoled by a wave. (Courtesy Royal New
Zealand Air Force)*

Destiny *alongside the* Tui Cakau III. *(Courtesy Royal New
Zealand Air Force)*

*The naval vessel Monowai's inclinometer showing a roll of 35
degrees. An electronic inclinometer aboard indicated a maximum
roll of 48 degrees—dangerously close to the point of no return.
(Courtesy Royal New Zealand Navy)*

*The Monowai rolls heavily to starboard as she approaches the
38-foot Australian catamaran, Ramtha. The yacht's mast is barely
visible, fine on the port bow. (Courtesy Royal New Zealand Navy)*

The crippled Ramtha *tries to motor toward the* Monowai.
(Courtesy Royal New Zealand Navy)

Ramtha's *crew awaits rescue. (Courtesy Royal New Zealand Navy)*

The crew of the Monowai *prepares to fire a lifeline to Bill and Robyn Forbes aboard* Ramtha. *(Courtesy Royal New Zealand Navy)*

The Forbeses, after abandoning their yacht, are dragged in helicopter harnesses through tumultuous seas to the Monowai. *(Courtesy Royal New Zealand Navy)*

Bill and Robyn about to be hauled aboard the Monowai. They did not have time to adjust their harnesses correctly before leaving Ramtha, and were dragged part of the way under water. (Courtesy Royal New Zealand Navy)

A rigid-hulled inflatable from the Monowai *warily approaches the disabled 32-foot American cutter,* Pilot, *in big seas. (Courtesy Royal New Zealand Air Force)*

The injured skipper of Silver Shadow, *Peter O'Neil, is hoisted aboard the* Monowai *strapped to a stretcher. (Courtesy Royal New Zealand Navy)*

Richard Jackson and John McSherry, crew from Silver Shadow, *share a helicopter harness as the* Monowai's *crew hauls them aboard. (Courtesy Royal New Zealand Navy)*

Perilous moments for the crew of the Mono- *wai's damaged tender— Leading Seaman Abraham Whata, Able Seaman Linton Hemopo, and Leading Medical Assistant Michael Wiig—as rough seas flood over the bow. All three men received official commendations for bravery after rescuing* Silver Shadow's *crew. (Courtesy Royal New Zealand Navy)*

Dismasted, and battered by storm-force winds, the 32-foot wooden double-ender Sofia *awaits rescue by the French warship,* Jacques Cartier. *(Courtesy Royal New Zealand Air Force)*

Following seas loom above Waikiwi II's *cockpit. (Courtesy Cath Gilmour,* Waikiwi II)

The New Zealand 44-footer, Waikiwi II, *drifts helplessly in violent storm conditions after being rolled and losing her mast. (Courtesy Royal New Zealand Air Force)*

A stern view of the disabled Heart Light *shows the large, open cockpit and vulnerable ports. She is taking on water through a crack in a hull. (Courtesy David Hughes, a crewmember aboard the* San Te Maru 18)

The final moments, as Heart Light *capsizes to port. She sank shortly afterward. (Courtesy David Hughes, a crewmember aboard the* San Te Maru 18)

Quartermaster's *empty life raft scuds along before heavy winds and seas. Evidence suggests that one or more of* Quartermaster's *three crew had been aboard the raft. No trace was found of them or the yacht. (Courtesy Royal New Zealand Air Force)*

CHAPTER 8

THOSE BEACONS ARE LIFESAVERS

As the Hercules C130 aircraft staggered through the squall, two observers searched the sea close below. They held on tightly as the old aircraft ricocheted off air currents.

"Five Squadron can keep their jobs," one of the spotters remarked. "I wouldn't swap with them for anything." The others on board agreed.

Number 40 Squadron was proud of its history of transporting New Zealand's military and peacekeeping forces around the world. The squadron had supported Allied forces during the Persian Gulf War, and had carried anything from troops to bulldozers. They had assisted in Rwanda, and were currently preparing to take a peace-keeping force to Bosnia. Next summer, they would fly to Antarctica. But, despite its versatility, the Hercules hadn't been designed for search-and-rescue missions. Its inadequacies in this respect were becoming acutely obvious as the crew peered through the rain to the tumultuous ocean below.

A few minutes earlier, as he'd taken the aircraft down to 500 feet, Sqd. Ldr. Peter Mount had depressurized the interior, allowing the observers to open the side doors and take their positions to hunt for the yacht *Quartermaster*. This was their first search-and-rescue mission and, although Number 40 Squadron had previously been placed on standby to back up the Orions, nobody on the flight deck could recall the Hercules actually having been commandeered for this work in the past.

"I can't see why they enjoy it," the spotter continued, pulling on the tether anchored to the floor of the empty cargo bay to ensure it was secure. "Bloody boring work."

Rivalry between the squadrons was keen. The 10 crew aboard the Hercules relished the opportunity to prove their squadron's search-and-rescue prowess to the Orion crews.

After the RCC had called him, Sqd. Ldr. Mount had searched the base for a crew. Eventually he cobbled together two copilots, a couple of navigators, and an engineer to fly the aircraft; and two load masters and two maintenance men to act as observers.

They'd prepared for the flight throughout the previous day. Thirty tons of fuel were taken aboard; by shutting down two engines and feathering propellers, the Hercules could remain aloft for perhaps 12 hours. Fuel was provided for the crew as well: bread, tomatoes, ham, cheese, and bacon for sandwiches. Cold food was all they'd get; the Hercules' galley facilities were primitive. In the conditions they were about to experience, they'd be lucky to get a hot cup of coffee.

The rescue coordination center summoned them at 0300 on Sunday. The RCC's instructions were to relieve the Orion monitoring *Destiny*, and to organize contact with a vessel heading to assist yet another stricken yacht.

By the time the Hercules was commissioned, the core of the storm was raging over an area approximately 300 miles in diameter. The crews of *Destiny* and *Ramtha* had been rescued, but skippers aboard other yachts reported being battered by huge seas. They estimated winds were gusting to 100 knots at times. The fate of *Quartermaster* particularly concerned the rescue center. Contact with her crew had been lost, and their plight was undoubtedly extremely serious.

The Hercules was ordered to search for another three boats in distress. The exercise was rapidly becoming one of the largest search-and-rescue missions ever mounted in the South Pacific.

Flying the Hercules for a search mission was a complex art. Its wingspan was greater than the Orion's, and the fuselage was considerably shorter. Consequently, as it rumbled and rattled 500 feet above the sea, the storm tossed it around much more vigorously than it would an Orion. Sqd. Ldr. Mount had reduced speed to 140 knots to allow the observers to watch from open doors, and it was difficult to maintain control of the airplane while flying at such slow speeds. With the ocean close below, Sqd. Ldr. Mount was on constant alert for sudden down drafts.

Their first search was for *Sofia*, the 32-foot double-ender crewed by Keith Levy and his 25-year-old companion, Uschi Schmidt. *Sofia*'s EPIRB was transmitting a distress signal. They soon homed in on her and saw that she had been badly damaged by boarding seas. Not even the mast remained. *Sofia*'s crew talked to the Hercules on their handheld VHF radio, and reported they were in reasonable condition, considering their ordeal.

When this news was passed onto RCC, the Hercules was instructed to leave *Sofia* for the time being, and to hunt for *Heart Light*, whose EPIRB also was transmitting. A short time later they found her. She appeared to be intact; at least the mast was still standing. But after contacting her by radio, they learned *Heart Light* had a cracked hull and was taking on water.

Her crew put on a brave face. They were confident they could ride out the storm. But, beneath the facade, there was obvious nervousness. They asked the Hercules crew how much it might cost them for a tow, and whether they might be able to repair the boat and save their possessions.

"All we want is for you to keep an eye on us so that if anything happens you know where we are," they informed the Hercules. "We reckon we can ride it out."

The woman aboard *Heart Light* was loath to stop talking. Reluctantly, the air crew explained they had to leave to check on other yachts requiring assistance. They sympathized with the woman and comforted her as best they could, assuring her they would maintain communications until assistance arrived. In fact, all the boats were so close to each other, they could easily keep in contact with everyone, even while they searched for other boats in distress.

The Hercules flew off in search of the sloop *Silver Shadow*. She had reported being rolled 360 degrees. But, while they were flying toward her, they picked up the signal of yet another EPIRB, and the vessel *Brigadoon* contacted them on VHF Channel 16. It was going to be a busy day.

Sqd. Ldr. Mount started the familiar grid-pattern search for *Silver Shadow*, starting from her last known position. Visibility was down to about 1,000 feet, and long before any of the spotters could detect *Silver Shadow*, the aircraft's direction finder locked onto the EPIRB. They noted its bearing and flew at it once more from a different angle. They repeated the exercise a third time and then plotted the three bearings. Within seconds they were flying directly over *Silver Shadow*.

"Those beacons are lifesavers," Sqd. Ldr. Mount said to his copilot. "No one should be allowed out without them."

They turned back for a second pass over the boat but, this time, she could not be seen. She was buried in the foam and murk. Returning for a third time, one of the observers threw a smoke flare out of the door, and it landed close to the boat. Turning back, they glimpsed the flare's smudge on the water in the distance but could not detect the yacht's white hull or gray decks as they passed over again.

There was no response to the Hercules' radio call. Only the clicking of a microphone switch could be heard. The yacht's radio obviously would not transmit voices, just the sound of the switch being depressed when a conversation began and ended.

"We can talk to them, but they can't talk to us," someone aboard the Hercules realized. "I think the clicking is their transmitter keying."

"See if they can click answers to us."

They asked *Silver Shadow*'s radio operator to depress his mike once to indicate "no," and twice to indicate "yes." And then began the most ingenious exchange of information of the whole rescue operation. For 20 minutes, the Hercules gathered information about the yacht crew's condition, using the code.

"Is anyone injured?"

Click. Click. (Yes.)

"How many are injured? Give one click for each person injured."

Click. (One.)

The air crew then called over the radio the various parts of the body that could be injured, receiving a single click each time until they mentioned "shoulder." Two clicks. A crewmember had a broken shoulder. They ascertained the victim was in stable condition, but not very comfortable. The rest of the crew were unscathed, and they had sufficient water and food on board.

"On a scale of one to five, how serious do you think your situation is?"

Click. Click. (Average.)

"We have your position and we understand you are reasonably comfortable. We have a lot of others to find and we'll be in the area until about 1600. An Orion will be back before we leave. We'll come back and talk to you before then to let you know what's happening, and when the rescue will be effected.

"It'll probably be lunchtime Monday before you can expect somebody in the area," Sqd. Ldr. Mount told them before leaving to search for *Quartermaster*.

Throughout its sortie, the Hercules kept in touch with the Rescue Coordination Centre, supplying them with information that determined the priority of each search mission. The RCC was controlling the whole rescue operation from an air-conditioned operations room more than 800 miles away. The air crews were their eyes, and the accuracy of their information was vital.

No one was sure how many yachts had actually activated EPIRBs because so many were transmitting simultaneously. It was possible that some of the signals they were receiving from EPIRBs were actually "shadows" of locater signals from boats they had already identified. The only way they could get a true picture was to ask some of the boats to switch off their EPIRBs briefly.

It was quite a lot to ask. The crews in trouble knew their boats were almost invisible from the air. The EPIRBs were their tenuous link with safety. If they turned them off, they risked never being found again. The air crew tried to allay their fears. They discussed the reasons for switching off the EPIRBs, and assured the yachts that the sonar locater beacons they'd dropped beside each vessel would still be transmitting strongly long after the EPIRBs had stopped. To their credit, the yachts cooperated.

The RCC was now so concerned about the size of the flotilla in the area, and the increasing number of distress calls being transmitted, that it seriously considered commandeering a New Zealand Navy frigate. The second Orion P3 that had overseen the rescue of *Destiny* was low on fuel and about to return to base. The crew of Kiwi 315 was recuperating in Fiji, its engineers dealing with the engine oil leak.

Instructing *Heart Light* and *Sofia* to turn off their EPIRBs was not the only tough call Bill Sommer and his team made that weekend. They evaluated the seriousness of each situation and allocated priorities. Was the injured sailor on *Silver Shadow* more of a priority than the crew of the *Mary T*? Should *Monowai* steam toward *Mary T*? How serious was *Mary T*'s leak, and how long could her exhausted crew continue to win their pumping race with the sea? The RCC staff had not only the yachts to worry about. Telephone calls flooded in from next of kin and the media.

After the media began publishing news of the havoc and destruction, inquiries came from as far away as Britain, Scandinavia, and the United States. Interpol was brought in to contact relatives of crewmembers, as were police in the United States, Britain, and Australia. And relatives of the Rimmers had to be kept informed about dwindling hopes for *Quartermaster* and her crew.

The RCC searched computer records to identify merchant ships in the area that might be able to provide assistance. A French naval ship, the *Jacques Cartier*, heading toward New Zealand on a goodwill visit, was asked to help *Sofia*, and a commercial fishing vessel, the *San Te Maru 18*, was requested to steam toward *Heart Light*.

Aboard the *Mary T*, spirits were low because of Kerikeri Radio's request for information about their next of kin. They could see no reason for informing family 6,000 miles away in America about difficulties they were encountering in the South Pacific. After all, what could their families do, apart from worry? It was not as if a Pan call was a sign that they were about to die. The next of kin request from Kerikeri Radio was chilling to everyone eavesdropping on the unfolding drama. It signaled hopelessness; after all, they wouldn't ask for that information unless they believed the *Mary T*'s crew was on the brink of death, would they? Carol's mother was a sprightly 76-year-old. They had talked a couple of days earlier on the ham radio. There didn't seem to be any justification for alarming her now. After some persuasion, Carol gave Jon Cullen Lianne's brother's phone number, knowing he wouldn't unduly concern her mother.

But without Carol's knowledge, police in the United States contacted Lianne Audette's brother. He, in turn, telephoned Carol's mother. Eventually, her mother did receive a message from officialdom: Carol was battling a Force 9 storm, *Mary T* was sinking, and it was not known whether anyone would be saved. She was not given the latest reports stating they were coping adequately and all aboard were well.

In fact, conditions aboard *Mary T* were improving slightly, as Jon Cullen found when he contacted them later in the day:

Jon: As far as your families are concerned, they have been contacted and as soon as you clear your Pan call we will also advise them. Over.

Carol: Thank you very much. We still would like to hold on that until the weather improves a little bit more. Over.

Jon: Roger. Okay. I understand. Okay now, the RCC would like you to check the stern gland and any internal possibilities for leakages and, if you're happy that it's basically on topsides, then we'd feel a lot happier about that. Over.

Carol: Roger. We have established the stern gland is secure. We also checked all the through-hulls. We checked all the internal leakages that we could think of. We think it's through the deck, possibly through the cockpit. We did reglass the whole of the deck, but didn't get as far as the cockpit, so there it is. Over.

Jon: Roger. Okay. I understand, so it's probably coming through your cockpit. Okay that's fine. All understood. Now, look, the update on the weather forecast, if there's nothing further from your end, I'll give you the weather. Over.

Carol: Roger. Thank you very much.

Jon: Okay. The update till midday tomorrow is for the low position, it's slowed down a touch, but is still moving southeast about 10 to 15 [knots] and its position is expected to be at 32°S, 178°—well, it's about halfway between 178° and 179°W. A pressure of 990 [mb]. It has, of course, the associated frontal systems with it as well, but it looks like for the next 18 hours, anyhow, you're going to have fairly severe conditions. The tendency by noon tomorrow will probably be southwesterly winds for you and I would expect them [to be] around about 20, 25, and gusts of 30. I doubt whether it will be 40, but certainly 20, 25, to 35. Over.

Carol: Oh! Very good. That sounds wonderful. We think that the seas will still be pretty big tomorrow. Over.

Jon: Oh yeah, the seas will probably be pretty big but at least they'll be rolling ones and not breaking. Over.

Carol: Oh, very nice. I'm very glad to hear that by midday tomorrow we can definitely expect better conditions. Over.

Jon: Yes. Okay. Well, if there's nothing further from your end, then, can we make the contact again in another three hours. The RCC wants updates every three hours. Over.

Carol: Roger. We will be delighted to update in three hours and thank you very much, and thanks to the RCC also. Over.

Jon: Okay, that's fine.

Carol: Well, thank you, Jon, and thanks to Maureen earlier with the weather. We were in a lull and we were hoping that it would have passed us, but she said to batten down the hatches, and she was right. Half-an-hour later it started to blow. Over.

Jon: Roger. She called me and I got up and made up the weather for you. Over.

Carol: Well, thank you. I hope we have a pleasant conversation in a few days. Anyhow, we'll talk to you in three hours. Kerikeri Radio, this is the *Mary T* clear.

Jon: Roger. *Mary T.* Thanks for that. Good luck with it, then.

They had become accustomed to their conditions and confident their boat would not let them down now that they had identified the cause of their problem, seepage from the cockpit hatches. Sigmund entered in the log that conditions had calmed down to a "very comfortable 45 knots."

They were exhausted from their battle with the sea and tried to snatch a little rest. Sigmund peered out a porthole, fascinated by the enormous waves, mountains of liquid indigo with rivers of white cascading down their faces. Their tops looked like snowcapped mountains, and at times the whole seascape turned a yellow-brown as if made of sandstone.

This is one of the most beautiful things I am ever likely to see, he thought. *I must not forget this image.* Even in the threatening storm, he saw beauty. How could this be? He was now totally without fear. He had become attuned to conditions that, hours earlier, had appeared ugly and destructive. Perhaps they had become normality. He seemed to have endured them for a lifetime.

Carol: Hello, Maureen, this is Carol on the *Mary T.* Our conditions are the same as last time. I was just on deck pumping and our situation is pretty much . . . I don't have an update on our position because I didn't take the GPS with me, but it's within a mile or two of the last one. The wind is 50 to 60, gusts to 65, and the seas are quite large. I would guess a good 20 feet. Over.

Maureen: Roger. So you've been pumping and it's under control for a time. You've got 50, 60 to 65 and large seas of 20 feet. And is everybody still okay there?

Carol: Ah, yeah, everybody is still okay. We're all quite tired. Our engine is not 100 percent okay. We're running it to make sure we can talk to you on the radio and it made knocking sounds. We shut [it] down, so we're saving it for emergencies, so I'd like to keep this transmission brief.

Maureen: Roger. That's okay . . .

Carol: We understand the ship is in the area and heard them talking to another vessel in far more difficulties than us. Over.

Maureen: Yes, there's a lot in far more difficulties than you. Some have had to leave their ships and some are in pretty bad shape in themselves as well, probably emotionally as much as anything, so just hang in there. At least you're still afloat and on your vessel, so hang in there. Over.

Carol: Roger. Roger. Thank you for being there. Thanks to the navy for being there, and we'll be clear until six o'clock.

Maureen: Roger. Look forward to it. Take care in the meantime.

Carol: Thanks. *Mary T* clear.

SUNDAY, JUNE 5, AT 1400

The crew aboard the Hercules C130 started a grid-pattern search for *Quartermaster*'s beacon. They locked onto it and were exhilarated when they saw a small red life raft scudding across the tops of the waves. They reported their find to the RCC, who were ecstatic. They were alive! They had abandoned their sinking boat and made it to the life raft. They were safe. Thank God!

As he took the Hercules closer to it, the life raft's condition concerned Sqd. Ldr. Mount. Its hood had collapsed and the gale propelled it across the waves like a beach ball. It would be difficult for anyone to remain inside the little capsule hurtling across the ocean. He took the plane down as low as he dared, to peer inside the life raft and to draw out anyone huddled inside with the sound of his engines. Nothing. Nobody popped a head outside the red cover or waved at him as he flew above, and none of the crew saw any sign of life. They were lost; nobody was there.

Everyone was deflated. Disappointment replaced the elation experienced a few minutes earlier when they'd first spied the life raft.

At Nadi, Kiwi 315's engineer could not cure the oil leak in the Orion's Number 2 engine. The crew discussed the problem and the dangers it posed. Then they decided to take their chances and resume their patrol over the yachts.

Aboard *Mary T*, the crew continued their long wait for the *Monowai*.

Carol: Kerikeri Radio, *Mary T* calling.

Jon: *Mary T*, Kerikeri. Good evening. I've got you there loud and clear. Go ahead.

Carol: Good evening, Jon. We are currently at 27° 42'S, 179° 44'E. The winds are from about 210 degrees magnetic, and 40 to 50 are the odd gusts of wind, so they're down quite a bit. It's overcast with some blue showing through. We're heading about 130 [degrees] and doing pretty well. We're a little low on electricity and we did run the motor this afternoon, but it was still making some interesting clunks, so we want to save it for emergencies, so instead of the tricolor [masthead running light] tonight we are going to run our mast strobe. Could you let the RCC know that we are not in immediate danger and that we are just running the strobe to save electricity and things are going quite well? We've cut our water inflow by making some homemade gaskets and lashing down the cockpit seat. Over.

Jon: Roger. Okay. Excellent. We'll advise the RCC that . . . they'll certainly appreciate the fact that you're in no imminent danger there. They've got two aircraft in the air that are probably buzzing in and around the area, anyhow, just about constant, and they've got warships and longliners in all directions assisting the ones that are in serious trouble. Okay, well, I think you're looking at improving conditions, anyhow, so if you've handled it up till now you should be fine. Over.

Carol: Roger. Roger, and thank you very much. I'm glad they're in the area. We can hear them on the VHF occasionally. That's why we want to make sure they don't think that our strobe is [flashing] because of danger. It's just that there are so many vessels out there we want to make sure people know where we are. Over.

Jon: No. I'm glad you told us that because they're definitely looking for another vessel still. They haven't located one of the vessels at all yet and a life raft they found, but they can't seem to get anything else together. The problem is there were so many EPIRBs running at the same time that we had to get some of them shut down so that they could isolate it, so it's been a real exercise. Okay. Well, I must leave you to it if you are all well. The conditions you've got will remain pretty much as I said. You've had the most updated information that I can possibly supply you with, and for your present locality they will remain south-southeasterlies or, um, say again, south-southwesterlies, and they're tending into the southwest, so that's the way they're going, and easing slowly all the time. Over.

Carol: Great. Well it sounds like we may be able to get under way for Suva, forgetting Minerva Reef is here. Over.

Jon: [He laughs.] Yes. Yes. I think so. Maybe give that one away. Okay. There might be a few spare anchors you can use in there, though, if you can find them. Over.

Carol: There possibly are. Well, okay Jon, we'll be looking at seven, so we can get a more long-range forecast. Are there any more lows coming along in the next few days? Over.

Jon: Well, I don't see them, and I hope not. Over.

Carol: I hope not, too.

Jon: Well, good luck *Mary T.*

CHAPTER 9

I'VE NEVER SEEN ANYTHING LIKE IT

≋≋≋

Greg Forbes heard the wave slam into the side of *Pilot's* thick fiberglass hull and felt her roll begin. She tilted with an unexpected gentleness. Loose food, utensils, crockery, books, and an array of noisy implements tinkled, clattered, and crashed as *Pilot* continued her roll. Greg fell from his bunk against a table, then he hurtled across the cabin, landing on top of his partner, Barbara Parks, as the yacht twisted full circle.

"What happened?" Barbara shouted in horror.

"We've been rolled!"

It happened so quickly and gently, it was almost unreal. The only confirmation that *Pilot* had capsized through 360 degrees was the noisy movement of everything below decks that hadn't been secured.

Earlier that day, they'd been knocked down. Greg had reduced sail, fighting in the screaming gale to drop the staysail, which was determined to remain aloft. Winning the battle, he returned to the stern to adjust the Aries wind vane, allowing *Pilot* to steer herself. *Pilot* settled into a course with the seas on the quarter. The wooden vane protruding from the top of the steering gear was the only semblance of sail she carried.

An hour later, *Pilot* was knocked down again. Greg arose from his bunk to consider tactics for dealing with the storm, and was still contemplating his options when they were rolled right over.

The boat's interior was a mess. Books and magazines were scattered throughout, smeared with spaghetti, mayonnaise, sugar, flour, and other food.

"Oh, great! Look at that." Greg pointed to a portlight that appeared to have been cracked by a blow from some flying missile. He methodically set about checking the rest of the interior. The hull was sound, there was no indication that water was entering; on the contrary, the boat was surprisingly dry. There was not even a sign that oil had spilled into the bilge.

Most of the loose food and provisions had, like Greg, ended up on Barbara, who shook herself free and joined him to assess the situation. Fortunately all the heavy gear—anchors, chain, batteries, and the like—were well secured and had not budged. Things below deck did not appear to be too bad; nothing a little tidying wouldn't rectify.

Greg struggled into his foul-weather gear and went on deck. The mast was still standing, but twisted into an "S." The boom was badly bent and was crashing about dangerously in the storm. Some of the standing rigging flapped about limply in the wind. The dinghy, which doubled as *Pilot*'s life raft, was still securely lashed on deck, but one of its four oars was broken. Astern, the Aries wind vane had been irreparably smashed.

Although waves crashed over *Pilot* and raced along her decks, Greg spent the next hour tightening the rigging turnbuckles to stabilize the mast and stop it from toppling overboard.

He returned to the shallow open cockpit, grabbed the tiller, and set about steering *Pilot* downwind. The waves mesmerized him. He had endured some memorable storms during the 23 years he had cruised the world, but none had been like this. The waves seemed to rise and tower almost vertically above him until the roaring wind bent their tops and submerged *Pilot* in a terrifying avalanche of churning foam.

Alone in the exposed cockpit, facing the greatest danger he had encountered in his years of wandering, Greg felt curiously elated. It was an elation kindled by the battle for control, as *Pilot* slid and stumbled down the steep faces of mountainous waves. They were united as one, he and his boat. He could feel the power of the ocean surging through *Pilot*'s sturdy rudder to the kicking tiller.

As he steered, he wondered whether he could have avoided the predicament in which he now found himself. After losing sight of his friend Keith Levy on *Sofia*, he had enjoyed excellent sailing with a following breeze until it had died away completely and forced him to turn on the auxiliary motor for four hours.

He had listened to the shortwave receiver on Thursday night, when he heard a warning about a deepening low-pressure system off Fiji. He estimated they were still 450 miles from it, and that he could safely continue sailing northeast. With luck, they might even get some fair winds. They sailed through that night and the next day without so much as a hint in the sea or the sky of the peril on the way. There was no significant swell or whitecaps.

Barbara, working down below, saw a warning in the barometer shortly after nightfall.

"It's the scariest thing," she called to Greg. "I wish I could say the barometer is on the way up, but it's not. It's falling."

As night arrived, she checked the barometer every 10 minutes. It fell steadily for seven hours. There was no doubting its message.

"I've never seen anything like it," she whispered, her apprehension growing. "It's frightening."

They reduced sail during the afternoon until only the staysail was left. Then *Pilot* had been knocked down. And knocked down again. And rolled.

Now, Greg knew, they were deep within the storm center. The wind was up to 90 knots by his estimate, and the seas were unlike any he'd ever encountered. In previous storms, he'd always found sufficient room in the troughs between swells to steady the boat and guide her back on course, but here the waves were so close there was little chance of shelter in the valleys. As he clung to the tiller, salt spray and rain doused him constantly, painfully lashing and burning his weathered face.

Phosphorescence streaked the dark waters like tracer bullets in a battle. Millions of microscopic marine organisms erupted into brilliance as the wind exploded the crowns of waves, and myriad illuminated fragments showered down on Greg.

Then, almost before he could comprehend what was happening, a huge roaring comber emerged from the darkness aft and swept aboard over the stern. Greg's hand was ripped from the boom gallows and he was tossed aside under the crushing weight of tons of water swirling over the boat. His safety harness and tether stopped him with a mighty jerk, and he splashed about in the submerged cockpit, not sure for a moment whether he was actually still on the boat or overboard.

As he rubbed salt water from his eyes, he saw that the mast had been carried away. He was incredulous. It was much sturdier than most masts, made of aluminum, $3/16$ of an inch thick. Now it lay across the cabintop, snapped in two like a matchstick a foot above the deck.

Greg figured the boarding sea must have wrenched the boom out of the gallows with such force that it shattered the mast below the gooseneck. The shrouds and stays that had kept it aloft all these years were intact. Not even a rigging screw had come undone.

Greg, one of the best dumpster divers on the seas, considered the mast still serviceable, even if it was broken in two, distorted into an "S," and missing its port spreader. He had to salvage it. But before he could work out a plan, it became apparent that the motion of the boat was hammering the mast against the hull. He was afraid that if he left it as it was, it would batter its way through and open the hull to the sea. He had no alternative but to abandon the mast before it destroyed *Pilot*.

He gathered some tools and crawled forward with water cascading over him. As the boat rolled and lurched viciously, he fumbled with the pliers, removing cotter pins and extracting the clevis pins holding the rigging to the chainplates until only a solitary fastening secured the mast to the boat: the pin holding the forestay.

The prospect of crawling out on the bowsprit plank to release the pin from the bow chainplate scared him. It was the most dangerous place on the boat, totally exposed and taking the full force of the waves. The mangled stainless steel pulpit was often fully submerged, and the prospect of working there as the bow was swept by combers scared him to death.

If I get washed off, I won't be able to get back on deck, even though I've got my harness on, he thought.

He considered his options and decided he had no choice. He had to remove the pin. If he didn't, the mast would eventually penetrate the hull. He slithered forward onto the bowsprit, bracing himself as the wrecked pulpit swung violently in the darkness. He reached the forestay and clung to a broken stanchion as the yacht lurched forward and buried her bow under tumbling water. He resurfaced and groped for his flashlight, shining it on the chainplate and searching for the cotter pin before another wave came. Fortunately, the pin came free easily. He withdrew the clevis pin, and the stay slipped over the side, freeing the mast from the boat. He crawled backward on his belly, elbows, and knees, determined to get away from the bow before another huge wave washed over *Pilot.*

"I wasn't able to save anything," he called despondently to Barbara when he arrived back in the cockpit. For him, the loss of valuable gear had been almost as painful as his ordeal on the bow.

It had taken him three hours to dump the mast, and he was cold and wet. There was little point in changing into dry clothes because the cockpit was exposed, and he had to stay at the tiller to protect the boat from another knockdown.

Barbara grew alarmed as she detected early signs of hypothermia in Greg—he was shivering. She felt useless. She was too weak to handle the heavy loads on the tiller, so she couldn't relieve him while he went below to rest and warm up. She rummaged through the chaos below and found a hot-water bottle, filled it, and handed it to Greg, who thrust it under his slicker. The warmth revived his chilled bones. Barbara was confident that if anyone could sail through this storm to safety, Greg could. Throughout the night, she refilled the hot-water bottle and prepared warm drinks for him.

He battled through the night to hold a course downwind. *Pilot's* natural tendency, if left to her own devices, was to lie beam-on to the seas, which was dangerous. He remained at the helm until midafternoon the next day, Sunday, when he finally surrendered to exhaustion and asked Barbara to take the tiller while he tried to sleep. By then the worst was over, but the sea remained confused, and swells traveled in all directions.

Without the steadying effect of a mast, the yacht's motion had changed drastically. Her normal slow roll had been replaced by a vicious, jerky motion that threw Greg and Barbara about violently and made it difficult to move, even to sit and steer. Greg rigged a control line on the tiller and secured it to the sides of the cockpit well. He hoped this would enable Barbara to steer the boat while he rested.

"I'd better get the engine going to keep the batteries up," he said as he went below.

It would not start. Despite his fatigue, he got out his tools and discovered water had entered the exhaust when the boat had rolled. He fixed the problem, and the next time he turned the ignition the motor fired into life. He collapsed on a bunk, totally exhausted. But it wasn't his night for rest.

"Greg! Greg!" Barbara yelled excitedly from the cockpit. "Greg! There's a plane out there!"

He could hardly lift himself from the bunk, but he forced himself out and into the cockpit. She was right. About five miles away to starboard, at about 1,000 feet, an aircraft was apparently searching for something.

"I can't believe it," Barbara said. "I thought they were stars, but they moved through the sky. Then they turned and I saw the afterburn," she said, referring to the plane's glowing exhaust. "I realized they were the lights of a plane. I wasn't sure it was a plane until it turned. You could see the burners, they were really bright."

"They're flying in a square pattern," Greg observed. His handheld VHF was not working, so he went below to fetch the parachute flares his friend Keith Levy had given him before he sailed from Auckland. Keith had warned him that they were old—their expiration date had passed. Greg hoped they would still work. His luck was good. The first flare he shot off burst into a bright red, glowing orb, but the plane did not respond. He fired off two more flares, with the same result.

The crew of Kiwi 315 had joined the search again and relocated the yachts the other rescue planes had been keeping an eye on. They had flown over *Heart Light*, *Silver Shadow*, and *Sofia*, talking to the crews, liaising with the RCC and rescue vessels, and establishing priorities for rescues. They were concerned that the injured person aboard *Silver Shadow* might be in much worse condition than anyone realized. They had also relocated *Quartermaster*'s life raft drifting by itself and confirmed there was no sign of life aboard it.

While they were talking to the *San Te Maru 18*, a fishing vessel on course to *Heart Light*, a spotter aboard the Orion saw a red glow below, about five miles away.

Sqd. Ldr. Yardley marked the sighting on his chart. They called on the radio but got no reply. As they flew closer, the cloud base near the yacht was lit up by a powerful searchlight.

Who could it be? *Quartermaster*! It had to be *Quartermaster*!

The RCC had no record of a yacht needing assistance at that location. They had not received distress calls from any boats other than *Heart Light*, *Silver Shadow*, and *Sofia*. Logic therefore suggested that the boat signaling the Orion could be *Quartermaster*. There was no reason why it should not be. After all, *Destiny*'s life raft had been ripped away, and if that had happened to *Quartermaster* it would explain the empty raft they'd sighted earlier. It probably took *Quartermaster*'s EPIRB with it. If the yacht had been rolled, it would explain why they'd lost radio communication.

The Hercules had searched all day for *Quartermaster* because nothing had been heard from the crew since Jon Cullen had spoken to them early Saturday morning. Everyone desperately wanted them to be found. They felt they knew them; they had heard their voices and felt their fear. Too much effort had gone into the hunt to lose them now, and no one wanted to believe they would not be found.

The Orion flew low over the yacht, but in the darkness it was impossible to recognize a name. The *Monowai* was requested to divert from the *Mary T* and steam toward the unidentified vessel.

When daylight came, the Orion flew low over the yacht and identified her as *Pilot*. The news had a curious impact on those involved in the search-and-rescue operation. Many were once again disappointed that it wasn't *Quartermaster*, whose predicament they'd discussed at length. The *Quartermaster*'s crew were familiar to them. Some of the search-and-rescue team felt confused and guilty about the emotions stirred by the discovery of *Pilot*; they didn't experience the excitement and satisfaction they usually felt when a vessel was found. They realized that *Pilot*'s crew also were in need of assistance, but they were greatly disheartened that *Quartermaster* was still missing.

Aboard *Pilot*, Greg wondered if the Orion had noticed the flares he'd fired. The plane was heading away from them when he ignited the first one, and cloud may have obscured the glow of the second, but it seemed likely that the Orion should have seen the third.

He and Barbara waved flashlights at the sky, hoping the Orion would notice.

"They might lose us. I'll get the searchlight," Greg said.

That seemed to do the trick. He played the beam on the clouds above, and the Orion flew directly to them. He was confident the Orion would arrange for assistance to reach them, and he and Barbara settled back into their routine of keeping the boat running before the weather on a safe heading until help arrived.

Barbara took the helm while Greg rested. She marveled at the conditions. The storm raged about her, roaring and howling and buffeting them to the accompaniment of flutes.

I must be hearing things. I must be cracking up, she thought, doubting her sanity as she sat alone in the dark. She knew about sailors hearing voices at sea, but she couldn't believe anyone would hear Mozart's opera *The Magic Flute*.

When she eventually discovered the source of the sound, there was nothing magic about it. The wind was playing haunting, melancholy tunes in the broken stanchions along the deck. The flutes kept Barbara entertained and distracted for hours. Not only did they accompany the crescendo created by the storm, they also attracted curious shearwaters. They flew about her in a frenzy, excited by the strange noise.

The Orion appeared frequently throughout the night. The pattern it flew indicated it was searching for something other than *Pilot*. They thought they saw lights flashing on the water at one stage and the glow of a ship in the distance, but in the heavy seas and howling wind they couldn't be sure.

They still hadn't decided whether to abandon *Pilot*. She was all they had, and she contained all their possessions. She was their home and their friend, and they had sailed the world in her. She had taken them from Miami to the Bahamas, through the Caribbean, and down to Venezuela before sailing to Colombia and Panama. They had been to Ecuador, remote Pitcairn Island, and the Society Islands. They had cruised the South Pacific from American Samoa to Fiji and New Zealand. They had lived aboard *Pilot* for six of the 23 years Greg had wandered the world in boats. If they abandoned her they'd have nothing, because she was not insured. It had taken Greg years to accumulate all the gear aboard *Pilot*, and it was unlikely he could afford to equip another yacht if he lost this one.

Daylight brought improving conditions and the return of the Orion. The plane startled them as it swooped low overhead and dropped a canister nearby. The instant it touched the water it exploded into yellow smoke.

Then the *Monowai*'s white hull loomed out of the murky gray horizon. They hugged each other and cried. Greg was too exhausted to continue the battle against the sea. Silently, they agreed to abandon *Pilot*, return to Maine, and start all over again.

They watched the *Monowai* as she drew closer and lowered a tender. Without hesitation, Greg went below, grabbed a carving knife, and slit the drain hose on the galley sink. He opened the seacock, and seawater started gushing in. When he stepped off *Pilot* for the last time, the water was over the floorboards.

CHAPTER 10

THE RIG'S GONE!

≋≋≋

Silver Shadow's crew was four experienced men who, in their years of racing, had weathered some of the worst conditions that New Zealand could throw at them. They were confident that their boat, a well-proven cruiser-racer, could easily continue in rugged conditions when other yachts struggled. They received warning of the low-pressure system that formed off Fiji, and they watched it track to the southeast without any indication it would develop beyond the 35-knot gale that was forecast.

But as they listened to other boats discussing weather conditions far ahead of them, *Silver Shadow*'s crew became concerned. Contrary to predictions, the low appeared to be taking a significant detour. *Silver Shadow* could find herself trapped directly in its path, so they decided to head west.

"Sail west," Jon Cullen concurred from Kerikeri Radio.

They altered course to reach west along the 30th parallel, from their position at 177.47°E. Normally, they would have been confident they could outrun the storm, but the conversations they listened to on the radio indicated otherwise. *Silver Shadow*, under storm jib and with three reefs in the main, raced along at 8 knots in the 40-knot gale. That evening, her crew realized an extraordinary storm was on the way, and they dropped the main for easier sailing during the night.

During the evening radio roll-call of the flotilla in the South Pacific, yacht after yacht had reported its struggle. *Quartermaster*,

Mary T, *Sofia*, and others recounted their ordeals, while *Silver Shadow*'s crew eavesdropped spellbound, concerned about how they would be affected when the storm reached them. They planned evasive action of their own, and considered what preparations they should make for the tough night ahead. They sympathized with Carol Baardsen on *Mary T*, and envisaged the crew pumping for their lives.

Although *Silver Shadow*'s crew realized they were in for a rough time, they remained relatively optimistic about the pending storm. Weatherfaxes from the New Zealand Meteorological Office did not indicate conditions as bad as the yachts were reporting, and conditions aboard *Silver Shadow* remained reasonably comfortable, although the barometer had started to fall. As they listened to the transmissions from *Mary T*, they even wondered if Carol was overreacting a little.

Silver Shadow's skipper, Peter O'Neil, tuned the SSB radio to pick up the next weather facsimile. He fumbled with a roll of new paper he was putting in the machine, and kept a wary eye on the whitecapped mounds that rolled past the portlight. Occasionally, he adjusted the autopilot a few degrees to keep the yacht on track.

Above him, John McSherry propped himself up on the companionway stairs and peered out into the darkness. His back rested against a washboard and he was well protected by the spray dodger. He was on a two-hour watch, but there was nothing to occupy him above decks; the yacht sailed well, the sea and wind were favorable, and there was not another soul around for miles. The weather certainly would not entice him outside. The gale carried driving rain, and it was so cold he anticipated an ice storm similar to one that had pelted the boat earlier.

The routine domesticity aboard *Silver Shadow* ended abruptly when a huge wave, unseen in the darkness, slammed into her with tremendous force, knocking her sideways like a ball smashing tenpins.

Richard Jackson, sleeping in the forward berth, shot through the air feet-first, smashing a starboard-side closet door. He appeared to hang suspended in midair for some time. Peter O'Neil crashed down on the starboard side of the boat, too. The whole action took only about 10 seconds until *Silver Shadow* staggered back onto an even keel.

"The rig's gone!" his son, Murray, shouted.

Nobody could believe it. The men below rushed out to see for themselves. Sure enough, only an 18-inch stub of mast protruded above deck. The rest of it dangled over the side, suspended by the rigging and wrapped under the hull in front of the keel. The dodger had collapsed across the cockpit.

Dressed in foul-weather gear and harnesses, Murray O'Neil and Richard Jackson set about cutting away the rigging to free the mast. They were amazed that one wave could reduce it to this tangle of cable and shattered aluminum. Although the 50-knot gale was producing waves 40 feet high, the tops of the swells remained surprisingly flat. Even so, they were afraid they would lose their tools if the boat rolled steeply, so Murray tied the bolt cutters to his harness. As he struggled to cut through the steel stays and shrouds, he peered warily into the darkness, watching for signs of another breaking wave. Each time the yacht rolled, he dropped the bolt cutters and grabbed a handhold to steady himself. After 45 minutes, he cut through the last shroud, and the mast and rigging slid 2,000 fathoms to the bottom of the ocean.

While Murray and Richard toiled on the rig, Peter O'Neil and John McSherry hunted out the Kenwood SSB radio's emergency antenna and attached it to the remains of the hydraulic backstay tensioner. But despite all their effort, it wouldn't work, probably because water had splashed the back of the radio during the knockdown.

"That really pisses me off," Peter grumbled. "I don't think an SSB should be susceptible to water. It was in the driest area of the boat, and only a couple of inches at the back of the set got wet." Now they were without long-range radio communications.

The crew gathered their wits and inspected the interior for damage. Only a few cans of soup had flown out of a locker; the double latches had kept the cupboards secure. The tedious and meticulous care they'd put into stowing gear and provisions before leaving New Zealand had proved its worth. Seeing the boat clean and tidy, despite the knockdown, was very satisfying. Peter was particularly pleased that he'd had the foresight to stow 200 feet of anchor chain beneath the floorboards near the mast, rather than leave it in the anchor locker. The weight of the chain so low down may have provided the extra stability that prevented the yacht's rolling over completely. The anchors remained securely lashed, and nine lead ingots stowed forward for ballast had not moved. The boat's structure remained intact. After completing his inspection, Peter felt very relieved.

Peter pulled a large Whale Gusher pump out of storage and placed it near the sump to empty the bilge. The pump was bolted to a plywood base to make it easier to use. "It should be a must on any boat," he said. The efficiency of the pump impressed them all.

Peter and John were about to tackle the SSB problem again when John yelled: "We're holed! Water's coming in!"

Peter rushed to the head and saw water gushing over the floorboards.

"Oh shit!" he exclaimed in horror. "The mast has holed us somewhere. Something's gone through and holed us." He called to Richard and Murray, who were working on deck: "We have a hole! Come down and help!"

The floorboard concealing the source of the leak was jammed in place and refused to budge at first. They struggled to pry the cover free, fearing the worst as water continued to pour over the floor. Eventually the floorboard gave way, and they peered into the bilge and groped about trying to find the hole in the hull.

"Okay guys, it's all right," Peter called after a few seconds. There was no mistaking the relief in his voice. "It's just the plug for the depth transducer."

Murray had got as far as the main hatchway when he heard the good news. He returned to the task of tidying up on deck.

"The transducer was actually pushed right out," Peter added. He screwed it down tightly into its skin fitting and the gushing water subsided.

After tidying up the boat inside and out, they discussed their predicament. They were not unduly worried. They were confident *Silver Shadow* was still seaworthy, even though her motion was distinctly different without the counterbalance of her mast. The seas were still huge, and they lay beam-on to them, but no breaking waves were hitting the boat—for the moment, anyway. Their options had narrowed because they had lost their radio as well as their rig, but their circumstances were manageable.

"We don't need to set the EPIRB off," Peter said. "Tomorrow morning the storm will hopefully die down, and we can jury rig with a spinnaker pole and make our way to Tonga."

They checked again and were satisfied there were no significant leaks, although there was still a little seepage into the bilge.

Contrary to Peter's hopes, the seas did not subside. As the wind rose to 60 knots, the swells became confused. Waves pounded the yacht with sledgehammer force, throwing her violently over on her side and tossing her occupants about wildly. The crew ripped up bedding and tied handholds to grabrails so they could hang on when the boat shook and shuddered. They were knocked down so many times that dark night, it almost began to feel normal.

Before dawn on Sunday, June 5, Peter left his bunk to make the crew coffee. He filled the kettle and was about to turn on the gas when an alarming roar gave a split-second warning of a wave that hurled the boat over until the keel pointed skyward. Peter stood in the galley, momentarily suspended in space, before crashing against the other side of the cabin. Murray was flung from his bunk, his head smashing against the floor. The others were also whipped from their bunks as *Silver Shadow* completed a 360-degree roll.

The sensation was amazing. Some of them had experienced rolling in a car but never in a boat. Unlike a car rolling, where the sensation is one of catastrophe in slow motion, the boat's movement was a blur of speed. The outcome was uncertain and confused as the crew hovered and spun and fell through space, colliding with bulkheads and furniture, and receiving blows from flying projectiles.

Floor-locker tops and bilge covers fell out during the roll, transformed into lethal missiles that hurtled through the cabin. One fetched a glancing blow to Murray's back, felling him and knocking him semiconscious.

Silver Shadow righted herself. Peter crashed head-first into the bilge, his shoulder smashing into the floor beams. A floorboard thudded down on top of him. Murray groaned. Peter screamed and shouted from the excruciating pain. As he lay wedged upside down in the bilge, Peter could feel one part of the bone of his shoulder blade rubbing against another. He was disoriented, and dread mingled with the pain. He could see nothing and feared the boat was sinking.

In a haze, Murray turned to help his father, but the exertion exhausted him and he grew faint again. John tried to pull Peter free, but he couldn't because Peter was jammed firmly between the floor beams. Gradually, they pried him out of the bilge, moved him to a bunk, and propped him securely against a bulkhead.

"I've broken something in my shoulder," he told them. The pieces of bone were still grating against each other. "But what the hell," he added cheerfully. "I actually thought we were going to Davy Jones's locker when we went over like that." He looked around incredulously. "We're still upright!"

While Murray and John put the floorboards back in place, Richard went on deck to see what had happened there. "The life raft is gone," he called down dejectedly.

After some discussion, Peter decided not to hesitate any longer. "No life raft, no SSB—we've got to set the EPIRB off," he commanded. Murray switched it on inside the boat, watching the indicator light pulsing with their SOS call.

Once again, they assessed their situation. Although Peter considered present conditions dangerous enough to warrant a distress call, he still believed that if the weather improved they could motor, and sail under jury rig, to Fiji. It was 700 miles away—200 miles farther than Tonga—but the repair facilities were better. They had plenty of fuel, and there were spare containers of diesel lashed on deck. The hull was still intact, although there was a puzzling tapping sound coming from aft that nobody could identify, and the bilge was collecting only about 8 inches of water every three hours. In the end, he reasoned, everything depended on the weather.

The pain in Peter's shoulder was agonizing. He refused to take morphine because he wanted to be alert if they had to abandon ship. He settled for pain-killing tablets to subdue the torture. But all the time, the yacht's violent rolling was threatening to catapult him out of his bunk and inflict further serious damage upon him. So his crew set about lashing him to a bunk with rope, and propped him between cushions to soften the blows to his crippled shoulder.

This concern for his welfare was a mixed blessing, however. Peter suffered severe claustrophobia. Attacks of panic hit him regularly during the next few hours, as the boat was knocked down time and again. He feared he would be trapped in the bunk if the boat rolled over and they had to abandon her quickly. He concealed his phobia from the others as they lay curled up in their bunks, flinching with every blow from the gale, but he couldn't help crying out in pain as he braced himself against every wrenching roll. They offered him morphine again; and again he declined because of the drowsiness it would induce.

Although he couldn't leave his bunk, Peter still managed to offer advice when they tried to get *Silver Shadow* to lie more safely, end-onto the swells, rather than leaving her to roll her beam-ends under. Peter gave them suggestions, but no matter what they did with drogues, they couldn't coax *Silver Shadow* to alter her beam-on position.

They tied lines to the corners of a small jib and formed a bridle. They attached 600 feet of warp, and got ready to feed the sail into the sea, hoping it would bite and gradually turn the boat's side away from the threatening waves.

But the howling wind snatched the sail out of their hands and dumped it over the leeward side. "That won't work," somebody shouted. "The boat will drift over it and we'll foul the rudder and propeller."

They got it back on board with a struggle and shoved it through the main hatch down into the cabin, where they kneeled on it and rolled it tightly into the smallest ball they could make. This time, with the wind unable to find a free edge, the sail sank in the water, and they made the bridle fast at the stern. But, for all their efforts, nothing changed. The boat continued to lie beam-on.

Eventually, they decided that only a sea anchor from the bow would do the trick. They attached a second line to the drogue and wrestled it with great difficulty to the bow. They then cut the stern line. This time the sail unfolded correctly and took a bite on the sea. They eased out more warp to coax the yacht to round into the waves, but the snubbing was vicious. After each snub, the line went slack and the bow blew off, gradually turning the yacht broadside-on, until the next wave suddenly jerked her head around again. No matter how the crew tried, they couldn't get *Silver Shadow* to lie consistently head-on or stern-on.

One of the major reasons for this difficulty was the confused seascape. Huge swells, with breaking waves riding their backs, lunged at them from practically every direction. It was time for another conference below decks about how to deal with the conditions. Between them, they had read a whole library of books on seamanship, but none had dealt with difficulties similar to these. Finally, they decided to set some sail aft, to bring her stern around in line with the wind.

Under the most atrocious working conditions, they lashed a reaching strut to the mangled remains of the aft pulpit on the port side, and hoisted the head of a trysail on it. They took the foot of the sail forward to the lifelines on the starboard side, where they fought to tie the clew far enough forward to make the jury rig effective.

The crude mizzen worked, at least partially. For some of the time, at least, it kept *Silver Shadow*'s bow pointed into the waves, with the improvised sea anchor jerking tight, and the bow lifting high on a crest before snapping down. But more often than not, the yacht stubbornly fell off the wind and exposed her beam to the waves.

While Peter was wondering what to do next, he looked through a portlight and saw a Hercules C130 aircraft approaching. The others scrambled out to the cockpit to wave furiously. From open doors on the plane, spotters waved back at them.

SUNDAY, JUNE 5, AT 1210

Murray grabbed the VHF microphone, depressed the button, and tried to make contact on Channel 16. But to his intense frustration he discovered that although he could hear the Hercules crew calling him, the radio operator could not hear his reply.

Then one of those minor miracles occurred. A voice from the Hercules said they could hear the clicking of the microphone button when Murray pushed it to transmit. From then on, all communication from *Silver Shadow*'s end was done with clicks—one click for negative, two for affirmative.

As they listened and answered questions with their simple code, *Silver Shadow*'s crew realized that the aircraft's crew was trying to establish their order of rescue. They listened incredulously as the pilot explained the mayhem surrounding them. EPIRBs were going off all over the ocean, he said, and *Silver Shadow* was only one of several boats in distress. In return, Murray indicated that although Peter appeared to be seriously injured, and was suffering considerable pain, they were coping.

"We have you positioned. We have a lot of others to find and identify. We understand you are reasonably comfortable, please confirm."

Murray pressed the button on the microphone with his thumb. Two clicks. Confirmed.

"Did you have an EPIRB on your life raft?"

One click. No.

"If we don't come back to see you, an Orion will come and talk to you and identify what is happening," Sqd. Ldr. Peter Mount told them. "You shouldn't expect any rescue before lunchtime tomorrow."

Before the plane flew out of VHF range, he added: "Is there anything else you want to try to tell us?" He knew they would have to play an electronic quiz game to elicit any such information.

One click.

"We'll see you later." The Hercules left them to search for *Quartermaster*'s crew.

The pounding sea continued to build all day, taking *Silver Shadow* for a wild ride behind her makeshift sea anchor. Sometimes she lay with the seas on her beam, and on other occasions she took them on her bow or her stern. When the underwater genoa filled, she snubbed severely. In these tumultuous, undisciplined seas, there was no way to make her lie quietly and safely.

Murray repaired the VHF radio, and when Kiwi 315 flew over them that afternoon he was able to talk to them.

"What is your overall situation?" they inquired.

"Medically we are stable," he replied. "Dad has been having Panadine and seems comfortable. Structurally the boat is okay but we've no life raft. The boat is not taking on water."

Sqd. Ldr. David Powell, the doctor aboard Kiwi 315, asked them to describe Peter's injuries. He inquired whether they could remove his foul-weather gear and inspect his damaged shoulder, but they declined. They thought it better not to disturb Peter because of the pain it would cause.

"On a scale of one to five, how do you rank yourself in terms of your safety?"

The four crewmembers looked at each other quizzically. They were acutely aware that their answer might determine whether they were rescued before someone else in greater need. They took their time to reply. They didn't regard the situation as life-threatening, but it had definitely deteriorated as the day had progressed.

"I'd say two," somebody suggested.

"Hang on," another said.

"Let's talk about this," Peter said.

The consensus was that if other yachts were in trouble, *Silver Shadow* was not in need of immediate assistance, and the rescue team's efforts would be better used helping others in more acute danger.

"How do you feel?" Peter was asked.

"I'm okay. I'm sore but okay."

They told the Orion that on a scale of one to five they would place themselves at two.

The crew of the Orion sounded grateful. That gave them the opportunity to send the rescue ship to a yacht in immediate danger. When the aircraft flew over them later, two-way conversation took place again briefly. Murray asked them about weather conditions. If the weather improved, he said, they would build a jury rig and motor to safety. The transmission died again during the conversation and the dialogue reverted to the clicking code. After the air crew had gathered all the information they needed, they announced that they would have to leave the area now.

"We'll be back tomorrow," Sqd. Ldr. Mike Yardley told them, little realizing how much that announcement would dash their spirits. That meant another night alone in a merciless sea that threatened their very existence. There were 13 hours of darkness ahead of them, 13 hours to lie rigid in a bunk, listening and waiting fearfully for the wave that would finally sink them.

The electricity supply began to fail. Dampness was seeping into vulnerable spots in the wiring, connectors, and fuses. Murray worked on the circuit board, disconnecting circuits not critical to the boat's survival. He isolated charged batteries to preserve their power. He rewired the gas cut-off switch so they could use the galley stove, and they boiled hot dogs for supper. They devoured them voraciously with lots of ketchup.

The night was bad. As the storm gradually passed over them, they clung to handholds and jammed themselves into their narrow bunks. The waves pushed and shoved *Silver Shadow*, rolling her and making her pitch and slam. She slid sideways down the face of breaking waves, almost tripping over her keel, but always righting herself at the last moment. It was a black, wild night, a violent night of extreme discomfort and danger, a night they all hoped they'd never have to live through again.

Throughout the darkest hours, John tried to ease Peter's pain. He fed him pills and tried, as gently and cautiously as he could, to move him about to relieve his cramps.

All night long, the tapping noise from the stern grew louder. Still nobody could imagine what it might be. Murray investigated once more but again failed to identify the sound. But as he groped about in the dark, he did find the cause of the seepage into the bilge. Water was coming through a gap in the deck where a post had held the radar antenna. He suspected the post must have been ripped out of the deck when the boat rolled. He made a crude repair, using a can and a tea towel to block the hole, and, sure enough, the water level in the bilge stayed steady.

MONDAY, JUNE 6, AT 0600

When the long-awaited dawn finally broke, it revealed an empty gray expanse of angry ocean with not a friendly sign anywhere. They looked forward to the return of the Orion, which had promised to be back at 0900, but it did not arrive. They listened, and scanned the horizon, and wondered where it was. An hour later they heard it overhead. Its message made up for the delay: the *Monowai* was coming to pick them up. She had two other rescued crews aboard.

The news greatly cheered everyone. They even made jokes. The *Monowai* had picked up three lots of Forbes, the air crew told them—Bill and Robyn from *Ramtha*, and Greg from *Pilot*. They hoped there weren't any more Forbes on *Silver Shadow*. The confusion would be too much to bear.

But the banter ceased when *Silver Shadow*'s crew realized the *Monowai* wouldn't reach them until 1730—almost nightfall. They knew the ship wasn't likely to attempt a rescue at night.

"This is no good, we're going to have to do something," Peter said. "Why don't we motor? There's no way I want to be taken off in the dark in these seas."

The plan was to motor directly toward the *Monowai* to reduce the distance she'd have to cover. But when they got under power, they discovered the source of the mysterious tapping beneath the stern: The steering was damaged. The rudder was swinging back and forth. Something else to fix.

The *Monowai* made radio contact at 1500. *Silver Shadow*'s crew had by then rigged an emergency steering system, and the yacht was motoring toward the ship, often at 7 knots, enabling them to bring forward the rendezvous time to 1600.

The survey ship had had a difficult time of it after rescuing *Pilot*'s crew. The sea ran high again and the wind gusted to about 40 knots. Cmdr. Larry Robbins was concerned about the conditions for his third rescue operation in as many days. It was getting dark, and the sea was too rough to let him place the *Monowai* safely alongside *Silver Shadow*. He experimented to find the course that gave his ship the most stable ride, but the sea was so confused it made no difference what track he laid. His options for a rescue were limited. He couldn't send over some harnesses, as he'd done for *Ramtha*. *Silver Shadow*'s skipper was badly injured and would not survive being towed through the sea. He really had only one choice. He would have to send the ship's 20-foot tender to the ailing yacht.

When the *Monowai* made radio contact with *Silver Shadow*, Murray was still not sure they should abandon the yacht. "Would you consider towing us to the nearest port?" he asked Cmdr. Robbins.

"We're 500 miles away from land and my first consideration has to be saving lives," Cmdr. Robbins replied. "We will take the skipper off and leave the others if you wish."

"We've got two days' fuel aboard."

"We can pass fuel, but we don't have any jerry cans as such, and it may be difficult to handle."

Murray paused, obviously feeling the burden of making the right decision for all those involved. "What do you want to do?" he asked the others aboard *Silver Shadow*.

"There's no hurry," Cmdr. Robbins assured him. "Why don't you think about it and let us know when we get there?"

Murray was thinking ahead. "If we're going to get off the boat let's take some basic gear with us," he suggested. "We've got some bags."

Considerable time was then spent discussing the possessions they intended taking with them.

"My father's cribbage board, I must take that," Peter said. "And underneath me are 12 bottles of rum. Put a couple of bottles in the bag."

"No, put four bottles in."

They grabbed them and wrapped them in a towel. *Silver Shadow* was well provisioned for the party they'd intended enjoying in Tonga. Four bottles were placed in the bag for the crew of the *Monowai* and to celebrate their rescue; a three-month supply of spirits remained on board.

The *Monowai* came into sight at precisely 1600.

"We have discussed our situation with the skipper and wish to abandon the boat," Murray informed them.

Cmdr. Robbins was ready. The ship's 20-foot, rigid-hulled inflatable boat (RIB or RHIB) was standing by with a crew of three: the coxswain in charge, Leading Seaman Abraham Whata; a bowman, Able Seaman Linton Hemopo; and a medical cadet, Leading Medical Assistant Michael Wiig. The *Monowai* steamed ahead at 5 knots as the RIB was lowered over the side. As soon as she hit the water, they unhitched the painters and shot off toward *Silver Shadow*, taking a wide berth around her to judge her roll and pitch before deciding on their best approach route.

Leading Seaman Whata stood at the craft's control center amidships. He nosed the RIB toward the *Silver Shadow*'s stern as she steamed straight ahead. Then he came alongside her port side. The medic jumped aboard, and Whata veered away from the yacht to await a signal that they were ready to evacuate.

"Okay guys, this is what we're going to do," the medic said breezily to *Silver Shadow*'s crew. "We're going to get you out of here."

"Oh yeah?" Peter responded testily. The medic looked altogether too young and too hyped up. But he quickly impressed Peter with his professionalism. He examined *Silver Shadow*'s injured skipper to see exactly what he was dealing with, and Peter forgave him his youth. The crew helped Peter up through the narrow companionway and held him steady on deck while they waited for the RIB to come back alongside.

"Wow, if I go in there with wet-weather gear on, I'm going to go down like a rock," Peter said, peering at the water.

The medic bent some stanchions that had been damaged in the rollover, so the lifelines wouldn't be in the way when they left. After several unsuccessful passes the two craft came together, and Peter was pushed over the side. He landed with a scream of pain on the RIB's solid floor, and the bowman dragged him onto the stretcher he'd prepared and strapped him down. Peter lay there awaiting the arrival of the others.

Leading Seaman Whata kept the RIB at a distance from the yacht until the other crewmembers were ready to board. His brow furrowed as he concentrated on the motion of the sea, trying to determine where the biggest waves were and when was the best time to go alongside the yacht. Once again he maneuvered in, just as smoothly as he had previously. John and Richard jumped aboard, leaving Murray alone on *Silver Shadow*. The RIB ran clear again.

Irritation gripped Whata as he waited for Murray to appear on deck. He was anxious to get the injured man to the *Monowai* while light still remained. Murray finally emerged, struggling to the deck, laden with bags that he waved at them, further exasperating Whata, whose instructions had been to evacuate the crew and three bags only, not the six that now appeared. He lost concentration, and the RIB lunged over the top of a wave. They hung suspended above its crest for a split second before gravity pulled them down, swamping the boat as water spilled aboard. Peter screamed in pain as his body lifted off the floor and crashed down again, grating one piece of shattered shoulder bone against the other. The medic sheltered him from as much water as possible, but Peter could not avoid swallowing some that came over his head.

Murray finally jumped into the RIB and Whata turned and headed away. He picked his way cautiously back to the *Monowai*, protecting his injured passenger as best he could, weaving in and out of the enormous waves.

Peter, lying on the floor and able to see only the outlines of the mountainous seas surrounding them, and the gray sky above, wondered whether he would have been safer remaining on *Silver Shadow*. The water the RIB had taken on earlier still splashed about him. He wondered if he might not drown sooner here than on his own boat.

Suddenly, the *Monowai*'s white hull loomed above him. From his supine position, the ship seemed to be rolling wildly. He wondered how they would ever transfer him across to her.

"Careful! Keep away from that side!" Somebody screamed a warning as the two boats slammed against each other.

Lines rained down on the RIB to secure her to the *Monowai*'s side. Another was fastened around Peter's stretcher, and he was swiftly hoisted skyward. The sailors above pulled quickly and urgently. There was a danger in this high swell that the rising RIB could smash into the stretcher from underneath. When they had him up to the torpedo davit, they swung him around toward the deck and lowered him.

To take the others off the RIB, the ship's crew sent down two helicopter strops, the same harnesses that had saved Bill and Robyn Forbes 48 hours earlier. John McSherry and Richard Jackson got into the harnesses and were hauled aboard, clinging to each other.

As they ascended, trouble struck the RIB. Black smoke suddenly belched from the inboard engine. It had worked under considerable stress throughout the rescue. Alarms screamed warnings about oil pressure, water temperature, and alternator output. Red panel lights came on as the dense smoke billowing from the craft's stern engulfed its crew.

All at once, the RIB plunged down a wave, and the straining painter pulled out the metal frame to which it was attached. Water flooded into the boat.

"We must have a hole in front!" Whata yelled to the bowman. "It must have pulled out the A-frame!"

Murray was hastily hoisted out of the boat, leaving the crew to assess the damage. They freed the painters and backed away from the *Monowai*. Whata called the ship on the handheld VHF, reported he suspected the vessel was holed, and said he intended running the boat at high speed to drive the water out through the self-bailers. The water was rapidly creeping up to their knees.

Cmdr. Robbins watched from the bridge. Dusk had descended and the light was rapidly fading. With a boat full of water, black smoke billowing from the exhaust, and all the RIB's alarms sounding, the likelihood of total failure was real. If the RIB's engine failed now, he would have a disaster to contend with. He did not relish the prospect of having to mount a night search for three of his men in one of the worst storms he had encountered.

The RIB lumbered around to the lee side of the ship to be hoisted aboard by crane. "We've lost about 60 percent power," Whata called into the VHF.

The RIB spluttered and coughed and chugged along in the swell until she crashed to a halt against her mother ship. Lines dropped from the deck, and they secured them to hold her alongside until the cable from the winch was within reach.

But the two boats pitched and rolled clumsily, and disaster struck again: The hoisting cable jumped its pulley and jammed in the block.

The RIB, now dangling on its cable, was a pendulum swinging to the rhythm of the sea, its arc blocked by the *Monowai*. Time and time again, she swung out and came back, each time ending against the ship's side with a violent jolt that could catapult the crew into the churning sea below.

Meanwhile, the hoisting team took the block apart and reassembled it. Cmdr. Robbins ordered two sailors to stand by with life buoys and smoke markers in case any of the RIB's crew were knocked overboard. When the swell lifted the RIB level with the deck, heaving lines were passed to the crew to tie around their waists.

Despite his military training, Whata feared he might not survive the pounding. He looked at the medic and noticed he was trembling. His face was blank and devoid of emotion. Affectionately, Whata cuffed him around the neck to shake him out of it.

"Just think, mate, in a few years you'll be bouncing grandchildren on your knees and telling them what happened," he joked.

The medic gave him an incredulous look. "It's no time to think about grandchildren," he said.

"Don't worry about it, mate, we'll get out of this, you know. Just hold onto the steadying lines."

Whata suggested to the hand in charge of hoisting the RIB that the medic should be taken off at the first opportunity. "He's quite shaken," he said.

The RIB moved upward, and as it paused level with the deck the medic stepped over the side to safety. The *Monowai* rolled to starboard again and the RIB lurched outward, only to smash back against the side again. Whata told the bowman to get off. They handed the bags belonging to the crew of *Silver Shadow* to the sailors aboard the *Monowai*, and it was over.

The ship steamed off to hunt for *Quartermaster* and *Mary T.*

CHAPTER 11

CAN YOU SHOOT A FLARE OFF . . . ?

KEITH LEVY AND URSULA ("USCHI") SCHMIDT WERE ENJOYING ideal sailing conditions as a 15-knot breeze sped the 32-foot cutter *Sofia* toward Tonga. This was the good life Keith had promised Uschi when they'd been planning their voyage. They couldn't imagine better sailing. Since they'd pulled away from their friends on *Pilot*, they'd averaged 100 miles a day for the past three days. They wouldn't see Greg and Barbara again until they reached Tonga.

"It's a pity their radio isn't working," Keith reflected. "We could call them up." He remembered that the radio had blown a fuse every time Greg tried to use it. That didn't surprise him. At one stage, before he'd tried to repair it, it had been so hot its housing melted and it almost burst into flames.

Although he couldn't contact *Pilot*, Keith spoke frequently to passing ships. During one of these sessions, the radio operator on a freighter alerted him to a storm moving rapidly through the South Pacific. The operator suggested he should head more to the west as a precaution, although there was really little reason for concern, because the system was 500 miles east of them.

Jon Cullen confirmed the ship's report when Keith made his next scheduled radio call to Kerikeri Radio:

Keith: Keri Radio, this is *Sofia*. How do you copy?

Jon: Roger there, Keith. Gotcha strength three and clear. Go ahead.

Keith: Great. We're at 31° 27'S, 178° 05'E. We have a moderate sea. A bar[ometer] of 1018. An easterly swell of 2 meters [6½ feet].

We have 20 percent cloud. We're on a heading of 019 magnetic at 3.5 knots, and we have winds from the northeast, 20, 25, Jon.

Jon repeated *Sofia*'s position and then gave them a forecast of the weather they could expect in their general vicinity during the next 24 hours.

Jon: East-southeasterlies, 20 to 25 knots, perhaps even 30 knots. You could do with slowing down, too, I think. I'd be a bit inclined to slow down and let the system go through, or else make your heading slightly to the northwest to avoid the severity of it. But at this moment I would definitely slow down, rather than run on straight into it. Over.

Keith: Okay Jon, that's fine. That's exactly what we'll do. Thanks for that. Will it be any worse tomorrow, or just the same? Over.

Jon: No, I don't really expect so. It might touch 35 by tomorrow evening, or overnight tomorrow night, perhaps. I'm a bit short on info, but at this stage I think 30 knots will be the top of it tomorrow, but perhaps by tomorrow evening or overnight it might get more. At this stage I'm a little unsure. Over.

Keith: Okay Jon. How far nor'west do you think we should head? Over.

Jon: Well, anything you do at all is easing the situation. I think that's probably the easiest way to explain it. I don't think you have to go to the extreme, but I think anything at all is going to help you if you go to the northwest. Over.

Keith: Okay Jon, look forward to hearing from you tomorrow night. This is *Sofia* clear.

Keith was unperturbed. The weather was well within his capabilities, and the yacht's. Still, he followed the advice from Jon and the freighter's radio operator, and changed *Sofia*'s course slightly to the west, although he elected not to travel directly west because that would take them too far out of their way.

The weather slowly began to deteriorate, and the sea started to build. Uschi placed an antiseasickness patch behind her ear, but Keith assured her there was no need for alarm. Both he and *Sofia* had coped with 50 knots before, and he couldn't imagine conditions deteriorating beyond that.

Shortly before nightfall on Saturday, a massive wave pooped *Sofia*, climbing over the stern, flooding the cockpit, and smashing the windvane self-steering unit.

Keith set about cleaning up the mess of tangled lines and broken pieces. He made fast two ends of a thick warp to the stern, and cast the bight overboard to make a drogue. *Sofia* settled down and appeared more under control as she ran before the wind.

Keith considered his options. He could lash himself at the helm, close the companionway entrance, and leave Uschi below. He could manage at the helm for a few hours until the storm blew itself out. But he might be injured, and he would almost certainly exhaust himself. Then Uschi would be at risk, because her bluewater experience was limited, and he doubted her ability to cope if anything happened to him.

He therefore decided the best thing to do was leave the boat to her own devices while they both sheltered below. He checked and tightened the lashings around the jerry cans holding fuel and water. The life raft appeared safe. The drogue appeared to be doing its job. It had slowed the boat to 3 knots, just as Adlard Coles's book *Heavy Weather Sailing* had promised. He'd been reading it just that afternoon. Satisfied that the yacht was safe, he retreated below, placed the washboards into position, slid the hatch closed, and settled down to weather the storm.

But the wind continued to rise, and there was no peace below, or anywhere on *Sofia*. The waves grew steeper and more out of control, and the yacht was thrown about wildly.

Keith wondered whether he should alter the drogue, perhaps fasten a trysail to it, to slow the boat further. But he was worried that the mess of lines might foul the propeller in an emergency, so in the end he decided to leave things as they were.

Uschi's composure impressed him. For someone without sailing experience, other than the cruise they'd shared off Tonga a year earlier, and a shakedown trip to the Bay of Islands, she showed considerable courage and knowledge.

Sofia was now being battered mercilessly. The storm's increasing power surprised Keith. It was completely out of character for this time of the year. Still, that might mean it would exhaust itself quickly. So far, thankfully, the boat was meeting the challenge.

They tuned into Kerikeri Radio at 2000, and listened to Jon read his weather forecast. Once again, they heard reports of the intensity of the low-pressure system blasting through the Pacific. But there was still no indication they were in its path, and the forecast warned of worse conditions farther out in the Pacific.

"I'm glad we're not farther east," he said as he waited, microphone in hand, to be called to broadcast his position.

Suddenly, the world turned on its side. Uschi flew through the air in front of him and landed on the starboard side opposite. Glasses, food, and utensils hurtled around the cabin and smashed at his feet.

"We've been knocked down!" he shouted. After *Sofia* righted herself, he checked that Uschi was all right, and then, still surprised, kneeled down to pick up the broken glass.

"*Sofia. Sofia.* Copy Keith?" He heard Jon's voice on the SSB radio as he tried to remove the jagged slivers littering the floor.

Keith: Yes, Jon. How are you? How do you copy? Over.

Jon: Roger, Keith. I've got you loud and clear. Go ahead.

Keith: Jon, we're at 30° 00'S, 176° 55'E. We've just lost our self-steering. We're under bare poles. The tiller's . . . we've just had a partial knockdown. We're okay. We're in very rough conditions, rough seas, things aren't very happy, but we can get through the night. Over.

Jon: Roger. Could you give us your wind direction and strength please? Over.

Keith: Yes, I think it's still from the southeast, Jon. We seem to be heading approximately sou'west at the moment, or something like that. It's hard to tell. Over.

Jon: Roger. Okay. You got knocked down, but you're all well? Over.

Keith: We're just coping here, Jon. There's not much anybody can do . . . just trying to get through the night. Over.

Jon: That's all you can do, I'm afraid. Okay. Well, I've got for *Sofia* east-northeasterly to easterly-quarter winds of 40 to 50 knots. Gusts of 60 with a tendency to the east-southeast for you by this time tomorrow night, Keith. I'm afraid your next 24 hours is going to be a pretty rough one. Over.

Keith: Oh well, okay. We heard an Orion was over this afternoon and we hope they will start looking for us like that too, Jon. I trust you will have your station on all night, Jon?

Jon: Roger. Roger. The Orion is actually going to be on standby over *Destiny* until midnight as well, so there'll be an Orion out there all night. Over.

Keith: Okay, Jon. Are they on [Channel] 16, or what are they on? Over.

Jon: Sixteen continuously and 2182 [KHz]. Over.

Keith: Okay Jon. Thank you very much.

The moment Keith signed off from Kerikeri Radio, two other voices urgently requested *Sofia* contact them on another channel. Keith was overwhelmed. Cruising friends he'd made in the past offered him encouragement. Their words did wonders for his morale. Even 500 miles out in the South Pacific, he was not alone.

He started the motor to charge batteries, and returned to the navigation station. Uschi was standing between the table and the galley bench, repacking loose gear, when she felt the cabin slowly rotate. She screamed. The carpet flew through the air, and the companionway entrance turned upside down. A mighty force grabbed her from behind and hurled her to the far side of the boat.

Within seconds, *Sofia* was completely inverted. She didn't right herself straight away. She just squatted there, the wrong way up, while cushions and locker lids and books and crockery rained down onto the overhead.

"We have to get out of here!" Uschi screamed from beneath the mess.

Keith didn't respond. He couldn't. He lay limp and unconscious on the overhead.

"My glasses. I can't find my glasses," Uschi sobbed, groping around in the mess. She abandoned the search and sat down in despair.

Sofia seemed to remain upside down for an eternity, but gradually she tilted over again, gathering speed as she completed her roll through 360 degrees.

Uschi rolled with *Sofia* as the yacht finally swayed upright. A moment later, Uschi felt water lapping about her calves. She grabbed the microphone. "Mayday! Mayday! Mayday!" she called, fearing she could die at any moment. Nobody answered her. She could hear other crews speaking on the radio, but they evidently couldn't hear her. The antenna must have been damaged.

She quickly calmed down and tried to think what to do. *Sofia's* motor had died when they rolled, and the terror of the moment was heightened by the scream of the engine's oil alarm.

She looked for her glasses again, groping for them in the water, but still couldn't find them. Eventually, she came across her camera bag, which contained a spare pair. The sight in the cabin was not reassuring. The boat was in chaos. Water swirled through everything, carrying papers, books, frozen food, and all sorts of gear in its wake.

Lifejackets! she thought. *I must get the lifejackets!*

She noticed the EPIRB fixed in its bracket beside the companionway and quickly read the instructions for activating it. They offered her three options, which totally confused her, so she decided to wait for Keith to regain consciousness.

While struggling into a lifejacket, she found her right shoe and a left boot. She pulled them onto protect her feet from the broken glass scattered under water on the floor.

Water pouring down from overhead made her look up. The skylight was smashed, and she wondered if she should get the life raft ready so they could abandon ship. The raft was stowed on deck, but when she tried the companionway hatch, it was jammed tight and she couldn't budge it.

Uschi returned to Keith, urgently struggling to get him into a lifejacket while he slowly regained consciousness. He awoke to the wailing of the engine alarm on the dead motor.

"Where are we?" he asked groggily. "What's happening? Where's the water coming from?"

She told him what had happened, but he didn't understand. "How dare water enter this boat?" he asked incoherently. "How dare it? How could it?"

Uschi waited patiently for him to recover. "What the hell happened?" he asked again. "I just can't believe it," he said angrily.

"We're on our way to Tonga in a storm and we have been rolled," Uschi told him.

Disorientated and dazed, he wondered if his ears were playing tricks. *Shit, she said we're on our way to Tonga. I don't understand. Maybe it's a language thing between us.*

She told him the same thing several times during the next 10 minutes, while he gradually regained his faculties.

"We're on our way to Tonga? What are we doing now?"

"Well, you know, we've been knocked over and we've been rolled around. The skylight is broken." She slowly spelled it all out in a matter-of-fact manner.

He looked up and saw the gap overhead where the water had washed in.

"There's water all over our beautiful new carpet and all over the place, it's just crazy," he raved, still stunned. But his mind began to clear gradually, and soon he was able to focus on their plight.

"Are you all right?" Uschi inquired anxiously.

"My back hurts," he said.

She showed him the EPIRB and told him she'd tried to activate it. "I was too nervous. I couldn't read the instructions," she admitted. "I tried to get a Mayday call through to Kerikeri. We could receive them, but I couldn't break into them. Jon just kept talking on and on, and I couldn't get through."

Keith struggled to the companionway hatch to put the EPIRB outside, but it wouldn't open for him either. Hoping the signal would carry outside the boat, he wedged the beacon in the companionway and switched it on. It was 2211 on Saturday, June 4.

"Grab your boots," Uschi warned, telling him about the broken glass hidden beneath the water swirling over the cabin sole.

Keith then started an inspection tour to find out what damage had occurred down below. The freezer had emptied its contents, and the coffee grinder had flown through the air, but he was relieved to find his careful stowage routine had limited the mess inside. He saw that plywood bunk tops in the forward cabin, which had not been locked in place, had fallen out, but others in the saloon had remained firm. Netting had restrained dozens of books, a computer, cameras, and food. He was amused that a heavy sewing machine had moved from the starboard side to the port side, while chain originally stowed on the port side now lay piled on the starboard side. The stove had slipped its gimbals and was inoperable. Water splashed about the cabin sole.

The water level did not seem to be rising, so Keith was fairly sure the boat wasn't holed. Something was knocking lightly against the hull, but it did not sound serious enough for immediate investigation. More worrying was the gap in the overhead skylight. The lid appeared to have been wrenched from its hinges, rather than smashed by some heavy object flying around outside. But, on the whole, they had escaped lightly, Keith thought. He was pleased that their thorough preparation for the trip had kept the damage down.

By this time, Uschi wanted desperately to lie down, but Keith was afraid shock and hypothermia would set in. Activity would be their ally, he reasoned. Work would occupy their minds and protect them from dangerous negative emotions. He insisted they busy themselves, so they started tidying the boat and finding a dry place to store valuable tools and survival equipment: flashlights, batteries, and food.

The driest place on the boat was the forward cabin. They cleared a space there and secured their survival gear so it would come to no harm if the yacht capsized again. The V-berth up forward was also the safest place for them, they saw, because if *Sofia* rolled again they wouldn't have far to fall.

How bad was the damage outside? Keith opened the forward hatch and stuck his head out. The mast and rigging were gone, and the boom gallows was crushed against the companionway. In the darkness, he couldn't tell whether the jerry cans of fuel and water were still there or not, but he could see the life raft. Thank God! At least they still had the security of their life raft. He shut the hatch to wait for daylight before making a closer inspection.

Meanwhile, they searched fruitlessly for the VHF radio. They'd need it to talk to aircraft or ships homing in on their beacon. They groped under water, obsessed with finding it, even if it was wet and useless. They searched cupboards, lockers, and the navigation station, and returned time and time again to inspect its usual home behind the shortwave radio. It should have been stored there, and neither of them recalled removing it. They stared despondently at the empty space as if willing the radio to materialize. Unbelievable! It was nowhere to be found.

The hunt consumed them for hours but the radio remained invisible until, just as they were about to give up, they discovered it tucked down the side of a cushion in the forward cabin. They turned it on. To their immense relief, it crackled to life.

Their next priority was the water. They had to get rid of it. Keith was scared that if they lay down in their bunks, they wouldn't want to get up again. They had to use buckets to bail because the bilge pump was clogged with debris. At first, Uschi handed full buckets to Keith, who emptied them through the forward hatch. But it was slow, tedious work that sapped their strength.

After a while, they opened a small hatch above the galley. It was a little larger than the book, *Heavy Weather Sailing*, he had read earlier. To get the water out, Keith had to meticulously maneuver a small saucepan through the opening, empty it, and twist it back inside the opening. They worked most of the night that way. Water splashed back over them all the time, and they had to stop and change into dry clothes several times to ward off hypothermia. It was exhausting, and neither of them knew what kept them going, but the water level continued to fall until it was all gone. And, thankfully, it did not rise again.

SUNDAY, JUNE 5, AT 0600

Eleven hours of toil passed slowly. Keith and Uschi grew to dread a hush that frequently descended on *Sofia*. They found the silence warned of the approach of a huge wave about to tumble over the boat, pushing her to the brink of another roll. Each silence warned them to brace for the inevitable blow that might push *Sofia* over for the last time. But each time, they came back upright, only to wait for the next hush to descend. When dawn did finally come, it brought no cheer. It revealed the biggest seas they had seen in their lives and kindled greater fear in them.

Keith had assumed that the knocking noise he'd heard all night was the mast hitting the hull. Now he had to find out for sure.

He climbed through the forward hatch, tethered by two lines, and hauled himself up on deck. His body was growing stiff from hours of bailing. He attached the tethers to both the port and starboard jacklines and slowly crawled along the bare deck with Uschi shouting warnings about approaching waves. He tied an orange rescue cloth over the broken skylight and stopped most of the water going below. From what he could see, the mast wasn't responsible for the knocking noise. The boom was hanging over the port side of the boat and was banging against the hull. Uschi handed him the wire cutters. He was concerned that the mast would pierce the vessel like a lance if she rolled over again, so he cut some shrouds and stays until it lay clear, although it was still attached. He chose to cut the wires where they lay across the deck, rather than unfasten the clevis pins at the chainplates near the gunwales. He felt it would be too dangerous to work so close to the sides of the boat.

He cut the shrouds and slashed the mainsheet, and the boom slipped from view. A 3-inch stump of mast protruded above the deck. He crawled aft to the cockpit and saw that the companionway hatch wouldn't open because the boom gallows had fallen against it.

Keith was concerned about the way the boat was lying. He thought that putting an anchor out might alleviate the problem. He let the 40-pound CQR run out its full 120 feet of chain. Then he unlashed the 80-pound Northill storm anchor, tied 330 feet of 1-inch nylon rode to it, picked it up with one hand, and tossed it overboard. A few moments later, when he thought about the feat he'd just performed, he was astonished. *Jesus, how did I throw that over?* he wondered.

While he was still marveling, the handheld radio burst into life with the voice of an RNZAF Hercules pilot. Keith scrambled back down below.

"Can you shoot a flare off in a couple of minutes?" the pilot asked.

Keith found the flares and fired one off. Within seconds, the Orion flew out of the gray shroud in which they were engulfed and passed low over them. Uschi and Keith hugged and cried and yelled, relieved that at least there were now other human beings nearby who knew where they were. As the emotion poured out of them, so did Keith's strength. He slumped, totally exhausted, into the cockpit.

The air crew promised to stay nearby, and to check on them every hour. Their presence eased the pressure on Keith, and for the first time since the capsize he felt able to rest. He climbed into the forward berth, but he was so stiff and tired that he couldn't undress. Uschi cut his wet clothes from him with scissors, and he drifted off into an exhausted sleep, which lasted only about 20 minutes.

As the day progressed, the weather improved and blue sky poked through the scattering clouds. When Keith woke up, they lunched on dried apricots and Coca-Cola. The future began to look a bit brighter.

"Hey, this is going to be okay," Keith told Uschi. "Maybe we won't have to get off. Maybe we'll be taken in tow." Some other "maybes" occurred to him, too: *Maybe Uschi will get on the rescue boat, and they'll put somebody on here. Maybe we'll get a jury rig up tomorrow if the thing is calming down.* The one thing he didn't speculate on then was that the weather might get worse again. But it did.

A few hours later, his delusions of remaining aboard were shattered. The wind rose slowly but inexorably, and the familiar roar of huge, breaking waves returned. They cried together again when the air crew told them their friends Greg and Barbara from *Pilot* were safe aboard the *Monowai*, and that the flares Keith had given them contributed to their rescue. In their tired, emotional state, the Orion stirred them each time it passed, and they grew to rely on sighting it every hour. They admired the crew's precision when they flew low over them and dropped a sonar buoy alongside to enable them to locate *Sofia* in the event their EPIRB failed.

On one run, the Hercules reported it was returning to New Zealand to refuel, and that another aircraft would replace them. Paranoia gripped Uschi when no plane arrived for three hours. It was the longest they had been ignored since the Hercules found them earlier in the day.

Keith had to deal with what was left of the rigging because of his continuing fears of the damage it could cause if they rolled. He now thought it best to ditch it completely, so he went to work with the wire cutters to free the roller-furling headstay and sail. For one brief moment he put the cutters on the deck while he shut the companionway. The boat rolled viciously. He watched helplessly as the cutters slipped toward the gunwales in slow motion. He grabbed at them, but it was too late. They slid over the side. He marveled at the sapphire-blue of the water that devoured them; it was as if he had never noticed it before.

I've lost the bloody things. I should have tied them to myself, he thought. *I just couldn't get there fast enough.*

He cursed his carelessness and fetched a hacksaw from below. Of course, it would happen now, just when he was tackling the most dangerous stay of all, the forestay. It would be much more difficult to saw through the wire with a hacksaw, and it would take much longer. But he set to determinedly, and finally the mast and rigging sank, free and clear of the hull.

That evening, in the gathering darkness, their old, familiar fears returned. They listened tensely for the unnerving stillness that warned of an enormous wave about to slam into their side, and perhaps capsize them. Each time it happened, *Sofia* teetered on the brink, but just as it seemed she would roll over, she steadied herself. Occasionally, they drank a little whiskey to warm themselves, but the night dragged miserably. They could only hope they would survive a few hours more, long enough to be rescued by the French warship that was on its way.

The French transport ship *Jacques Cartier* left Brisbane, Australia, for Tauranga, a lumber port on the east coast of New Zealand's North Island, on Tuesday, May 31. It was an important assignment: She was the first French naval vessel to visit New Zealand since French commandos mined the Greenpeace antinuclear protest vessel *Rainbow Warrior* in Auckland harbor nine years previously.

The *Rainbow Warrior* had spent several years protesting French nuclear tests on the South Pacific atoll of Mururoa, tests that New Zealanders thought should have been conducted in France's own backyard, not theirs. The *Rainbow Warrior* had been in Auckland only three days when French Navy divers attached a limpet mine and sank her, killing a Portuguese photographer, Fernando Pereira.

Relations between France and New Zealand were severely strained.

The ship's visit to the quiet little port was planned as a low-key public-relations exercise, part of the delicate process of rebuilding relationships with New Zealanders, who'd been outraged by the blatant French terrorism.

The *Jacques Cartier*'s crew were well aware of all this, and conscious of their important public-relations assignment in New Zealand. Auckland, the country's largest city, was obviously out of bounds for the vessel because of possible objections from local residents, so she planned to call at Tauranga instead.

As they steamed across the Tasman Sea they ran into the storm. It slowed them down to 8 knots, and they feared their arrival at Tauranga would be delayed. The *Jacques Cartier*, lightly laden and with a shallow keel designed for beaching the bow on atolls, was not comfortable in the tempestuous conditions.

The order to help the New Zealand search-and-rescue teams came from their headquarters at Noumea. The information was surprising: eight yachts in trouble, some already abandoned. Their task was to save the crew of *Sofia*.

They altered course and headed into the storm for 36 hours, experiencing increasingly harsh conditions. The RCC and the Orions kept them updated on developments in the disaster zone, despite occasional language problems.

MONDAY, JUNE 6, AT 2030

The Orion dropped flares to light the way for the French ship. It was pitch-black and blowing a strong gale.

The ship's spotlights finally found *Sofia* in the darkness, playing on Keith and Uschi as they stood waiting in the cockpit. The Frenchmen were alarmed at the conditions. Huge waves pounded *Sofia* and threatened to capsize her at any moment. Breaking crests crashed over her decks and rolled her so vigorously they exposed her keel.

"I'm so happy, I can't believe somebody has come to get us," Keith yelled with relief on the radio. He seemed so emotional, the

Frenchmen believed he was about to burst into tears. "We've had a plane over us for two days, but a plane is not the same as a ship. The plane can't do anything except talk," he explained.

The officers aboard *Jacques Cartier* grew concerned they would lose the little boat behind the towering walls of water concealing her from their spotlights. If they lost sight of her, they would have to start the operation all over again, relying on the Orion to guide them in, and then scanning the sea to pick up a speck in the darkness. Transfixing *Sofia* in their lights, they searched for the best course to carry out the rescue—a mission that would require precision sailing and one that could jeopardize the safety of both vessels. The waves were so threatening, the captain endeavored not to take them abeam. If the *Jacques Cartier* came too close, *Sofia* could be crushed by a collision with the transport ship.

The captain and crew had a bold plan. They would lower a Zodiac and send a team of divers to evacuate *Sofia*'s helpless crew.

The French officers pitied Keith as he waited numbly in the cockpit. They could imagine what he and his companion had already endured, and they suspected he was too exhausted to cope any longer. With help at hand, Keith's last vestige of strength had ebbed.

Aboard the *Jacques Cartier*, the atmosphere was electric. Despite the danger, all 70 sailors aboard would likely have volunteered to join the rescue party. They felt an affinity with *Sofia*'s bedraggled crew, whom they envisioned as close to death. They knew they had to act swiftly. The storm was suspected of having taken three lives already.

When she hit the water, the Zodiac inflatable fought and strained against her painter, but she quickly got under way with a coxswain and three divers aboard.

Although the sea had abated somewhat since the height of the storm on Saturday night, it was still tumultuous. The wind roared at gale force, and combers rumbled and rolled around the inflatable as she picked her way carefully through the darkness to *Sofia*. There, a diver rolled over the side and waited in the roiling water, hanging onto the Zodiac's lifelines, in case Keith or Uschi fell into the water during their transfer.

Aboard the *Jacques Cartier*, the five officers on the bridge were concerned when *Sofia* disappeared from the 1,600-foot range of their spotlights. The yacht was drifting rapidly away from the ship.

A wave lifted the Zodiac above the yacht. The rescue crew jumped aboard *Sofia* and found Keith and Uschi exhausted, almost incapable of helping themselves.

"Is anyone injured?" they were asked. "Can you move?"

"We're all right," came the response.

"The bags, throw the bags over!" Uschi yelled to Keith as she passed their belongings to the rescuers.

"No, you go first," the Frenchman insisted.

Keith shut the companionway hatch.

The Frenchmen threw some of the gear into the Zodiac, explaining they could not take everything because, with six people in the rubber boat, there was little space for baggage. They ordered Keith and Uschi to wait for the moment when the two craft were level and then to jump into the Zodiac.

Keith called farewells into the handheld radio to the circling Orion. "Don't leave. Don't leave. Thank you very much, I'm grateful for what you did. We'll see you in Auckland."

"Go! Go! Go!" the Frenchman ordered. Uschi unclipped her harness, stepped over the lifeline, and jumped into the Zodiac. She clung to one of the divers as the bobbing craft moved away from the yacht for safety.

"We have to hurry!" the coxswain shouted to Keith as he brought the Zodiac back alongside the yacht. But Keith was too tired to jump. With two divers helping him from *Sofia*'s deck, he struggled to board the Zodiac. The men below pulled at his legs to drag him into the inflatable, and he tumbled among them.

As the coxswain maneuvered the Zodiac alongside the *Jacques Cartier*, a line with a harness was dropped into the boat. A ladder stretched up the ship's side.

"We'll put a harness around you to help you climb up the ladder," the coxswain told Keith. "Go up as fast as you can."

God, how am I going to do that? Keith wondered. It was all he could do to stand up.

He needn't have worried. The crew on deck pulled him up quicker than he could climb. He fell onto the ship's deck head-first. Swiftly, hands scooped him up and led him, dazed, toward the sick bay. He turned back, wanting to see if Uschi was all right, and then watched her scramble up the side of the ship.

While they were examined in the sick bay, the ship aimed her guns at *Sofia*. They'd received a request from the RCC to sink the yacht, so she wouldn't be a hazard to shipping.

The ship's captain came and told Keith and Uschi what he was about to do. They cried at the news. Before he'd left *Sofia*, Keith had written a note on the main bulkhead in the cabin:

"Thank you for being such a lovely lady. We'll be back for you."

Now they were betraying her. They were going to be party to her destruction. As they showered, they listened for the 20 mm cannon fire that would signal *Sofia's* last moments. But it never came.

The captain of the *Jacques Cartier* had had second thoughts. *Sofia* was registered in New Zealand. Shooting a New Zealand yacht out of the water might not be a diplomatic move, considering the reasons for their visit.

The *Jacques Cartier's* captain contacted the RCC and asked for confirmation that he was to sink *Sofia*. When confronted with the request, Bill Sommer issued a reprieve. He told the Frenchmen that if they could get an accurate fix of the yacht's position, the RCC would issue a Notice to Mariners, and *Sofia* could be left afloat.

Instead of continuing her trip to Tauranga, the *Jacques Cartier* steamed with the rescued crew of the New Zealand yacht directly to a berth at the Devonport Navy Base in Auckland, the home of the Royal New Zealand Navy. The Frenchmen tied up within gunshot of where their compatriots had mined the *Rainbow Warrior* nine years earlier, but the locals made no objection. The French Navy had acted very bravely to save one of their sons.

CHAPTER 12

TO THE EDGE OF PERIL

THE MESSAGE DIVIANA WHEELER RECEIVED, THAT THEY WOULD travel to the edge of peril, could have persuaded *Heart Light*'s skipper to abort the voyage to Fiji. But the weather improved after the storm they encountered off Great Barrier Island, near Auckland, and Darryl Wheeler insisted on continuing. Diviana was unhappy with his decision, and considered it irrational that after 25 years of marriage, during which the accuracy of her clairvoyance had been proven time and again, he should ignore her premonition. But she could not sway his judgment. She felt Darryl was at a crossroads in his life, confronted with making a significant decision involving his consciousness. She believed Darryl's usual faultless logic had been eroded by materialism resulting from his business success. When his decision was made, however, she was obliged to support him, even though she had been warned of the consequences. Besides, because of her faith in God, she knew how to cope with the threat of death.

Darryl, meanwhile, was trying to decide whether to sail the 60 miles back to New Zealand's Bay of Islands to repair the broken pole for *Heart Light*'s wind generator. The equipment had cost $2,000, and his worry was that it might be lost overboard if conditions deteriorated during the passage.

The weather was so beautiful that it was inconceivable the wind would blow harder than 40 knots. After all, the cyclone season was over, and Diviana's warning about traveling to the edge of peril had been fulfilled by the experience off Great Barrier Island. Neither he nor Diviana had told their son, Shane, or his wife, Stephanie, about that warning, and it didn't seem to matter now.

"Conditions are perfect," Darryl said. "It's a sailor's dream."

So *Heart Light* pressed on, sailing away from New Zealand toward Fiji, passing first *Quartermaster* and then *Silver Shadow*. Darryl was anxious to reach latitude 29° south, the magical border that divides the stormy outskirts of the Roaring Forties from the gentle trade winds.

Diviana relished the wonderful sailing conditions as much as Darryl, but for a different reason. She felt that previous bluewater excursions had enhanced her clairvoyant and telepathic powers. Sailing the ocean, she was free from the clutter of polluting energy forces generated by electricity transmission lines, television sets, telephones, and other electromagnetic debris in the atmosphere.

Her pursuit of personal fulfillment had evolved into contact with the extraterrestrial. Before starting this trip, she had received a message that she would be contacted at sea by another dimension. On Thursday, June 2, the contacts were so real she underwent experiences she referred to as altered states of consciousness.

She told Darryl that she had first experienced contact with beings from another world when she was 4 years old, but she'd not spoken about it for 32 years.

As the trip progressed and the weather patterns changed, she once again felt in contact with these alien visitors. Darryl was used to his wife's experiences and took little notice as he went about the business of keeping the boat on course in deteriorating conditions.

While she meditated, a particular mantra played in Diviana's mind: "The Kingdom of Heaven is near at hand. The Kingdom of Heaven is near at hand. The Kingdom of Heaven is near at hand." She could not stifle the communication. As she continued, Diviana received a clear feeling about the message, although she still did not receive a full picture of its meaning: They were going to the edge of peril.

The deteriorating conditions plunged everyone aboard the catamaran into a state of foreboding. Darryl spent much of his time on watch, getting little sleep after Thursday evening. Neither Shane nor Stephanie had much bluewater experience, and Darryl sat dozing beside them as they stood their watches.

"A container ship, when it comes on the horizon, can hit you within 20 minutes if you are not paying attention," he warned them.

Stephanie was seasick, but she stood the watch from 2100 to 2400, and Shane did the next three hours. They rotated the watches over a 24-hour period, and although she felt ill Stephanie always surfaced for her shift. Diviana tried to feed her yogurt, but Stephanie couldn't keep anything down. She kept a bowl beside her throughout her watch. All she wanted was to finish her watch and go to sleep.

Diviana wasn't able to help Darryl much. She often meditated on her watches. She discovered she could endure up to eight hours scanning the ocean in her semialert state and, remarkably, complete her stints feeling as refreshed as when she began. Darryl, on the other hand, needed his rest because fatigue took its toll. But as Diviana meditated, Darryl found himself being required to keep watch almost around the clock.

FRIDAY, JUNE 3

They tuned in the SSB radio and learned that several yacht crews were becoming alarmed about the threatening weather. They contacted *Quartermaster*, and sensed that Bob and Marie Rimmer were scared. Bob sounded very tired. "We'll just keep hoping for the best," he said.

Darryl decided to slow the boat, to let the depression pass ahead of him. He lowered all sail and motored under bare poles. They discussed their changing weather with Kerikeri Radio that evening.

Jon: Heart Light. Copy Darryl?

Darryl: Good evening, Jon. This is *Heart Light.*

Jon: Roger. Got you there, strength two to three. Go ahead.

Darryl: We're located at 30° 05'S, 179° 30'E. We're on a heading of 020 magnetic. We're steering at a slow speed of 6 knots. Easterly winds, 20, 25. We have 100 percent cloud cover, we have 2-meter swell of confused seas and a bar[ometer] reading of 1025 and all's well. Over.

Jon Cullen repeated the information to ensure he'd recorded it accurately, and then delivered the 24-hour forecast he'd prepared for *Heart Light's* area.

Jon: Easterly-quarter winds, predominantly. Twenty, 25, may rise to 30. You could also expect gusts of 40. I have that with a question mark, so you may not get them, but I'm warning you anyhow. It could happen. You're certainly fairly well across and you could just catch the edge of it, with the tendency, of course to the southeast, as the system goes past. So it's a day of caution tomorrow . . .

Darryl: Roger, Jon.

Jon: If I was you I'd be a little inclined to slow down a tad. I know that's a bit of a shame, but I would be inclined to just slow down a touch because the system . . . you don't want to go right into the middle of it. Over.

Darryl: Yeah. Roger. I think that's good advice, Jon. We appreciate that. At this point, we'll endeavor to slow her down to about 4 knots. This is *Heart Light* clear. Over.

Jon: Yeah, that would be the move all right. About 4 knots would be just about right, and let it go through ahead of you because it's unknown the speed that it's traveling, so I wouldn't like to see you in the middle of it. Okay. Do take care then. We'll catch you tomorrow. Good night.

Darryl: Good night, Jon.

Darryl decided to head west, and used a small parachute sea anchor as a drogue streamed aft to slow her further. During the night, both *Quartermaster* and *Silver Shadow* passed them. Next time they heard them on the radio, they were 60 and 70 miles ahead of *Heart Light.*

Jon: Heart Light. Good morning.

Darryl: Good morning, Jon. Our position is 29° 28'S, 179° 30'E. We're steering due west with a southeasterly [wind] of 30 to 40 knots. Sea's confused and rough. About 10-foot swell and the barometer looks like it's about 1018, and we're making about 4 knots. Over.

Jon: And all okay?

Darryl: Yeah, okay, Jon. We saw a boat light about 10 miles north of us and heading northeast, so we decided to head west and maybe the system will pass over the top [to the north] of us and we're trying to decide whether that's the best option. Over.

Jon: Yes. Well it [the weather map] doesn't look a very good one this morning, I'd have to say that. Unfortunately the low pressure, for midnight tonight, is expected to be about 27° south and 178° east, and that, with the opposing high pressure down south, at 43° south or 44° south, and 173° east, with a pressure of 1034, is creating a very strong sou'easterly flow between the two systems. It looks like it's going to just about come over the top of you, unfortunately, but you're going in the right direction, anyhow, to ease it, if you can. That's all you can do. Over.

Darryl: Roger. So heading westerly is right tactics?

Jon: Yeah. That's right. Well, you don't have a choice. If you want to ease it at all, that's the only way you can really go with some ease, otherwise you're going to tend to sail straight into it. It's still going to catch you. I'm afraid you're probably going to have to just heave-to, in the final analysis of it. The day is going to get extremely boisterous by the look of it. You'll have 30 to 40 [knots] and it looks as if it may even go to 40 or 50. Over.

TO THE EDGE OF PERIL   179

Darryl: Okay. Roger. Is it going to go through in 24 hours, do you think, or are we going to have it with us for a couple of days? Over.

Jon: I would think it's going to go over you probably during the next 24 hours and then start to ease slowly on the back of it with southerly-quarter winds. Over.

Darryl: Okay, Jon. Appreciate that. We'll get off the air 'cause there are others that want to talk to you. This is *Heart Light* clear.

Jon: Okay. Good luck for the day then. Take care.

As Darryl listened to the reports from the other yachts calling Kerikeri it was obvious the weather forecasts supplied by the meteorological office in New Zealand had not kept up with the storm's increasing ferocity. Boat after boat reported a rough night, with conditions continuing to deteriorate. Few of the yachts now had an opportunity to avoid the weather, and Jon advised them to prepare for a rough time.

Diviana was concerned that Darryl was growing frightened by the conditions and that fear was draining his energy. "You sound and look very tired," she said sympathetically.

She pulled out charts and searched for a haven in which to shelter from the storm. There was nowhere to hide. New Zealand's shores were more than 400 miles behind them, the Kermadec Islands were even farther away to the east, and Fiji was still about a week away.

They changed course to run to the northwest, which was a little closer to their desired course. Darryl doubted whether the wind would build much beyond the 40 knots forecast by Jon, although he expected it to swing around to the northwest eventually when the system passed over them.

Stephanie valiantly tried to stand her watch at 2100, but the seas and wind built to a strength she could not manage, and Diviana relieved her. Watches were not physically onerous aboard *Heart Light*. The boat sailed permanently on autopilot, and the duty crew had only to sit in the helmsman's chair inside the spacious cabin, scan the horizon, and keep an eye on the instruments above the wheel. It was so pleasantly simple to control the boat from inside that they had never manually steered her during 16,000 miles of ocean passages. The only time they ever took her off autopilot was when Darryl maneuvered her into a berth, picked up a mooring, or eased her onto a beach.

"If we have to steer this boat by hand you may as well kiss your ass good-bye, because I don't know how to steer her," Darryl admitted as the wind reached 60 knots later in the morning, and the sea grew accordingly. "I've never done it in calm weather, let alone in a storm."

Because of their lack of experience at the helm, Diviana spent her watch concentrating on the three dials displaying information about the autopilot's performance. She watched how "George," as they dubbed it, steered the boat. The seas had risen to 25 feet, and were very confused. *Heart Light* slid down the waves, her stern sliding sideways as if it were trying to overtake the bow. The autopilot screamed its protest at the stern's disobedience and changed the angle of the rudder. Diviana noted the degrees of correction on the dials and the rudder-angle display. George always brought the stern around slowly, she discovered. They would rise to the top and rush down another wave, only to have the same motion repeated as the stern tried to have its way. But George always won. Diviana learned his rhythm and figured out how to steer the boat manually, if necessary. God forbid!

"What the hell was that?" Darryl yelled as the boat shuddered under a wave.

"The bulletproof glass has gone!"

"Jesus Christ!"

He had secured the clear acrylic storm covers over the large cabin windows before they'd left New Zealand, and now one of them had been wrenched off by a large sea. Diviana decided to make sure others knew of their predicament. She called Kerikeri Radio.

Diviana: Kerikeri Radio, this is *Heart Light.*

Maureen: Ah, *Heart Light.* Kerikeri. Go ahead.

Diviana: Good evening. It's *Heart Light. Heart Light.* L. I. G. H. T. We've got a bit of a situation here, so we thought we would try and check in early. We're on a catamaran and we're not able to heave-to. We've been running before the storm. We have 60-plus knots of wind and we have a confused sea, so I thought I would give you a location.

Maureen: Roger. Yes. Go ahead.

Diviana: We are now at 28° 53.96'S, 178° 40.55'E. We are steering approximately, at time to time, 300 magnetic. Our speed varies from 6 through to 12 knots. Our wind speed at the moment is 49, 53, well, it's running up and down. Over.

Maureen repeated the coordinates to verify she had recorded them correctly, and then asked them to stand by while she checked whether Jon had compiled a forecast of the conditions they could expect.

Maureen: Easterly-quarter, 50 gusting 60, tending to the east-south-east, and into the southeast and east-southeast by tomorrow evening's sked. Over.

Diviana: Can you give us any kind of hope on when it might ease? We're having a hard time steering and we're getting awfully tired and we'd like to know when it might start easing up a bit.

Maureen: Just stand by. I'll go and ask Jon. He's having his dinner . . . No, that's the best he can do for you, I'm afraid. That's the best he can do. Over.

Diviana: Thank you. Could you please write this phone number down? Only call it if it's irreversible that we can't make it back to land. My family in the United States don't know where we are. Please contact Ester Watson [she gave a New Zealand number]. My mother's phone number in the United States is [she gave a number on the West Coast] and she should also be told that her grandson was with us also.

Maureen: Roger. Okay, I've made a note of it and we'll hear from you tomorrow morning on the high-frequency. [Maureen seemed shaken by the request, which seemed a stark indication of the seriousness of the drama being enacted on the sea.]

Diviana: We hope so. And please don't call that number unless you don't hear from us. Thank you so much. Bye-bye.

Maureen: Yeah. Okay. Take care out there. Hang in. It will improve.

But it did not. The ferocity of the wind and sea continued to increase throughout Saturday night, sapping their strength. Even George found it too much when *Heart Light*'s stern was whacked by a huge comber that slewed her around with irresistible force. Diviana felt a sudden change in rhythm. She responded quickly, switching off the autopilot and steering the way it had shown her. She taught Darryl to do it, too. When *Heart Light* straightened out, she turned the autopilot back on, and George took over again, only to die 10 minutes later. After two more attempts, it became obvious that George could no longer cope.

Darryl grabbed the wheel from Diviana and took control. The sky flashed with lightning, and thunder rumbled and cracked across the ocean. The yacht shuddered, and cracked, and shrieked.

For the previous 48 hours, Diviana had been meditating, and now she felt an intensification of the whole cosmic conflict swirling about her. She received powerful messages that involved everyone aboard *Heart Light*.

At the wheel, Darryl was not certain they'd survive. He fought to keep *Heart Light* from toppling over, but he had no real faith in his ability to stave off capsize. He had several verbal exchanges with Diviana, who believed he was undergoing a significant transformation of his state of consciousness.

Concerned that he was being too negative, Diviana pulled the cushion off the helmsman's chair and made him sit on the hard bucket seat. And she fought to change his attitude, and instill some confidence in him.

"Don't you forget you were born and raised in Fairbanks," she said. "You're one of the best drivers I've ever known. Ever since you were a kid, you've done wheelies on the ice. Be a kid again. Pretend you're on ice, driving your car. There's no difference! Drive by the seat of your pants. Feel it. Become one with it."

Both of them had spent much of their early lives in snow country: Alaska, Colorado, and Idaho. They knew how to drive in treacherous weather. And Diviana had shown complete faith in Darryl's driving skills.

"I never thought twice about it when we were driving in that car," Diviana told him. "So keep your butt on that seat, and it will be like doing the same thing out here."

She stood behind him, massaging the tension from his neck and shoulders, and caressing his cheek. She tried to calm him and assure him they were not alone. She was aware that other beings were with them.

Diviana succeeded in raising Darryl's spirits. He kept both of *Heart Light*'s engines running, and used them to maneuver the catamaran to avoid broaching.

He would turn the wheel one way, then the other, level off, and then catch her again as the twin rudders bit and responded. He would thrust the throttles fully forward, and the engines would scream when the propellers came clear of the water. He held her steady, concentrating on the compass, trying to keep her between 300 and 330 degrees. The wind, now 60 knots, continued to rise.

Diviana was impressed. It appeared to her that Darryl had mastered the boat's motion, and *Heart Light* could not turn one way or another without his controlling her. Outside, the night was bleak. The darkness was impenetrable. The cabin windows were constantly under water, lashed by spray and swamped by breakers.

Darryl was glad he'd fastened the thick, bulletproof sheets of acrylic plastic over the large windows. *Heart Light* was submerged so often, it seemed more like they were traveling in a submarine than on a catamaran.

A banging noise on the port hull attracted his attention. The dinghy was loose. They had paid $3,000 for a new hard-bottomed inflatable dinghy before leaving Auckland. They'd lashed it securely after the wind had loosened it earlier, but now it was a flying missile in the cockpit, banging about and threatening to puncture a hull. Darryl dared not leave the helm. Shane would have to go outside into the darkness and secure it before it caused serious damage.

Diviana clung to Shane's shaking legs to help calm him before he opened the door to the cockpit to assess the situation. The waves crashed in heavily and poured through the door. She couldn't keep it open for long, so she had to abandon Shane outside. He had no harness or tether to secure him to the boat. Grabbing a flashlight, she shone it through a portlight as he worked to lash the dinghy down. A wall of water crashed over the stern, knocking Shane flying.

"Is he still out there?" Darryl screamed. "Is he still there? Get him in! Get him in!"

A second wave crashed over the boat with such force that Darryl felt the steering bulkhead buckle forward a good 2 inches.

Then they heard Shane outside. "Fuck you! Fuck you!" he screamed at the waves.

"He's still there! Thank God he's still there!" Diviana shone the flashlight and saw him clinging for his life. Tons of water had picked him up and hurled him against the companionway door. He'd grabbed hold of the line he was cutting, and clung to it as the water receded and sucked at his legs.

"You go out there next time," Shane told his mother when he returned, slamming the companionway door behind him. They all laughed as the tension ebbed.

Diviana kept working on Darryl to keep him from yielding to exhaustion. She asked Shane to massage his father's head, so he beat Darryl's brow lightly with his knuckles, and rubbed hard to keep him stimulated.

"We've got to keep him going," she warned Shane. "We've got to keep him going."

Darryl battled throughout Saturday night, totally focused on the challenge of holding the boat upright, but his energy was waning. He complained he could hardly keep his eyes open, they were becoming blurred and heavy.

Diviana clung to him from behind, holding him in the seat, comforting him and talking to him as they hurtled down wave after wave at speeds of between 6 and 13 knots, pulling their drogue behind them. Darryl was amazed that they traveled so fast. The 6-foot-diameter sea anchor they were using for a drogue should have slowed her almost to a standstill.

As he thought about it, the catamaran broached. The stern shot around and she rose up on her starboard hull. The force was so great, it snatched Diviana away from Darryl and threw her down onto the cabin side, slamming her into a wooden lip that bruised her hip and ripped open flesh on her ankle and leg. Darryl was snatched from his seat, and crashed on top of her. *Heart Light*'s engines screamed and wailed a dirge of death until the port hull plunged back down into the sea. Dazed, Darryl scrambled back to the helm to regain control.

"That was the most godawful screaming sound I've ever heard," he said.

The boat was in terrible shape. Shifting bulkheads had jammed some doors shut, while some lockers had burst their locks and sprung open, spewing their contents into the cabin.

Stephanie was thrown 4 feet from the forward bunk. She landed heavily on the floor and was badly bruised. She didn't bother to climb back into the bunk, but sat sprawled on the cabin sole, clasping her bowl.

"You all right?" Diviana inquired.

"I'm fine. As long as you're fine, I'm fine," she responded gamely.

Diviana's leg swelled and stiffened, so she could no longer stand up and keep Darryl from being thrown out of his seat. She called Shane, and he wrapped his arms around his father to hold him down. The buoyant catamaran was bucking violently under the constant bombardment of the growing sea. Even with Shane's sturdy 6-foot frame holding him, every third or fourth wave managed to throw Darryl out of his seat.

"You're not coming out of that seat!" Shane shouted each time the boat shuddered. "You're not coming out of that seat!"

The glow on the anemometer told them the gale had reached 75 knots.

"Oh, for it to go down to 60. Wouldn't it be nice if it was only 60?" Shane said.

The noise of something flailing about outside warned them of another problem. Switching on the spreader lights, they saw a coil of 650 feet of nylon line poised to topple off the port hull.

"That could foul the props," Darryl observed. "We're going to have to secure it."

Despite Shane's harrowing ordeal in the exposed cockpit earlier that night, there was no alternative to sending him out again. He gathered his nerve and disappeared out the companionway door, again without the security of a lifeline. He had to crawl to the extreme end of the port hull, to the diving ladder. Water crashed over him, flattening him against the coaming, but he managed to retrieve the line and drag it into the cockpit. There he had to cut the line free, as it was hopelessly tangled with the mainsheet.

Darryl, aware of the danger Shane was in, couldn't wait to see him safely inside the cabin again.

"Is he still there? Is he still there?" he shouted, his voice showing his concern.

Diviana carefully opened the cockpit door to check on Shane's whereabouts, only to be swamped as a wave poured inside. Then Shane rushed through, and a second wave followed him.

Stephanie, filled with relief at his appearance, shouted: "God-damn it, I've scrubbed and cleaned this boat for two days. Close that door behind you. Look at the mess you're making." They all burst out laughing.

But the worst wasn't over yet. The windspeed indicator rose to

90 knots, and then a huge bomb of water exploded against *Heart Light*'s side, throwing her up onto one hull, where she hovered a few seconds before falling down, upright. Shane, still clutching his father in a bear hug, was hurled across the cabin. They crashed into the wall. Darryl freed himself and quickly dragged his tired body back to the helmsman's seat, steering the boat back on course.

"The window's broken," Shane yelled as the boat came upright. Water gushed in through the open portlight as they all looked on in horror. Closer inspection revealed that the aluminum-framed window had flexed out from the cabin side, then popped back into place under the force of the wave, but not before gallons of water had gushed through.

An avalanche of water poured through the flexing windows and ran down into *Heart Light*'s hulls. They watched the flexing windows with horror. The frames gaped about an inch, and then closed, each time the boat was buffeted by the wind on the crest of a wave, or when a sea struck her amidships. Darryl switched on the electric bilge pumps and hoped they could suck the water out fast enough to save their lives.

The catamaran was tilted high again, this time on the opposite hull. Everything spilled across to the other side in a crashing, splintering crescendo of destruction. Drawers flew out, and glass and crockery broke. Water poured into the boat, filling cupboards and drawers, and flooding the carpets. This time, the boat seemed to teeter on the brink of capsize before eventually plunging back.

I've got to get back on the wheel. I've got to get us headed in the right direction, Darryl told himself as he struggled once more to his chair.

Jon: Kerikeri, [we receive you] loud and clear. Go ahead.

Darryl: We just want to give you our position. Luckily we're still upright. We came down on a wave pretty hard. We're 28° 22', 178° 08'. We're in about 80 knots of wind and it's pretty nasty out here, so I just wanted to give you a position in case . . . [He did not finish the sentence.]

Jon: Roger. All copied *Heart Light.* Over.

Darryl: Ah, hold on a second. I'm still fighting out here on the wheel.

Jon: Roger. Those minutes of latitude. Were those definite: two two? Over.

Darryl: Two eight two. Two eight, two two south.

Jon: Roger. Roger. All copied. And you've got about 80 knots of wind at the present moment? Over.

Darryl: Yeah, well, we have a steady 65, 70, gusting to 80. Over.

Jon: Roger. Copy. What is your heading at the present moment? Over.

Darryl: Ah, we're trying to maintain a heading of about 310. Over.

Jon: Roger. Thanks. Heading of 310. Okay. Will you check with me every hour, please? Over.

Darryl: Roger. If we can, we sure will.

Jon: Okay. We'll look for your call every hour. Okay. Good luck there. Over.

Darryl: Thank you, Jon. *Heart Light* clear.

There was no respite. The horror of the night continued hour after long hour, during which they continually reenacted the same scene of knockdowns, invading water, and the struggle at the wheel to keep *Heart Light* heading the right way. Often the boat was suspended in midair as she catapulted from the crest of a wave, her fiberglass hulls cracking and shuddering as she fell back down into the water.

During the night, *Heart Light* once again passed *Silver Shadow* and *Quartermaster*, unseen in the darkness, as the catamaran ran before the wind and seas at great speed.

Twenty-four hours earlier, Diviana had shared a chilling message with Darryl, and now it was being fulfilled: "I have been told we are going into a vortex, that is where we are being taken. The boat is going to go to her spot and your job is to keep her moving."

Diviana thought they might leave their bodies when they reached the center of the energy field in which they were traveling. She could feel the rising apprehension in her children and wanted them to be prepared.

She took Stephanie and Shane by the hands and sat them on the floor in the cabin near Darryl's seat. In the midst of the intense energy generated by the storm outside, she felt the four of them bonding into a state of consciousness that was extremely peaceful. As she concentrated, the motion of everything about her slowed, and a calmness descended upon her.

She instructed Shane to keep a hand on the handle to the companionway door, so that if the boat capsized he could open it, enabling them to float free to the ocean outside. She did not want anyone to panic, or to be trapped in the boat. They should all maintain a peaceful state of consciousness in which they would swim together.

"Before you were born into this world, you were in your mother's womb, which was filled with salt water. You were safe, cradled, and loved in that environment. Your bodies have that memory stored in them. The minute you release your clinging to them, they will immediately go into a state of joy, not fear. You will inhale water, which will shock you, because it will be cold, but it won't hurt you. All of a sudden you will be free, swimming. As you swim, you will become aware you are leaving your bodies," she explained.

The wind instrument was reading 86 knots by now, and the waves appeared to be more than 100 feet high. Darryl concentrated on maintaining the catamaran's course as best he could while his family sat on the floor before him. He, too, experienced the peacefulness that befell them as Diviana led them in meditation. But there was nothing gentle about the next knockdown. It was in violent contrast to the peaceful slow motion of their meditation, and snapped them out of their placid state with a jolt. Shane leapt to his feet instinctively to catch his father catapulting through the air, and they crashed once more against the side of the boat.

Diviana remained in her trance. To her, the whole action was occurring in slow motion. Stephanie was clinging to her, and she saw the boat lift, and Darryl slowly fly through the air. Shane appeared to be lifted off his feet three times. The port side rose higher and higher as the boat scudded along on one hull, to the accompaniment of the shrieking of the engine, a sound reminiscent of the death cry of a hawk.

"I'm sorry, I did the best I could!" Darryl yelled apologetically as he tried to regain a footing.

"No!" Shane bellowed. The massive voice rose from the depths of his soul. As he protested that he was not ready for death, *Heart Light* fell heavily through the air and crashed back down, throwing them all to the port side of the cabin.

"I've had enough. I want my soul mate. I want my lady. I want to live my life," Shane pleaded, "I'm not ready for this."

"Sit back down and move back into meditation," Diviana commanded sternly.

"I don't know if this stuff really works," he retorted.

Diviana noticed he was trembling. She had schooled him in her beliefs until he'd left home at 18. Ten years later, he'd returned and told her he was ready to learn more. Now he had doubts again.

"It's all right," Diviana said soothingly. "It isn't you. It's only your body's response, for survival. It's okay for you to be having this response."

"I'm not afraid to die for you, Mom. I'm not afraid to die. I'm just not ready for it."

He calmed down, and Diviana felt compassion for him. He was exhausted and angry that he was in this predicament. He had survived two other major knockdowns and exposed himself to death twice outside already. It was understandable that he was angry and doubting.

Diviana noticed a strange whirring sound coming from the

instrument panel and asked Darryl what he thought it might be. He noted the engine alarm light glowing dimly as the sound increased in strength.

"I hate that sound. What is it?" Diviana asked. It was coming from an engine.

"I think we're taking salt water into the engine," Darryl suggested. Without further warning, the port engine died.

Without the port engine, *Heart Light* was less maneuverable and therefore more vulnerable. Darryl had to devise a new strategy. As the yacht started careening down the waves he swung the wheel to starboard to hold her stern into the waves while keeping his bow pointed downwind.

The starboard engine suddenly shuddered, then died. Frantically, Darryl tried to restart the lifeless engines, but with no success. Diviana called to him, "Darryl, stop fighting it. *Heart Light* has found her spot; we are at the center of the vortex."

He immediately turned the wheel hard to starboard and lashed it in place, hoping to hold *Heart Light* sideways to the stacking seas so she could slide down them. He was afraid she would surf out of control if he kept running with nothing but a tangled drogue to slow her and no engines to help with the steering.

SUNDAY, JUNE 5

Darryl's other great fear was that the weakened cabin windows would be punched out by the charging waves. When he finally left the wheel temporarily to inspect the boat in daylight, he was surprised to find that the yacht was structurally sound.

But the interior was a wet, smelly, tangled mess beyond his wildest imagination. The engines were still inoperable. The batteries had broken their restraints and moved around on the engine-room floor. The port hull was cracked, possibly by the propeller shaft being pulled out of line by the tangled drogue lines. He pumped it dry, only to see it fill again. The sea seeped in every time the boat fell down a wave.

While Darryl was inspecting the port engine compartment, which was partially full of water, the first Orion rescue plane had located them. He had discussed these problems with the crew aboard the Orion, and later with the crew aboard the Hercules. Battery acid had spilled, and the crews told Darryl to clean up this potential bomb.

He then made a patch for the cracked hull out of linoleum from the galley and marine epoxy. Luckily, this reduced the seepage to a minimum.

On deck, it was also a mess. The headsail sheets were tangled with the shrouds and the halyards, and he confirmed that the line leading to the drogue they streamed astern had worked its way around the rudders and propellers.

Darryl did not doubt their situation was far beyond the dangers he'd encountered when he challenged nature on the icy slopes of Alaska. He was exhausted. He had been at the helm for 36 hours. They had faced death several times throughout this marathon watch. Now *Heart Light* was damaged, and they would need help cutting the line free from the shafts.

Resigned to defeat, Darryl switched on the EPIRB.

CHAPTER 13

WE'RE ALL IN SHOCK

≋≋≋

On Monday, June 6, at 0810, a satellite picked up another cry for help from a 406 MHz EPIRB. It belonged to the 44-foot New Zealand yacht *Waikiwi II*. An Orion P3 was immediately diverted from its patrol to search for her.

The 406 MHz EPIRB was the only communication *Waikiwi II* had with the outside world. Her radio had been knocked out of action when the yacht pitchpoled, then rolled back upright. Their 243 MHz EPIRB had been swept out of the cockpit by breaking seas.

"Are you sure this thing is going to work?" someone quizzed the skipper, John Hilhorst.

John wasn't sure the EPIRB would work if kept down below, but after losing the other, he was afraid to put the 406 in the cockpit. Eventually, they lashed it in place outside and hoped for the best. Cath Gilmour's father had given them the beacon as a Christmas present, believing it would be the most important piece of equipment aboard their boat if they fell victim to the sea.

John recalled that the instructions were to activate the beacon in a place where its radio signal to an overhead satellite wouldn't be obstructed. He vaguely remembered that the EPIRB should be placed in the water, but he feared that if he offered it to the sea, it would rip free from its tether. It was far too valuable to trust to the waves that mauled *Waikiwi II* in the darkness.

The EPIRB tested their faith in technology. Cold, lifeless, and inert, it was small—only the size of a plastic milk bottle. Could it save them? Was it actually transmitting, or was the flashing light that crowned its plastic case simply teasing them? John told the others the light meant it was, indeed, transmitting its vital message. He hoped he was right. Inside this small yellow device were circuit boards capable of performing the miracle of beaming a signal far into space to a COSPAS-SARSAT satellite that, in turn, would relay it to the nearest receiving dish on land. From there, the EPIRB's location would be calculated and its code deciphered. The information would then be relayed to a mission control center, which would use the identification code to determine boat ownership, size, and an emergency contact. The appropriate search-and-rescue forces would then be alerted, and rescuers would be sent to scour the ocean for the source of the signal. John hoped the process would unfold as smoothly as the promotional material promised.

He was tired, and he felt that his crew had not been as much help as he had hoped. He had found himself doing most of the work alone when they sailed into the second storm. It seemed unfair; they had sailed in and out of storms ever since leaving port, and now the sea had given them a brutal beating. They had been pitchpoled, and endured several knockdowns. Their mast was gone, and they were in dire straits.

They had been too far south to experience the warm gentle breezes that, prior to the storm, the other yachts had reported during the schedules with Kerikeri Radio. Aboard *Waikiwi II* they wore woolen balaclavas, scarves, gloves, and thick sweaters under heavy foul-weather gear to keep out the Antarctic chill in the 50-knot winds that lashed them. Their fingers and faces stung from the cold as they worked in driving rain to untie the lacing holding the spray dodger over the companionway entrance, so they could remove the canvas and reduce windage.

As evening fell on Thursday, June 2, they rolled in the storm jib, in keeping with John's practice of reducing sail during the night. They tied a car tire to some line and streamed it aft, to act as a drogue. John and his old hiking buddy, Geoff Spearpoint, sat in the cockpit for almost an hour, trimming the boat and trying to get her to settle safely stern-on to the waves as she ran under bare poles. But no matter what they tried, she simply lay ahull with her starboard beam presented to the 30-foot waves. In the end, they let her have her way, and at 2200 they went below.

They had a relatively comfortable night, and when they got up at dawn, the wind had fallen slightly, to 40 knots, hinting that the storm would continue to abate during the day. They set the storm jib and sailed comfortably with the wind aft, confident that having managed the unpleasant conditions on the way from Lyttelton, they had little to fear.

On Friday, June 3, they heard over the radio that another low-pressure system was forming, this time off Vanuatu. It was hundreds of miles away, however, and unlikely to threaten them. In any case, the winds the other skippers described were no worse than those *Waikiwi II* had already endured on her stormy passage from New Zealand.

Over the next 24 hours they maintained three radio schedules a day with Kerikeri Radio, one in the morning and two in the evening. The news about the weather did not improve. On Saturday night, confident with the boat and now more familiar with its rhythm, they ate a meal of steaming-hot lasagna. But while they ate, the wind intensified and they decided to reef down to storm jib again before they talked to Jon Cullen on the evening radio schedule.

The news was not good as they plotted the progress of the low-pressure system. It was moving south at about 10 knots, but it appeared to be on a track that could sweep around in front of them. If they continued on their present course, they could sail straight into it. But if they slowed down, there was a chance the storm might pass to the north of them.

"Blow this. Let's make ourselves comfortable for the night and lie ahull," John suggested. "Why bash our heads by sailing into it? Let's slow down a bit."

They dropped the storm jib, streamed their drogue, and settled in for the night with one person at a time standing a lookout watch.

The next morning, Sunday, the radio revealed the full extent of the havoc wrought by the storm. They heard that the sea ahead of them was littered with yachts in trouble, sparking the South Pacific's largest search-and-rescue operation.

"Wow, I'm glad we're not out there," Cath said as they listened to one skipper after another recounting the horrors of the night they had endured. At the same time, she felt secure knowing that they had already survived 50- to 60-knot gales on this trip. "We've been hove-to in worse than that, and been okay."

Outside, the waves had grown to well over 20 feet, a warning that their strategy of slowing down might not be enough to avoid the new storm. These building seas clearly indicated deteriorating conditions.

"Either we turn west and go up the side of it, or we stay here and wait for it to blow out," John reasoned. "I think it's more logical to stay here." He anticipated that the heavy winds now sweeping down on them would abate as the storm center passed by to the north of them.

Staying in their bunks, they remained ahull for the day, reading magazines and books, but it was uncomfortable. *Waikiwi II* took the confused seas on her beam and rolled viciously.

John felt satisfied with their storm precautions. He had screwed down floorboards and hatch covers, and strengthened the catches on cupboards he suspected could burst open. He had screwed plywood storm covers over the windward portlights, but he left the leeward side exposed, to allow some light into the cabin. Fastening storm shutters on both sides would plunge them into darkness.

On the radio broadcast that evening, all the boats north of them reported gales of between 50 and 60 knots, with seas of about 30 feet.

John: Hello, Jon. We have stopped running north and hove ourselves to, so we are presently making about 1 to 2 knots on magnetic 204 degrees. The winds are gusting around 30. Seas around about 1 meter to 2 meters with overcast, and the barometer is on about 1013. Over.

Jon: What have I got here for you for weather? It's not looking so good. Southeasterlies of 30 to 40 knots, maybe plus at times, for you. Southeasterly quarter. Is that what you've got, southeasterlies now?

John: It's east to southeast at the moment, over.

Jon: Roger. Yeah. Okay. I actually had east-southeasterlies jotted down for a start-off, and tending to the southeast for you tomorrow. Over.

John: Roger. Can you tell us, is the system passing overhead of us? Over.

Jon: Umm, the system is expected to be in a position, at noon tomorrow, of 28° south and 180°, so it's going off just to the . . . oh, you're at west. Blimey, you're at west! No, it's going to go straight over the top of you, by the look of it. Over.

John: We're likely to be sailing into the proverbial maelstrom? Over.

Jon: I'm afraid so. Yeah, it's going to go straight over the top of you, with your westerly coordinates there. Over.

John: Roger. So if we actually made westerly [a course to the west] now, would we be able to sneak out behind it? Over.

Jon: No show. No, I'm afraid not. It's moving on you at 15 knots, and I'm afraid there's very little you can do about it at all. You'll just have to prepare yourselves to heave-to, and hang on, and settle down for it. Over.

John: Roger. Thanks very much. And I can expect that for 24 hours? Over.

Jon: Yes. Yes. You will do, for 24 hours, and the winds will . . . I've put you on the wrong side of there, so you'll be looking at 50 to 60 knots of wind, probably, increasing tomorrow. Over.

John: Roger. Thanks, Jon. That's twice in a row, isn't it?

Jon: Yeah, yeah, [he laughed] I'll say. Blimey, you could do without that. Okay. Well, good luck with it then, and we'll look for you in the morning on sked [schedule]. Over.

Jon Cullen's message was chilling. It sent a wave of apprehension through the crew. Had they prepared adequately for the approaching storm? What more should they do? Was everything secure?

Jon's predictions were accurate, and while they lay in their bunks listening to the building crescendo outside, and feeling the buffeting from the rising sea, they heard a foreign sound, a shotgun blast that repeated itself over and over. The mainsail had carried away its lashing to the boom, and the staccato roar of flogging Dacron reverberated through the boat.

With the gale building in the pitch darkness, John didn't fancy the idea of going on deck to stow the wildly flogging mainsail. But there was no option, so he and Geoff donned harnesses. Geoff stayed in the cockpit while John gingerly made his way forward in the beam of a spotlight held by Cath.

John wrapped his arms around the boom, hugging the flaying sail, and fumbled to secure it while the boat rolled and pitched dangerously. Walls of water collapsed on deck and cascaded over him. For a moment, he froze with fear, realizing he had no help. Then he simply got on with the job.

"It's obvious we're in a significant storm," he said, stepping into the safety of the cabin.

As the night progressed, the growing seas slammed *Waikiwi II* alarmingly. She reeled before the onslaught under bare poles, lurching and stumbling drunkenly in the face of roaring breakers.

"We'd better get the life raft blown up and ready," someone suggested. Morale was deteriorating. The British couple, Merve and Shirley Bigden, stayed in the forward cabin, probably the safest place in the yacht if she rolled or pitchpoled. Everyone took turns pumping the bilge. It filled each time a wave flooded the cockpit, forcing water through the ventilation louvers in the companionway hatch. Although John fastened washboards on the outside and plastic on the inside, water still cascaded down below.

John and Cath felt sorry for Geoff, the odd man out. They could comfort each other, as could Merve and Shirley, but Geoff was alone with his fears. John wedged himself in at the foot of Geoff's bunk and tried to cheer him up with recollections of their hiking and climbing adventures in New Zealand.

Suddenly, John was facing downhill as a giant hand seemed to lift *Waikiwi II* in the air and slam her down brutally.

"Are you all right?" they shouted at each other as the boat steadied herself.

John picked himself up from the floor several feet from where he'd been sitting, and inspected the bilges.

"We're okay," he told his crew calmly. "Nothing is leaking. There's no water coming in."

By this time, walking around inside the boat was extremely difficult because of the violent and unpredictable pitching and rolling. The safest place to be was in a bunk.

But John sat on the floor and wedged himself between a bulkhead and a cupboard, while he pumped the bilge.

"John, I'm not enjoying this," Cath called. It was an understatement. She was surprised at her own calmness, given that she had been afraid of the sea long before they set out on this voyage.

It's like when I was working on the ambulances, she thought. *I was always scared of the first time I would come across death, but when I did, I automatically played my role and the fear went away. The same is happening here.*

While Cath was pumping, the handle broke off the bilge pump. Clearing the bilgewater was vital, so John took over and pulled the diaphragm in and out with his fingers. It was awkward work. Geoff relieved him after a while. Push, pull, push, pull. It was difficult and tedious to maintain the rhythm without a handle, but it was as vital as a heartbeat.

About 20 minutes after Geoff began pumping, another enormous wave slammed against the yacht's side, knocking her over to the very edge of her balance. But her ballast keel did its work again, and pulled her back from the brink of a complete roll. Water rushed down below, and it took Geoff 40 minutes to pump her dry again.

John found the hull still apparently intact. All the seacocks were turned off, everything was closed, so he assumed the water had entered through the companionway hatch again.

The boat was a mess. Food had spilled from the freezer, and a shampoo container had leaked all over the cabin. John decided to call Kerikeri Radio.

John: We're at 33° 05'S, 178° 09'W. We're making about 2.5 knots on a magnetic course of 274 degrees. The wind speed is still about 60 knots, gusting upward of 70. The sea is still rough. We are still hove-to under bare poles with tires out. We're still comfortable. Barometer is about 1001, and it's obviously cloudy and raining. Over.

Jon: Roger, that. Wind direction for you, please? Over.

John: Roger. I'm not sticking my head out to the steering compass, but I think it's still from our easterly quarter. Over.

Jon: Roger. Okay. So . . . apart from getting the hell bounced out of you, you're pretty happy with everything? Over.

John: Roger. That sounds very good. Over.

Jon: Okay. Your next 24 hours, John, is much the same, unfortunately. You've probably gathered the position of that system, and it's going to go right over the top of you. Tomorrow is going to be a bit of a mixed bag, but at least it shows signs of improving by tomorrow evening at this time. Over.

John: Roger. So we can't expect the system to have passed us until midafternoon tomorrow, is that correct? Over.

Jon: Yeah, that's right. Yep. It shows it right over the top of you for noon tomorrow. The low pressure is shown at 32° south and 177° west, so, you know, it puts it just about over the top of you . . . so it's going to be pretty boisterous. Over.

John: Roger. We'll just stay sitting tight. Over.

Jon: I think so. That's definitely the way to play it. Play it slow. Okay, good luck. We'll look for you in the morning, John. Have a safe night. We will be on all night, of course, if needed. Over.

"At least if anything does go wrong, he knows our position," Cath said as John climbed into the bunk beside her. They had never imagined nature could be this violent.

The giant wave that hit them was silent. It approached in the darkness like a torpedo tracking its victim, and they felt the liquid bomb explode against their side before they actually heard it. The boat cracked with pain and pitched forward. John and Cath fell onto the cabin ceiling a few feet above their bunk. They sprawled awkwardly across each other as the boat silently floated upside down.

Okay, I've got to lie here now, and then move fast when we come upright, John told himself. He was surprised at the silence, as if the sea had paused to contemplate its next act of brutality.

The weight of the keel eventually prevailed and pulled *Waikiwi II* back upright. As she rolled back and righted herself, the silence ended. The boat filled with the sound of rushing water, falling crockery, straining rigging, and bodies falling and hurting themselves. Anchor chain shot out of its locker. Yogurt containers shattered against the roof, dripping their contents throughout the saloon as they tumbled.

"Shit! The boat's gone!" somebody shouted. Everyone was uncertain about what would happen next, what they should do.

Floorboards fell from their hatches, and lockers spewed bottles of wine, peanut butter, syrup, flour, sugar, salt, and pasta. They smeared the bulkheads, covered the floor, stuck to cushions, and clung to the ceiling.

John scrambled up from the floor to inspect the boat, but he didn't get far. His cabin door would not open. He heard Geoff outside groaning in pain.

As he struggled with the door, John felt water lapping about his calves. He became even more alarmed after he did finally wrench the door open: He felt wind blowing through the cabin. Deep bilgewater and wind! She must be holed.

He found Geoff in the darkness, groaning with pain from back wounds he'd suffered as the boat went over.

Flashlights! Where were the flashlights? None could be found.

Groping in the darkness, John became even more alarmed when he discovered that the floorboards throughout the entire boat were under water, and the wind continued to blow across his face. He found some light sticks that he had stored for an emergency, and snapped them to start the chemical reaction. They emitted an eerie incandescence.

"I think I'm in shock," Geoff muttered as he bumped against John in the galley.

"We're all in shock," John said. "We've got to find out what's happened, how bad the damage is."

They snapped more light sticks and discovered that two windows on the boat's leeward side, which hadn't been covered with storm covers, had smashed, letting in wind and water.

"I don't know whether the boat will go down or not," John told his crew. "We'd better all put lifejackets on."

John climbed over the washboards into the cockpit, and pulled lifejackets out of a locker. He handed one to everybody below and they donned them in case *Waikiwi II* foundered.

John took a sharp knife stowed at the aft pulpit and tied it around his calf. Then he gathered buckets from a locker and handed them below. Everyone started bailing, hurling the water out of the broken ports.

When John looked forward for the first time, he was startled to see that the mast was gone. The stanchions all along the starboard side were also missing.

Unsure about the extent of their damage and their ability to remain afloat, John inflated their four-person life raft, leaving the eight-person raft in reserve. The wind lifted the inflated raft and fought to pluck it free.

God, no way, he thought as the wind tossed it about, *there's no way we'll survive in that.*

He went below, gave Geoff a container of emergency flares, and tried the radio. It was dead. They decided to switch on their EPIRB. It was just after 8 AM on Monday, June 6.

They bucketed water out through the smashed cabin portlights for three hours. They also tossed out a battery that had come adrift, and then they blocked the broken portlights with waterproof pants and plywood boards.

John was concerned that if they rolled again, these wouldn't be able to stop water rushing into the boat as they hovered upside down. Their chances of survival next time would then be slim. But there was nothing to do about it now. Exhausted from the bailing and lack of sleep, they slumped into their bunks, still wearing their lifejackets.

The storm continued its attack. Every time the bow pitched, they could hear something solid hit the hull. It had to be the mast, still attached by its rigging.

"Oh God, do I have to go out there again?" John asked, as he contemplated having to go on deck and cut the mast free. He wondered if the mast might somehow free itself and save him the ordeal of working in the dangerous conditions outside. He was exhausted. He had not slept for two nights and he felt weak and cold.

But he knew in his heart that he'd have to go, like it or not. The mast could sink them. He gathered a hammer, pliers, and screwdrivers, and cautiously climbed outside. The mast was broken in many places and lay across the deck. A tangle of electrical wires protruded from its base. The boom was still intact. First he tackled the backstay turnbuckles, which turned easily and were quickly freed. He was surprised that it was quite warm, even though the wind howled and the waves dumped over him. He could not tell whether it was raining: Everything was gray, and white, and full of spume. The noise of the wind and crashing waves was deafening. Merve watched him helplessly from the cockpit.

Having freed the backstays, he checked the rest of the rigging and planned how to tackle it. Most of the pins securing the wire rigging to the boat were attached to chainplates, so he would be working precariously close to the side. He moved cautiously, tethered to the jackstay, but he did not trust it and feared it could give way under his weight. *If I go over the side, I'm dead,* he thought. He stopped at the first chainplate and doubled his harness around a handrail, taking up the slack so he couldn't fall too far. He attacked the cotter pin with pliers, then a screwdriver and a hammer.

He freed all the rigging until the only pin remaining was that holding the forestay. Although it was only a few feet away, it might as well have been the length of a football field. There were no handholds across the foredeck, and the bow bit deep into the seas, scooping up torrents of water that rushed along the decks. The force of the water was enormous. It could sweep him away as easily as it washed a leaf from a shore. He waited for a chance, and scrambled forward on all fours to the plunging pulpit.

Wedging himself in as best he could, he worked on the cotter pin holding the rigging in place. The forestay was under great strain as the bow rose and plunged. Waves broke over him, and he clung to a port stanchion until the water subsided sufficiently for him to attack the cotter pin again.

His reaction to this danger surprised him. The adrenaline pumping through his veins warmed his body, and he actually experienced a perverse pleasure from being at the very front of the boat, surrounded by danger, risking his life to save everyone. He was acutely aware that one slip, one mistake, and he would be dead.

But his exhilaration changed to gloom as he watched the forestay fall from the boat, carrying with it a brand-new furling headsail they had paid $3,000 for only a couple of weeks earlier. The storm's noise was so intense that he didn't hear the Orion as it flew only a few hundred feet above them. Merve saw it and started shouting from the cockpit. John momentarily forgot about his precarious position on the bow, and raised his arms and waved and shouted.

"Here I am!" he cried.

He worked his way back to the cockpit, bitterly disappointed that the rough sea had prevented him from saving the mast and sails. "I managed to save only the spinnaker pole and some of the halyards. But I got all the sheets," he reported breathlessly to the others.

The Orion's visit lifted morale considerably. *Waikiwi II*'s crew were also relieved that continuing checks revealed no damage to the hull. She was not taking on any more water. They began to wonder if they really wanted to abandon the yacht.

"Shit, we're going to be rescued in the next hour or two," John said. But they had no radio contact with the air crew, so they couldn't confirm it.

As the afternoon progressed, and there was no sign of a rescue vessel, they took stock of their situation. They couldn't start the motor for some reason, they had disposed of one of their batteries, and they couldn't turn the rudder. They had no sails and no communications. But they still had a spinnaker pole and, if the wind abated to about 20 knots, they might be able to make a jury rig. They estimated it was still blowing at 50 knots, so they could only wait patiently for the storm to pass over them or for a rescue vessel to arrive.

"We've got to keep the EPIRB on, because that's our bottom-line defense," John said.

Darkness came without any sign of a rescue vessel, nor any indication the storm would abate. It had raged now for 36 hours without appearing to lose intensity. The sea was still running at 40 to 50 feet and huge curling waves surged against the side of *Waikiwi II*, throwing her sideways each time they crashed into her.

Bright light suddenly pierced the darkness, and they heard the drone of the Orion's engines penetrating the howl of the storm. They rushed on deck and saw the Orion's searchlight beam lighting the water 600 feet from the boat, moving away from them, appearing not to know where to find them in the dark. Disappointment consumed them as they heard its engines drone fainter in the distance. But it returned, homing in on the EPIRB's short-range signal, and John fired a flare. The Orion spotted it and dropped a sonar buoy to mark the yacht's position. The Orion had not dropped a locater buoy the last time it passed overhead, so they took it to be a sign that rescue was imminent. They waited expectantly for the rescue vessel, but again it didn't materialize out of the darkness. The Orion returned again later in the night, and then again the next day, and each time they repeated their ritual of setting off flares and anticipating rescue.

Visibility was so bad, the Orion disappeared from view when it flew past them at about 400 feet, and, without communications, *Waikiwi II*'s crew experienced the frustration of mutes.

TUESDAY, JUNE 7

"Shit, we're going to have to leave our boat," John murmured, the consequences of rescue dawning on him for the first time. Lose the boat? That was not part of the plan. Perhaps they could tow it to the nearest port, where they could tidy it up, rerig it, and get under way again.

"I wish we knew what was going on out there—how we'll be rescued," sighed Cath.

The loss of communications was the most frustrating aspect of their ordeal. They could see the aircraft, and wave and shout, but there was no way of knowing what plans were being made for their rescue. They couldn't be confident there was a ship nearby, nor could they be sure help would arrive before the storm abated. They couldn't plan for assistance, because they didn't know what form it might take. Would they be able to take any personal belongings with them? How much could they take? How would they get off the boat? They had no answers.

"Who knows where we'll end up?" John said, suggesting that whoever rescued them could be going to any port in the world.

"Perhaps we'll end up in Tonga," someone joked.

The Orion returned and began circling overhead, indicating that at last something might happen.

"There's a boat! I can see it!" Merve yelled excitedly from the cockpit.

They raced up from the cabin to join him, but they could spot the ship only occasionally as she rose and fell in the huge seas. It was about five minutes before they all identified the black hull.

"God, look how it's rolling," Merve cried, as she grew on the horizon.

The 30,000-ton Norwegian bulk carrier *Nomadic Duchess*, carrying a cargo of steel to New Orleans, staggered over the ocean toward them, her superstructure swinging like a metronome in the massive seas. *Waikiwi II*'s crew returned below to gather together possessions they hoped they could take with them.

"Should I take this?" John asked, holding up the portable drill Cath had given him.

"What about electrical gear, like the computer, and that kind of thing? Is there any point in taking that?" Cath asked. "My grandmother's locket. I must take that," she said, hastily stuffing a few changes of clothing into a bag at the top of Geoff's pack.

She added credit cards, passports, and the boat's documents. John snatched the New Zealand ensign and packed it away.

"Will the captain let us take all this?"

"It'll get saturated on the way."

On deck they let off a smoke flare to help the *Nomadic Duchess* identify them.

The ship grew larger until they could clearly see her four cranes and five hatches. When she was about a quarter-mile away, she slowly circled them. Again they felt mute and helpless without a radio.

As the *Nomadic Duchess* maneuvered alongside them, they spotted three rope ladders dangling over her port side, down to water level, and a large net clinging to another part of her hull. From about 400 feet, the ship fired rocket lines at the yacht, but the wind caught the missiles and carried them away. Standing in the unprotected cockpit of the yacht was still hazardous, and the possibility of running along the yacht's deck to retrieve and cleat a line did not appeal to anyone, particularly since one side was without stanchions and lifelines. But in the end, the rocket lines weren't needed.

The *Nomadic Duchess* hove-to and drifted down onto *Waikiwi II*. The ship's crew shouted and yelled in a foreign language, adding to the confusion as ropes and lines rained down her side.

Without further warning, the two vessels collided, smashing and grating against each other. It was difficult keeping a foothold on the yacht. The noise, the huge, black steel sides, the unpredictably violent motion, cast a spell of fear upon *Waikiwi II*'s crew. This was more intimidating and fearful than anything they had endured previously. They were so close to being saved, and yet it seemed impossible that this enormous ship could offer anything other than destruction as it crashed and bumped against the little yacht.

The water between the vessels swirled white with rage. They moved toward each other and then away again as waves smashed into them and sucked them apart.

Disembarking was a terrifying prospect. The steel cliff face, veiled in rope netting, towered over them, waiting for them to lunge toward it. Their escape would require precision judgment, and had to be timed for the exact moment the two vessels rose in unison. A mistimed lurch at the rope would plunge them between the two vessels, where they would either be crushed or sucked into the turbulent ocean. The result would be the same in both instances: death.

Terrified, they studied the motion of the two boats as the Filipino crew above shouted encouragement in a language they did not comprehend. They would prepare to make the desperate jump, only to find themselves knocked off-balance by the yacht's violent lurching. Or the rung of the ladder they targeted would suddenly shoot upward or downward as the ocean swell deprived them of their opportunity and their resolve.

Until now, they had survived their ordeal in storm-force winds and giant seas by exercising extreme caution in everything they'd done. They'd insisted that everytime somebody went on deck, they remained tethered to the yacht by their lifelines. Now, while they stood exposed to the elements, they had to unclasp and remove their safety harnesses so they could make this terrifying leap of faith to safety.

Cath and John were experienced rock climbers and had no apprehension about scaling the side of the ship. Their legs were strong and the height would not bother them. The obstacle was the constantly changing chasm that separated them from the steel cliff face. Geoff, also a climber, was not in great shape because of the back injuries he'd received when the boat rolled.

With a timely push on the buttocks from John, Cath was suddenly over the side and scrambling upward. Strong hands grabbed her and pulled her to safety, where kindly crewmembers rushed toward her and wrapped her in blankets.

"I want to see. I want to see," Cath protested as the crew nudged her away from the rail.

She looked back and saw Geoff appear over the side. They had pulled him up by a line attached to his harness.

John was peering up at the ship when the painter attached to the bow snapped. All of a sudden the yacht was atop a wave, perfectly positioned for evacuation, and John leapt, shouting to Merve and Shirley: "Jump! Jump!"

The yacht fell away as quickly as it had presented the fleeting opportunity for escape. Merve and Shirley were still aboard.

"Shirley can't climb ladders!" Merve shouted.

John felt guilty. He, the skipper, had left the yacht while they were still aboard, but it was too late to change his mind, and he continued to climb the net to safety.

Without the restraining influence of the painter, *Waikiwi II* drifted toward the ship's stern, where the transom rose and fell menacingly in the swell, and the propellers sucked and lured the yacht into the lair beneath the ship. John rushed up to the bridge to talk to the captain.

"We'll go round again," the captain said calmly as he commanded that the ship power ahead. Merve and Shirley huddled in the yacht's cockpit. John had placed an orange distress sheet on the cabintop, and the splash of color illuminated the yacht like a beacon in the gray, storm-tossed sea. The color, so foreign in this vast, drab environment, had assisted the air crews aboard the Orions to locate the boat, just as it now helped the ship's captain,

Harald Moegster, to keep *Waikiwi II* in sight.

"Can we save the boat?" John inquired, knowing what the response would be.

"The crew said you've got cranes," added Cath, who joined them on the bridge.

The captain agreed he would consider taking the *Waikiwi II* in tow until the weather improved and they could hoist the yacht aboard by crane.

The crew excitedly ran about the deck, selecting a warp that could be streamed off the stern to tow the yacht. John watched them preparing slings for hauling Shirley aboard.

As the two vessels approached, they shouted instructions to Merve about where to tie a painter to secure the yacht, and told Shirley how they would get her aboard.

"Turn the EPIRB off," John yelled to Merve. "The Orion says we must turn it off."

"Should we take it with us?" John asked Cath.

It was much more than a normal EPIRB. Cath's father had died since he had given it to them and, as it turned out, it was probably the most important gift he'd ever given her. It saved her life. Unfortunately, they were unable to recover it.

"Go! Go! Go!" they called to Shirley as she secured the sling about her. This line would prevent her falling into the sea if she mistimed her lunge at the net. "Go! Go Shirl!"

John pulled on the rope and dragged her onto the ladder. She grabbed it and the crew hauled on the end, pulling her aboard. Merve lunged at the ladder and started climbing as Shirley toppled onto the ship's deck, crying with relief.

"I'm okay, I'm okay," she said agitatedly through her tears, a stark contrast to the stoical British calmness she'd exhibited throughout her ordeal aboard *Waikiwi II*.

The ship's crew ran around readying the lines for towing *Waikiwi II*, but the painter snapped again and the yacht drifted toward the ship's stern, where the transom rose and fell on the swell.

Waikiwi II could not escape its lure. She sat there, under the ship's huge buttock, and the *Nomadic Duchess* crashed down on top of her, punching a 5-foot hole in her cabintop.

Capt. Moegster called for full speed ahead, leaving the yacht to the sea, which already licked at her wounds.

CHAPTER 14

JUMP! JUMP!

≋≋≋

THE FISHING ABOARD THE *SAN TE MARU 18* WAS APPALLING. THE
young crewmen deftly flicked the mackerel off the hooks as the long
line came in. Occasionally, they paused to pull stubborn squid off
the bait barbs and toss them overboard. Eight-and-a-half seconds to
unhook each bait before the next one arrived. Two thousand hooks
to unbait on 36 miles of line. Not a tuna in sight. Nothing. Not a live
fish to be seen anywhere. So much for this, one of Captain Bruce
White's favorite and most reliable fishing banks.

The new crew were doing all right, Bruce thought. Two of them
had never fished commercially before, and the other two had not
fished in blue water. They seemed to have learned the knack of
quickly baiting and unbaiting the hooks, however, and showed no
signs of wilting under the pressure or the monotony of the job.

Bruce White was hunting bigeye tuna for the Japanese market.
Really big ones could fetch $15,000 each. "We had a pretty good
season this time last year," he told the ship's engineer, who was in
the wheelhouse with him. "We were getting quite a few fish up here
this time last year."

But not now. Still nothing. The men kept flicking the whole fish
off the bait hooks, and letting the line fall through the sea door on
the starboard side below the wheelhouse.

It was his second attempt to find tuna on this trip. Earlier, he
had fished closer to the New Zealand coast with as little luck as he
now experienced off the Kermadec Islands. He had hauled in the
line and left the New Zealand coast when he decided the *San Te*

Maru 18 was too big to compete with the 10 smaller coastal boats working the area.

"They're doing close to a thousand hooks each. We've got something like twelve thousand hooks in this small area," he explained. "I mean, the fish are gun-shy, they have so much to feed on. We just can't compete."

Having decided to leave the coastal fishing grounds, Bruce ordered his crew to recover the orange buoy that marked the end of the 36 miles of line, and to start unbaiting the hooks as the line wound in.

He headed north for the next 30 hours until he passed over a bank off the Kermadecs that had yielded thousands of fish a year previously. The water temperature was favorable, and he was optimistic he might repeat his good luck as they rebaited the hooks and dropped the line. When the set was complete, he steamed farther north and dropped another set line, but neither yielded anything, and he was now retrieving the second line.

A day earlier, while he steamed toward the Kermadecs listening to Kerikeri Radio, he heard that a boat had broken down and required assistance. He offered his services but was told another yacht was on its way. Now, on Saturday, he overheard Jon Cullen mention during a noon bulletin that yachts to the north were experiencing severe weather.

Bruce found it curious that he enjoyed lovely conditions, a 15-knot breeze, and flat seas, while farther north yachts battled a storm. But he was not concerned; none of the usual warnings of inclement weather were obvious. He checked the sea state, which he regarded as the first sign of a change, and saw nothing untoward. He was confident that changes in the sea patterns would be the first signals of bad weather moving toward him. The sky revealed nothing; it contained neither streaks nor cumulus, the telltale signs of approaching wind.

But, four hours later, the sea finally sent its signal. It became short-tempered and irregular. Sudden whitecaps sprang up to greet a swell rolling in from the southeast beneath a wind of 30 knots. A gray blanket of cloud gathered on the horizon and drew a shroud across the sun to herald an early evening and put a premature end to Bruce's fishing operations. He left 12 miles of long line down for the night, attached to a beacon, because he was concerned about damaging it by working in the dark in the deteriorating conditions.

"The weather's getting shitty," he said. "We'll sit here and dodge and get it in tomorrow." He intended to maintain a speed of about 4 knots, riding into the approaching waves throughout the night. "We'll dodge our way up into them, just gently," he explained. "We'll just cruise up in the swell—a piece of cake."

The sea had other ideas. The gale intensified as the night wore on, and huge seething crests mounted giant waves that slammed heavily against the ship's bow and shook her as she fought her way through them.

They had completed two 10-mile circuits around the long line suspended in the ocean when Bruce, eating dinner in the mess in the aft quarters, became concerned about the amount of vibration caused by the propellers cavitating in the heavy swell. He left his meal and returned to the pilothouse.

"What's going on?" he asked. "There's something wrong here."

The duty crew were watching the huge crested waves charging the bow. The power of the impacts reverberated through the ship's 22-year-old steel hull. The crew appeared apprehensive, particularly those who had not been to sea before.

"Right, we're heading north. We'll run with it," Bruce said decisively. He explained to the two crew on watch the angle at which they should keep the vane on the wind-direction indicator to make sure the San Te Maru ran with the storm, emphasizing they must not take water on the starboard side because if it entered the sea door beneath the wheelhouse, the boat could list and capsize.

Bruce retired to his bunk, only to be physically lifted out of it at 0600 when a huge wave smashed its way on board, seemingly hitting the boat right against his cabin, which was below the pilothouse, adjacent to the vulnerable sea door.

He scrambled into the pilothouse, shouting at the watch: "Can't you see that?" He pointed to the vane on the anemometer that stiffly saluted to port. It was contrary to the direction he had instructed them to follow. They should have altered course on the autopilot to maintain their angle to the wind.

He could hardly believe the vista the weak dawn light revealed. The crests of the waves curled above him, creating a yawning black cavity in their center. These were hollow waves, with plunging crests, like surf pounding on a beach.

Surfing was his passion. When he wasn't at sea, Bruce spent most of his time riding the waves on Auckland's west coast. He read magazines and books on the subject, and studied the nature of the waves that crashed upon his beach. Now, in the middle of the South Pacific Ocean, he saw hollow waves.

He marveled at it. He had often ridden inside them, feeling them cascade over his body as he rode through on his surfboard, but out here in the Pacific? He shook his head.

He studied them warily. They charged upon the *San Te Maru* in clusters of three, about 15 or 20 seconds apart. It was always the middle comber that threatened to swallow the boat. He remained on the bridge throughout the day, fascinated by their rhythm and character. The first wave of the cluster was always full and flat. It ran so fast it sucked the substance from the wave that followed, as if it were trying to catch up to the preceding wave. The escaping water hollowed the face of the second comber, allowing the wind to mold a rolling top at least 5 feet high. The distance between the waves was about half the length of his 180-foot vessel.

The curling combers hovered above the *San Te Maru*, sometimes breaking to port, sometimes to starboard. Only occasionally did they crash right on top of her, forcing the boat's stern down into the sea.

He had never sailed in these conditions before, and this sea was the biggest he'd experienced in 20 years of fishing. He had to keep up a speed of 10 knots or more to maintain control. Sitting in his chair in the pilothouse, he contemplated the tactics he could use;

he discounted the possibility of using a parachute anchor because its tendency to pull the boat down would drive her bow under water.

His concern was that if they veered to starboard, water could enter the sea door, through which, on good days, they pulled the tuna and their gear and worked with their catch. Unlike the rest of the hatches, the door was wooden and vulnerable. If it crumbled under the sea's onslaught, the main deck would flood and the boat would list. If another wave then attacked while she lay vulnerable, the *San Te Maru* would undoubtedly capsize. Hence his anxiety when the watch allowed their concentration to lapse, and the boat wandered off course.

As the storm grew worse, he insisted the crew check that the scuppers were free of debris. It was important to allow water taken on deck to drain overboard quickly. If it were trapped, it could make the boat top-heavy and liable to capsize.

They were all grateful the worst of the cyclone passed over them in daylight; even for Bruce the darkness held fears. He remained in the wheelhouse throughout the day. He monitored radio traffic to and from Kerikeri Radio, the yachts to the north of him, and the Orion aircraft. The yachts were certainly in trouble; they were not coping well with this storm. He contacted Kerikeri Radio and gave them his position to alert them that he was available to provide assistance.

Looking outside, he could understand why the yachts were in difficulty. The *San Te Maru*, running from the swell, slid off the tops of the waves and raced down their faces for 50 feet at a 45-degree angle. Instead of the water peeling away at the bottom of her flared bow, it plumed at the top, 20 feet above the waterline.

Bruce preferred his own company in these conditions and he dismissed the crew, telling them to remain in their bunks; but they returned to the wheelhouse throughout the day, anxious about the conditions. He permitted them to remain there briefly, one at a time, and got them to fetch bedding to block water oozing under the door.

The wind strummed the *San Te Maru*'s rigging, plucking the radio antennae, the cables supporting the forward and aft masts, and the triatic stay joining their tops. The vibrations sent a constant hum through the boat, forcing the crew to raise their voices, and blocking the sound of the charging waves.

Bruce was full of admiration for this Japanese longliner. At 360 tons, she was the smallest of her class. A Japanese fisherman with whom he had worked had unstintingly praised her, recounting tales about her sister ships' abilities in storms and hurricanes that could snap the backs of bigger vessels. He felt comfortable in her; her only failing was that her propeller continued to cavitate when she flicked her stern up into an air pocket. Apart from those little self-indulgences, she relentlessly pursued her northerly course as if she were fully aware of her responsibilities.

The crew visiting the bridge informed Bruce that food and other goods stored aft had fallen from lockers, and the lashings on a canvas awning on an aft deck had come undone. The cover was flapping wildly in the wind. He didn't mind losing it, he said, and insisted everyone remain inside and keep the watertight doors firmly locked.

"What the hell are you doing there?"

The voice on Channel 16 startled Bruce. It was from an Orion that was obviously nearby, although he couldn't see it.

"Man, I've been coming this way for the last 24 hours. The storms got us down the bottom, and we're shifting to the north. We haven't got any choice."

"Why don't you tell anybody?"

Bruce bit his tongue. He wanted to say that Kerikeri Radio was aware of his position, and if no one told the Air Force he was in the vicinity and available to provide assistance, that was their problem. But he kept his silence.

"Well, we need your assistance."

"Are you calling me in?"

"Yeah."

"Well, okay. Where do you want me to go?"

The voice from the Orion told him about *Heart Light*, which was about 63 miles to the north with four people aboard, taking water through a cracked hull and broken portlights. Bruce recorded receiving the message at 1800 on Sunday, June 5, and advised them it would be midnight before he reached the stricken catamaran.

He was below eating dinner when the cook, who'd been on the bridge with the watchkeeper, dashed into the mess and blurted out excitedly: "We've just seen a portlight!"

"Where'd you see it?"

"On the starboard side."

Bruce leaped up from his meal, ran to the wheelhouse, grabbed the binoculars, and searched for the red light.

"It's moved to the stern," the watchkeeper said; but Bruce didn't see it.

He plotted the position and radioed the Orion circling over the disabled yachts. They flew to the position he gave them and called back confirmation that they had discovered a yacht, with a broken mast, that was unable to communicate. They didn't yet know they had spotted *Pilot*, and they requested the *San Te Maru* turn around to take a look.

"No way. I'm not turning this boat around, I don't care what you say to me," he said after checking the coordinates they gave him.

Bruce's prime consideration was the safety of his 10 crew and his ship. He was prepared to run toward *Heart Light* because that was the course he considered safest. He feared that if he tried to turn the fishing boat around in the dark, she could broach to and capsize.

The Orion made another request: "Will you go and see *Silver Shadow*?"

Had he been asked earlier, he would have considered altering course, but he was reluctant to change his heading now; *Silver Shadow* was 23 miles to the southwest. He had followed the Orion's conversation with *Silver Shadow* earlier and heard them respond with two clicks when they were asked to assess the urgency of their condition on a scale of one to five. To him, it meant they were reasonably safe. Bruce thought that if *Heart Light*'s crew had been asked the same question, they would have responded with five clicks, since they reported they were sinking. Even if he did go to *Silver Shadow*, he would be unable to transfer the injured yachtsman to his boat. Had he gone to either *Silver Shadow* or *Pilot*, there was little he could offer them before daylight except to sit and watch them in the dark.

"Well, will you go back to see *Silver Shadow*?" the Orion asked.

"No. The *Heart Light*'s taking water, and to me, that's telling me the vessel's sinking, and I'm goin' straight there."

He had only another 33 miles to run to her, and he had a vision of *Heart Light* having only one hull above the water, with her occupants huddling on it awaiting his arrival.

"Okay, that's up to you," the Orion's radio operator said.

"Well, those other people are okay; you know they're not in difficulty."

About 80 minutes later, Bruce had his first radio contact with *Heart Light*. Bruce told Diviana he had a dog called Storm, and Diviana said her nickname was Storm. Bruce kept the banter going because it seemed to comfort them. When he was six miles from them he saw their light, and at 0020 on Monday, June 6, he pinned *Heart Light* in his powerful spotlights.

Her condition surprised him. She didn't have one hull under water as he'd imagined. She looked seaworthy still, and she appeared to be riding comfortably in the improved weather, although the occasional wave still crashed over her cabintop.

Bruce asked what damage they had endured, and Darryl told him a hull was cracked and both engines were out. The portlights were still leaking, and the drogue line had tangled the propeller shaft. The line had also caught in the rudders and put them out of action, though they did not know this at the time.

Bruce held his spotlights on the yacht and wondered what to do if a serious problem developed before dawn.

He decided to lie downwind of them, so that if they had to abandon their boat and get into a life raft, they would blow toward him. He continued to hold *Heart Light* in his two bright searchlights and, when he was confident both vessels were secure, he switched one light off, set watches for his crew, and fell into his bunk for his first rest in 20 hours. He slumbered fitfully while rogue waves occasionally curled into the *San Te Maru*'s side.

He returned to the wheelhouse at 0600 on Sunday, relieved the mate, and sat pensively in his chair as the weather eased, revealing a friendly blue sky between the gray clouds. *Heart Light* did not appear to be in immediate danger, and he discussed various options with Diviana. Their life's belongings were aboard *Heart Light*, and they had no insurance. The company that employed Bruce was adamant he shouldn't attempt to tow *Heart Light* because of the legal liability that could arise from a failed salvage operation.

"That's the situation, I will not tow that vessel anywhere," he had stated with absolute finality after explaining the company's policy.

"We'll pay you."

"I don't care. Once I put that line on, I'm liable, and I'm not going to commit to that," he had told them.

Diviana became adamant that she would not leave *Heart Light* until Bruce agreed to sink her, but he refused because he feared losing his license. Suddenly, *Heart Light*'s drogue line snapped and the catamaran began to drift rapidly, but Diviana refused to leave until Bruce agreed to her request. Finally he gave in, and she and her family began packing their belongings. As they did this, the wind and seas calmed surprisingly, giving the *San Te Maru* a good opportunity to move in for the rescue.

As the *San Te Maru* rolled across the waves toward them, Darryl feared she would slam into *Heart Light* and shatter her fiberglass hulls before they could get off.

Bruce was not perturbed. When he was fishing, he frequently maneuvered the *San Te Maru* in gale-force winds alongside buoys and beacons. Not that it was easy. Her 22-year-old motor had to be stopped, and started up again, each time Bruce wanted her to go astern. It was an operation demanding timing and forethought, particularly in a wind that was still blowing at gale force.

Sitting on the bridge, Bruce watched *Heart Light* carefully. He brought his fishing boat to weather of the 41-foot catamaran. He stopped the engine, placed the gears in reverse, started the engine again, and then gunned her astern to prevent her 360 tons from overshooting. He wanted to create a lee for *Heart Light* to shelter in while the two vessels moved together.

"Little bitch. She's jumping all over the place," he grumbled in frustration as he watched the catamaran. "She won't let us get close." *Heart Light* drifted downwind faster than the *San Te Maru* did. The distance between them grew, so Bruce decided to go around to the yacht's weather side again, approaching more closely this time, so she would fall into his windshadow, and not drift away.

Once again, timing was critical. Bruce had only six seconds in which to stop the *San Te Maru*'s engine, change the gear to reverse, and fire her up again, giving her full thrust to stop her dead where he wanted her. *Heart Light* danced about on the confused sea, refusing to lie still even when the fishing boat finally stood between her and the wind.

The *San Te Maru* drifted down onto the yacht, smashing into *Heart Light*'s stainless steel dinghy davits.

The impact of the collision knocked *Heart Light*'s crew off their feet. When they recovered their balance, they waited for a chance to jump across to the *San Te Maru*. It was a time of great danger, because none of them was wearing a lifejacket or a harness. Stephanie was the first to go. She jumped toward the cargo net dangling down the fishing boat's side at precisely the moment *Heart Light* fell down a wave and the *San Te Maru* rose upward and moved away from the catamaran. Stephanie snatched at the cargo net with her fingertips and hung in space for a second before two strong pairs of hands grabbed her and pulled her up to safety.

"Jump! Jump!" the *San Te Maru*'s crew shouted at Diviana.

"Wait a minute," she said, waving them away.

Her inner voice told her to return to the companionway door and wait. She obeyed, and waited a few minutes until a wave lifted *Heart Light* level with the *San Te Maru*'s bulwark. The two boats moved together and Diviana stepped off *Heart Light* into the crew's arms.

"Hi boys. Good catch!" she said.

Darryl and Shane threw a dozen or more plastic garbage bags containing their most valued possessions onto the *San Te Maru* and effortlessly joined the women, only to realize they had left some of their belongings behind. They asked Bruce if they could return and retrieve some more.

"No, now I've got you, you're not going back," he responded firmly.

With *Heart Light*'s crew safely aboard, Bruce turned the *San Te Maru*'s bow toward the catamaran. He would complete his part of the strange bargain with Diviana.

The New Zealand Air Force had requested Bruce pick up *Quartermaster*'s life raft, which was scudding across the sea with an activated EPIRB inside, making it easy to find. Now, having completed the *Heart Light* rescue, the *San Te Maru* stood by, waiting for the Orion to return with the raft's updated position. Meanwhile, *Heart Light*'s crew went aft and maintained a death watch over their boat. She was gradually filling with water, slowly going down to the place Diviana had foreseen in her meditation. Heartbroken, they stood by helplessly. Bruce, aware of their state of mind, sent his cook to keep an eye on the boat's mourning crew.

Heart Light rolled over as the hulls filled with water. From his station, Bruce saw the warps wrapped around both her propellers and the rudders. One shaft was bent so badly he could see the kink in it from the bridge. As her cabin filled with water, she slipped away from view.

As *Heart Light* sank, dozens of items began floating to the surface. Bruce slowly cruised around the flotsam while his crew scooped up what they could. Finally, satisfied they had retrieved as much as possible, they turned in the direction of the last known position of *Quartermaster*'s life raft, 21 miles away.

The wind had eased and the sun was shining when the *San Te Maru* reached the position given. But they saw nothing, and steamed past the life raft for another seven miles before an Orion gave them new coordinates. Turning back, Bruce spotted it bouncing along on top of the waves like a bright orange beach ball.

The wind started blowing again, cresting at 40 knots when he tried to retrieve the life raft. When he put the *San Te Maru*'s motor through its awkward reversing maneuvers it stalled, and the raft bounced past out of reach.

The possibility of discovering bodies inside the life raft worried one crewmember. He protested about the task of recovering corpses and taking them aboard.

"We're committed to doing this, whether you like it or not," Bruce snapped impatiently. "You don't have to be there to help pull them out."

He banished him to the stern, away from the sea door where other crew waited with grapnels. "We're not going to leave them there, we're going to take them back if that's the situation," Bruce said.

Eventually he succeeded in stopping the boat so that the life raft blew against her side. The wind and sea had mauled the raft. The canopy, which was intended to shield its occupants from the harshest environment, was shredded. Only about a foot of the orange cover remained above the raft's buoyancy chambers. Nobody was inside. There was clear evidence, however, that one or more of *Quartermaster*'s crew had been in the raft at some stage. The EPIRB one of them had placed inside still emitted its distress signal, and a little kit of emergency rations told of somebody's vain hope for survival. They took the raft aboard and headed back through the storm toward the long lines they'd left off the Kermadec Islands.

Diviana took her bruised and aching body below to a little berth behind the engine room, but the stench that permeated the boat disturbed her. For two decades the *San Te Maru 18* had caught and carried fish and squid. For 20 years, successive crews had left a legacy of filth and untidiness in her cramped quarters.

The cabin was so small that Diviana and Darryl could not stand together in the close confines designed to accommodate small Japanese bodies. To her, the bunk was a coffin. She couldn't get comfortable, despite her exhaustion. Her head hit against the wall at one end and her feet touched the bulkhead at the other. The engine next to them groaned so loudly she couldn't sleep.

Moreover, she was famished. She had not eaten during her ordeal aboard *Heart Light*, and she found the food aboard the *San Te Maru* nauseating. The crew heartily consumed large helpings of sausages and other meats, all of which were repugnant to Diviana, a vegetarian. During the three days it took them to return to Auckland, she ate only a few slices of white bread with tomatoes.

As soon as the *San Te Maru* got under way from *Heart Light's* position, the storm began to rage again. Most terrifying of all, Diviana felt trapped as she lay in the boat's belly, listening to the waves slamming the ship's steel sides, and feeling her lurch off course and then veer back. She considered the *San Te Maru's* chances of sinking in the storm were probably higher than *Heart Light's* had been, because the fishing boat's motion through the waves was foreign and obscenely crude compared to the catamaran's. She wondered if she should have stayed on board her own boat.

Here she was trapped in a steel tomb, and if the *San Te Maru* capsized, there would be no easy escape for herself or her spirit. Here she was ensnared in the filthy belly of a stinking fishing boat, and this was more unpleasant than anything she had endured during her ordeal aboard *Heart Light*.

CHAPTER 15

THE VACATION FROM HELL

≋≋≋

AFTER THE *MONOWAI* RESCUED *SILVER SHADOW*'S CREW, SHE still wasn't able to get on with her original task of helping *Mary T*. Instead, she was diverted yet again to join the search for *Quartermaster*. The naval survey vessel spent two days scanning the oceans for her, dispatching her Wasp helicopter to fly low over the sea when conditions allowed. She liaised continually with the Orions above, meticulously working a grid pattern to cover the area in which the yacht was last reported. Meanwhile, in improving weather conditions, *Mary T* had canceled her Pan Pan call.

Everyone involved in the search—the team at the RCC, the Cullens, New Zealand's air force and navy, and all the listening yacht crews—willed the searchers to find the *Quartermaster*. The rescuers had performed remarkable feats during the four days of a storm that was to become known as the "Pacific Fastnet." They had shown stamina, dedication, bravery, and ingenuity in saving 21 souls from seven yachts. Only three people remained unaccounted for: Robert and Marie Rimmer, and Marie's son, Jim Anderson. Everyone wanted to see them come home safely from the sea.

The *Monowai* searched for flotsam that might reveal *Quartermaster*'s fate one way or the other, and hopes were raised when floating wreckage was sighted. But the bits and pieces they fished from the sea baffled them. One piece bore the name *Pleiades Child*, but no yacht of that name had been reported in the area. Only later did they discover it to be the previous name of *Heart Light*. The Wheelers had changed the name of their catamaran before leaving New Zealand.

No sign was found of *Quartermaster*. The search was called off, and *Monowai* headed toward Tonga.

"I don't expect anything unusual, but keep a good lookout just in case," Cmdr. Larry Robbins instructed the watch officer.

At 2200, the officer of the watch summoned Cmdr. Robbins to the bridge after he identified a white strobe light. They were puzzled; no vessel appeared on their radar screen.

"It could be a strobe light on a lifejacket," someone suggested. They turned the *Monowai* toward the light, their hopes again soaring with the prospect of solving the riddle of *Quartermaster's* fate.

Determining its distance in the darkness proved difficult until eventually they got a radar reading, indicating a vessel five miles away. The *Monowai* called on VHF radio without eliciting a response. When they came up to the light, they found a 40-foot yawl with sails flogging limply in the wind. The *Monowai* called again on the VHF, but again they had no response. Cmdr. Robbins nudged *Monowai* to within 200 yards and then sounded her horn. The mystery boat immediately came alive, and a voice crackled on the VHF radio.

"This is the *Mary T*. This is the *Mary T*," Carol called.

Sigmund was greatly embarrassed. It was his watch, and he'd fallen fast asleep. He'd succumbed to exhaustion after the long storm. Not even the blare of the *Monowai's* horn, nor the bright beam of the spotlight, woke him up. Carol had to shake him awake.

"You scared the hell out of us," Carol told the navy.

"If truth be told, we were really hoping you were *Quartermaster*," Cmdr. Robbins said, still slightly disappointed.

The *Mary T*'s crew felt a curious mixture of sadness and gratitude. Sadness for the loss of the gallant crew aboard *Quartermaster*, who had acted as a relay for them with Kerikeri Radio during their desperate attempts to stop *Mary T*'s sinking. Bob Rimmer had been so helpful, so confident at a time when it appeared that they, *Mary T*, would not survive. For Sigmund and Carol, the episode starkly illustrated how insignificant and powerless they were, and how unable to control their destiny.

Their gratitude was for the arrival, at last, of the *Monowai*, which had been dispatched to assist them four days earlier. At that time, they were pumping for their lives. How ironic that, after all they'd endured, the *Monowai* should wake them from their first sleep in more than 96 hours. Where was she when she was really needed?

They held no bitterness nor resentment that their promised rescuers had not reached them in their desperate hours of need. They understood the realities of the sea, and accepted that their plight was less serious than that of *Ramtha*, *Pilot*, and *Silver Shadow*. Once *Mary T*'s crew had found and fixed the cause of their flooding, things had taken a turn for the better. Other crews were less fortunate.

Hearing another human voice so close stimulated *Mary T*'s crew. Anna and Lianne wanted to join in the conversation with the *Monowai*, too, and they took turns at sharing their saga on the VHF.

Crew exhaustion wasn't the only reason *Mary T* was drifting aimlessly. Her steering was damaged, and they wouldn't be able to proceed until Sigmund went over the side to make repairs. They'd have to wait for the swell to subside before he could do that.

The *Monowai*'s arrival signaled the end of what they'd dubbed the "vacation from hell." The sea, for many years a good friend as they cruised the world, had terrorized them with its relentless brutality and violence. For 96 hours they'd been on their own against the savage sea. They'd relied entirely on their own resourcefulness, and survived probably the worst conditions they were likely to encounter anywhere.

They had faced periods of self-doubt, panic, anger, and tension. They had fought for their lives, and they had won. Like all the crews involved in the storm, they'd had to conquer their own frailties, solve problems, and make choices people ordinarily do not confront.

There were some regrets. Sigmund felt he had driven his crew relentlessly, seeing them as resources for survival rather than as sensitive human beings. He particularly regretted not being more available for his daughter, Anna, and not understanding her needs and fears as she faced death in the leaky boat.

"I was perceiving the people like winches or sails, nothing else. That is not a nice thing," he admitted candidly. At the same time, he bore the full responsibility of any skipper to use all means at his disposal to save his crew and his ship in an emergency. Even now, as they sat passively upon the ocean with their sails flogging, he still worked on their survival, preparing a plan to fix the engine and get the tangled propeller to turn.

Despite their reluctance to say good-bye, the Monowai had to leave.

"Wouldn't it have been grand to get one of their divers to help us get things sorted out?" Carol said as the ship moved away.

The thought that a naval diver could have helped them untangle the lines from the propeller and its shaft hadn't even entered Sigmund's mind.

"Why didn't you ask them for a hand?" Lianne asked.

"Truth be told, it never occurred to me," Sigmund admitted. "Should I have asked for assistance?"

His crew stared at him quizzically. Here they were, on a yacht wallowing on the waves, 500 miles from Fiji. She was without propulsion, she had no steering, and nobody knew whether the wind vane was repairable or not.

Gee, have I done right? Sigmund wondered.

EPILOGUE

Mary T received a hero's welcome from the other yachts anchored at the marina at Latoka, Fiji. Sigmund had managed to repair the Hydrovane self-steering gear, which was able to substitute as a makeshift rudder. He had freed the line around the propeller by winding an end around a winch and turning the propeller shaft with a wrench until the obstruction untangled. Then he set sail for Fiji.

Crews from the other cruising boats sheltering in Fiji followed the *Mary T*'s ordeal over their radios, and when they learned she was outside the reef off Latoka they eagerly offered assistance. A Florida yacht, *Strider*, met her a mile outside the reef, threw her a line, and towed her through the passage to a safe anchorage.

Sigmund had mixed emotions. He gratefully cleated the line when it hit his deck, but he was disappointed that after a voyage that challenged the seamanship and resourcefulness of everyone involved, he should be towed into port.

He and Carol shed tears of joy as they moved toward their anchorage and saw a crowd ashore holding a banner proclaiming: "Welcome Survivors of *Mary T*."

They were overwhelmed when they went ashore and were greeted with plates of food from neighboring boats. The welcome epitomized the spirit of the rescue: People really cared about them, and wanted to help them overcome their ordeal.

Sigmund admitted that previously he had been oblivious to the caring nature of the teams of people involved with the sea.

"What those rescue people did . . . it's very touching that people are prepared to do that for each other," he reflected. He admits to learning several seamanship lessons from the storm. He was particularly grateful that he'd had the foresight to stow earplugs aboard. They blocked out the violent noise of the storm. Yellow-tinted ski goggles enabled him to work on deck unhindered by the blinding spume and driving rain. Using the tricolor light at night produced enough glow for them to work under, and was more satisfactory than spreader lights. The GPS and ham radio were vital.

They were not able to set a trysail from the mainmast, but they found the fourth reef in their mainsail served them well, as did the Hydrovane self-steering gear, which they used as a jury rudder to steer them to Fiji. He thought it was much easier to handle than an emergency rudder created from a spinnaker boom and a table top, which would have been his only other option.

The rice in the pressure cooker provided the sustenance they needed throughout their ordeal. Bags of sails placed on the wet, slippery cabin floor protected them when they fell during the precarious rolling, and provided soft areas in which to rest when bunks became too wet.

The glass bowl of a Racor fuel filter enabled them to see that the problem with their engine was water in the diesel fuel. The drogues created a threat because they did not stream out away from the boat. The warp was sucked into the propeller, where it entangled itself.

They learned that despite all their work in New Zealand preparing for the cruise, their boat was still not "roll-over ready." Dorade ventilators could not be blocked to keep water out, and Sigmund intended to make plugs to make them watertight. Hatch slides allowed water to enter, as did the lack of gaskets around the hatches in the cockpit.

He found his floorboards did not open sufficiently to allow the bilge to be bailed with buckets, and he intends to ensure all hatches have latches that will remain closed in the event of a 360-degree roll.

Before setting sail again, he intended to have each of the crew test various seasickness medications, so they could assess their effects on land or in calm water. That way, they would learn the extent of any adverse reactions before they encountered high seas.

During the storm, they suffered considerable gear failure, including the emergency tiller, steering, propeller, binnacle, engine, mizzen sailtrack, self-steering vane and rudder, boathook, and cordage. Jerry cans were washed overboard and stanchions snapped.

Sigmund regarded the voyage as a turning point in their lives, a time for reflection and recommitment. Their last communication with the author was from Port Vila, Vanuatu.

Ramtha

Windora, one of the last boats to reach Tonga after a stopover at Raoul Island, overheard another yacht reporting the sighting of a strange green ball of light in the sky. The storm was long over, but they thought it could be a flare from a vessel in distress, and they asked the Royal New Zealand Air Force if they had an Orion P3 in the area to investigate.

The Orion crew could not discover any sign of a vessel in distress, but they did find the abandoned *Ramtha* bobbing about on the Pacific Ocean, the second time an inexplicable orb had drawn her to the attention of rescuers.

The *Monowai* had landed *Ramtha*'s owners, Robyn and Bill Forbes, at Nuku'alofa, Tonga. They received the news about the sighting of *Ramtha* as they were about to leave for the airport to fly to New Zealand to reestablish their lives, having accepted the loss of everything they possessed.

Ramtha was towed into port by another New Zealand yacht, and after a difficult negotiation over salvage rights, Bill and Robyn were reunited with her. They have since returned to Australia, where Bill has resumed commercial flying to build up a cruising kitty.

Bill did not carry parachute flares on the voyage but would include them as an essential part of his safety equipment on future voyages, because handheld flares were inadequate for the conditions.

Scuba suits would also be an essential part of their kit in the future, and the rule would be to don them when the weather deteriorated.

"If you fall in the water, foul-weather gear is cumbersome," he explained. "But if you have wetsuits on, you maintain your body heat and it is easy to move about. When we were taken off *Ramtha*, other clothes might have got tangled up in the lines and other gear. We also didn't feel the water or any coldness in them."

They will also ensure everything aboard is adequately marked as belonging to their boat. That results from lessons they learned while retrieving wreckage from *Heart Light*. The flotsam confused the search party because most of it was unidentifiable except for the item containing the catamaran's previous name, *Pleiades Child*. It was only when a bottle containing medicine was fished out of the water that they found information enabling the RCC to confirm they had found the wreckage of *Heart Light*.

During the storm, the Forbeses lost a lifering that was not marked. They will ensure this doesn't happen again.

They emphasized the importance that stress management played in their ordeal, and the way in which they maintained mental discipline, blocking out fear and imagination.

Silver Shadow

A helicopter pilot spotted *Silver Shadow* lying on a reef off Maewo Island, about 200 miles north of Vila, Vanuatu, five months after Peter O'Neil and his crew abandoned her.

The pilot noticed 10 local residents cavorting drunkenly around her, obviously partying on the liquor they'd found aboard. *Silver Shadow* had only a small hole in her port side, but her fin keel was broken, and she had washed so high up on the reef that freeing her was impossible.

A few months earlier, she'd been spotted 250 miles east of Noumea. Peter O'Neil set out to intercept her with a salvage vessel, but she disappeared. Peter suspects she was towed by an unknown vessel in anticipation of salvaging her. When he eventually found her on Maewo Island, she had been stripped, not by the local natives but by yachtsmen with a discerning eye for anchors, chain, shackles, fishing gear, the barometer, clock, and other equipment.

Peter was confident his yacht was well-found for going offshore, and the way she handled the conditions supported that. There were still systems that could be improved, though. For instance, a fully waterproof electrical system for the high-frequency radio would have been of considerable benefit, if such a thing were possible.

The extra-large bilge pump they carried earned its passage, and he regarded it as an essential extra for bluewater cruising boats because smaller pumps were inefficient and energy-sapping.

Sofia

After the French Navy decided not to blow his boat out of the ocean, Keith Levy was determined to keep his pledge and bring *Sofia* home. As the months passed, however, the chances of her being found grew dim, so Keith hit upon a novel way of getting back to sea: He asked friends and acquaintances for contributions toward pieces of marine plywood for a new boat to be called *Shoe String*. He thought the name was very apt. That's what she was to be built on.

Shortly after Ursula ("Uschi") Schmidt's visa expired and she left New Zealand, *Sofia* was found. The anchor that Keith had thrown over the side had hooked onto a submerged obstruction 230 miles northeast of where he abandoned her. She was found by the crew of an Australian yacht, *Gafia II*, six months to the day after she suffered her first rollover. Keith kept his promise to her and towed *Sofia* back to Auckland. At the time of writing, he was preparing *Sofia* for sale.

If he were to equip her for another bluewater cruise, he says he would keep as little gear as possible above decks, and whatever was there, he would lash down as securely as possible.

His list of essential gear would include a waterproof, handheld

VHF with a lead that could be attached to a 12-volt motorcycle battery reserved exclusively for the radio. Cyclists' helmets would also be included, and worn during extreme conditions to avoid head injuries such as the one that rendered him unconscious.

Essential tools, such as wire cutters, would have lanyards, so they could be secured on deck when the yacht is pitching and rolling.

He would seriously consider painting the deck a bright orange, so it could be seen more easily by searching aircraft.

Destiny

Though *Destiny* was abandoned with her main hatch open, and the broken mast still pounding her hull, she remained afloat. She was found washed ashore in the Banks Group of the northern Vanuatu Islands six months after she was abandoned. Local inhabitants stripped her of all equipment and then burned her in a dispute over salvage rights. Several small items were returned to Dana and Paula Dinius by a missionary stationed in the area, confirming the identity of the wreck.

Dana and Paula returned to California for surgery to reconstruct Dana's shattered femur. If they venture into bluewater cruising again, they will give special consideration to the restrictions imposed by shorthanded cruising, planning particularly for the incapacitation of the stronger crewmember, not the weaker one. They regret not having thought through a plan for Paula to handle some of the emergency procedures alone, but they don't think they're unique in this respect. It's probably one of those subjects few cruisers discuss.

If they're caught again in deteriorating weather, they'll plan for the worst possibility, rather than for the 45-knot gale everyone in the South Pacific anticipated on June 3, 1994.

Dana believes that apart from not rigging for the worst possible situation, they handled the conditions satisfactorily. The Sea Squid drogue could have been rigged to bite deeper by letting out more than the 200 feet of line they did. They would also like to carry hydraulic bolt cutters next time and have a prerigged emergency antenna for the SSB radio. It would also be nice to have radios that could withstand the moisture associated with extreme conditions.

Despite the loss of *Destiny*, the ordeal they endured, and the injuries they suffered, Dana felt they had gained considerably from their Force 12 experience.

He recalled that when he first started sailing, he needed four crew to help him take a boat 80 miles from San Diego to Long Beach. It had seemed the most frightening experience of his life. The same was true when they sailed in their first 40-knot gale. Now, if they are unfortunate enough to again find themselves in hurricane-force winds, they will be better mentally prepared to deal with it.

"I think we developed a lot of confidence, even in losing the boat. We were at least able to learn how the boat handled in such conditions," he said.

On the subject of drogues, and the boat's sliding down extremely steep waves, he added: "I've read about people able to do it, but I'd never had an experience like it. The boat kind of takes care of itself in a lot of ways." His biggest concern was getting caught sideways, which could lead to the boat's being rolled.

While impressed with, and grateful for, the capabilities of the rescue teams, he believes the real hero of the weekend was the 406 MHz EPIRB that enabled the U.S. Coast Guard to contact their family literally within minutes of its being activated. It also dramatically reduced the search time of the Orion aircraft. He would give a 406 greater priority when equipping a yacht than he would a life raft.

Pilot

Greg Forbes and Barbara Parks flew home to Maine after unsuccessfully trying to work their passage to America on a freighter. They have since bought a hull and deck in Maine, which they are now fitting out in Florida.

After their rescue, they felt any new boat would have to have a good seagoing cockpit providing shelter from the weather and good back support to suppress fatigue. Their 32-foot Westsail cutter, *Pilot,* lacked both these features. They felt exhaustion was their undoing during the storm.

They also thought their ideal boat should have a well-sealed companionway hatch to keep water out if the yacht floated upside down.

While there was criticism that they did not have a life raft, Barbara said she would not have wanted to get into one in those conditions. The peril in doing so was demonstrated by the fate of *Quartermaster*'s crew. *Pilot*'s dinghy was, in fact, fitted out as a lifeboat, with food for several months and sufficient flotation to support two people, even when it was flooded.

The fact that the four boats that remained afloat—*Ramtha, Silver Shadow, Sofia,* and *Destiny*—all turned up after they'd been abandoned, supports the advice that one should not leave a vessel for a life raft until the water is around one's knees.

Greg and Barbara also recommend carrying a good searchlight, with backup batteries, over expensive flares. They've found flares to be unreliable and less visible than advertised.

Heart Light

Diviana Wheeler has written a book about the extraterrestrial experiences she encountered during the storm. Its title is *Heart Light: Rescue at Sea.*

Her husband, Darryl, believes it is essential to have a handheld VHF radio for short-range communications, and to have a handheld GPS that will still work if the ship's battery power is lost. He also advocates an EPIRB as essential.

"Those are the three most important pieces of equipment, because if something happens, those are your lifelines," he said.

After seeing *Quartermaster*'s life raft scudding across the ocean, he feels a raft is suitable only for relatively calm weather. A raft would have been unsafe in the conditions they encountered.

After they disembarked from the *Nomadic Duchess* in New Orleans, John Hilhorst and Cath Gilmour drove through the United States and Mexico to make up for the trip that was interrupted when *Waikiwi II* capsized. They had just set out on a planned five-year circumnavigation. The others in their crew returned to New Zealand and Britain.

Like Darryl Wheeler, John considers a handheld radio to be essential in case the yacht's electrical systems fail. Their rescue would have been easier, and salvage a possibility, had they been able to talk to the rescue aircraft and the *Nomadic Duchess*.

John believes it important to get to know other crewmembers properly before setting off on a bluewater cruise, so that capabilities and compatibility can be assessed.

He would include light sticks in his kit again because of the handy illumination they provided after their 12-volt power failed, and he would make sure he once again had bright-colored canvas to display on deck, because of the help it gave the air crew during the search.

He, too, believes a 406 MHz EPIRB to be essential.

RESCUE CREW RECOMMENDATIONS

The military personnel involved in the rescues recommended the following as essential for offshore cruising:

406 MHz EPIRB
Handheld VHF radio
Brightly painted boat (orange or red)
Bright sail or other material to stand out at sea
Parachute flares

METEOROLOGICAL REVIEW

≋≋≋

THE NORTHERN FORECAST MANAGER FOR THE NEW ZEALAND Meteorological Service, Bob McDavitt, has had extensive experience analyzing weather for yachting folk. He is responsible for predicting weather for the popular sailing waters at the top of New Zealand's North Island, and he has also had extensive experience forecasting offshore weather. He called the weather for New Zealand's America's Cup challenges in 1987 and 1992, and for the country's yachting team at the Barcelona Olympics. This is his analysis of the weather that caught the yachts unprepared during the June 1994 storm:

The Birth of a Bomb

What occurred was a subtropical low that deepened rapidly; that is, its central pressure fell more than 14 mb in 24 hours. At 30 degrees latitude, this is described in meteorological terms as a "bomb."

During the cruising season in the South Pacific (May to October), weather systems to the south can be anticipated from a long way off as they travel the midlatitude roller-coaster. In the tropics, the convergence zone goes through irregular cycles of building and breaking up. This plays games with the trade winds, but nothing very dramatic happens.

The main problem is caused by lows that form in the tropics and deepen in the subtropics ($22\frac{1}{2}°$ to $30°$ south). These lows can form quickly (in less than a day) and maybe even develop a small area of gale-force winds around them in the tropics. As they leave the tropics, if the timing is right, they sometimes encounter conditions that help them to deepen rapidly, and then their gales expand into a storm covering a large area for several days. Seas can build to 33 feet or more.

Any well-found cruising vessel equipped with stormsails, and able to heave-to, should be able to cope with a gale for a day or so. After several days of being in gale or storm conditions, with waves of 30 to 40 feet, equipment starts to break, and crew get worn down. If at all possible, it is best to try to avoid subtropical lows by keeping abreast of the latest weather reports and by using the proper evasion tactics.

Tropical lows can occur at any time of the year. They are least likely at the end of the southern winter, during September and October, when "high-index weather" is at its peak. They are most likely at the start of the southern cruising season (May and June), when the sea is still ripe for forming tropical lows, but not warm enough to develop them into cyclones.

The Bomb Explodes

On Thursday, June 2, 1994, conditions were almost perfect for the voyage across the South Pacific from New Zealand to Tonga or Fiji. A high-pressure area was stuck over New Zealand. Steady trade winds blew between the Kermadecs and Tonga.

But on Friday, June 3, a tropical depression started to form between Vanuatu and Fiji. It was *not* a tropical cyclone, because it did not have the symmetrical warm central core that characterizes such systems.

Only when this depression moved south, out of the tropics, did it deepen rapidly. This is because it started entraining very cold air that had been brought all the way from 60° south by that high-pressure system over New Zealand. When cold air meets warm air, the warm air is bumped upward out of the way. If, as in this case, the upper winds remove the rising air faster than the lower winds can replace it, then the surface pressure in the immediate area falls rapidly.

Central pressure dropped 15 mb, from 1,001 mb at 0000, Friday, June 3 (noon local time), to 986 mb on Saturday, June 4, making this system a meteorological "bomb." Clockwise winds around

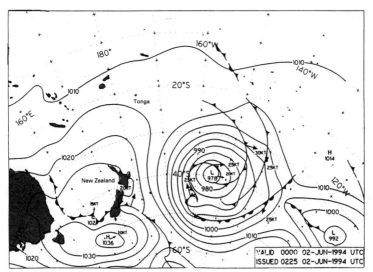

Noon, Thursday, June 2, 1994 (New Zealand Standard Time,
NZST) (Courtesy Ocean Navigator)

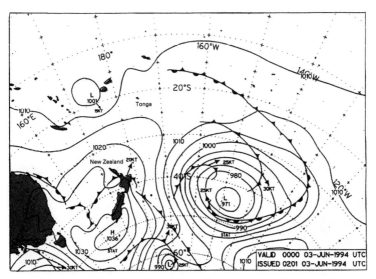

Noon, Friday, June 3, 1994 (NZST) (Courtesy Ocean Navigator)

the low center accelerated to more than 50 knots during Saturday, creating a confused, tossing sea with steeply sloped waves. Conditions near Raoul Island turned from fair to foul within 24 hours.

The weather system reached the peak of its development at about 0600 UTC, Sunday, June 5 (6 PM local time), with central pressure about 978 mb, generating a swell judged by rescue aircraft to be 30 to 45 feet high. A senior pilot of the New Zealand Air Force No. 5 Squadron, with 10,000 hours' experience, commented that he had not seen anything like these wave conditions before.

In more ways than one, that high-pressure area over New Zealand was an accessory to the storm. Since the pressures remained high (more than 1,030 mb) on the south side of the depression, isobars there bunched together into a squashed zone of accelerating wind. Because of the high pressure holding on in the south, it was difficult for anyone in the path of the approaching low to detect its approach simply by watching the barometer. Vigorous winds came before the barometric warning

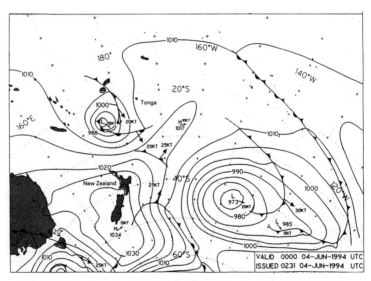

Noon, Saturday, June 4, 1994 (NZST) (Courtesy Ocean Navigator)

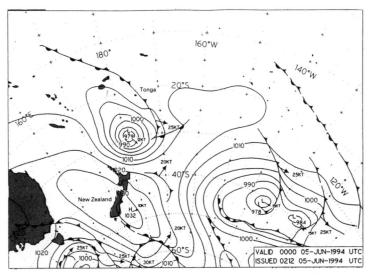

Noon, Sunday, June 5, 1994 (NZST) (Courtesy Ocean Navigator)

The Bomb on Paper

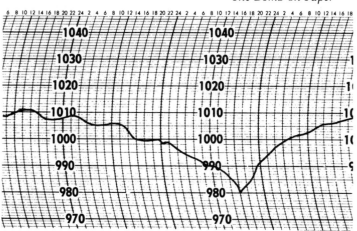

This barograph recording was made aboard the Tui Cakau III,
which rescued the crew of the yacht Destiny. It vividly demonstrates
the rapid fall in pressure (20 mb in 24 hours) that created a
weather "bomb." (Courtesy Tui Cakau III)

PARTICULARS OF VESSELS AND CREWS

≋≋≋

Destiny

Registered in the U.S.A. A Norseman 447 cutter, 45 feet overall, designed by Robert Perry. She carried SSB and VHF radios, a six-person life raft, a 121.5/406 MHz EPIRB, and a 10-foot Avon inflatable dinghy.

Crew and experience. Dana R. Dinius (skipper) and Paula D. Dinius. Each had more than 20,000 miles under sail, mostly offshore.

Heart Light

Registered in the U.S.A. A Catalac, 41-foot, sloop-rigged catamaran, designed by Tom Lack. She carried SSB and VHF radios, a six-person life raft, an inflatable dinghy, and a 121.5/243 MHz EPIRB.

Crew and experience. Darryl Wheeler (skipper): More than 16,000 miles of bluewater sailing. Diviana Wheeler: Also 16,000 ocean miles, with her husband, Darryl. Shane Wheeler: Retired U.S. Coast Guard. No sailing experience. Stephanie Wheeler: No sailing experience.

Mary T

Registered in the U.S.A. A 40-foot, Cheoy Lee Offshore 40 yawl. She carried SSB radio, a six-person life raft, a 10-foot inflatable dinghy, and a 121.5/243 MHz EPIRB.

Crew and experience. Sigmund T. C. Baardsen (skipper): Sailing since 1944, including two races to Honolulu, several trips from California to Mexico. Sailed from Mexico to New Zealand in 1992. Carol B. Baardsen: Sailing since 1950, including several trips from California to Mexico. Sailed with husband, Sigmund, from Mexico to New Zealand 1992. Anna K. Baardsen: Sailing since 1978. Two trips to Mexico from California. Mexico to New Zealand, 1992. Lianne Audette: Ocean races and many delivery voyages.

Pilot

Registered in the U.S.A. A double-ended Westsail 32 cutter, designed by William Atkin and William Crealock, 32 feet in length. They carried a ham band receiver, a handheld VHF, and 12 hand-held flares. They carried no EPIRB or life raft, but the dinghy was equipped with flotation, to be used in the event of an emergency.

Crew and experience. Gregory Forbes (skipper): U.S. Coast Guard captain's license and 25 years of deep-sea sailing. Barbara Parks: Ten years of ocean sailing.

Quartermaster

Registered in New Zealand. A 40-foot sloop with VHF and SSB radio, an eight-person life raft, and a 121.5/243 MHz EPIRB.

Crew and experience. Robert G. Rimmer (skipper): Restricted Launchman's License. Total sailing experience 35 years, including two years offshore. Marie L. Rimmer: Boating for 25 years. Three years of coastal sailing. James M. Anderson: Five years of boating experience.

Ramtha

Registered in Australia. A 38-foot, sloop-rigged catamaran designed by Roger Simpson. Fitted with VHF and SSB radio, a five-person life raft, a 10-foot plastic dinghy, and a 121.5/243 MHz EPIRB.

Crew and experience. William Forbes (skipper) and his wife, Robyn: Five years of coastal cruising off southeast Queensland. A trip from Australia to New Zealand via New Caledonia, and 20 months' sailing between Whangaroa and Tauranga.

Silver Shadow

Registered in New Zealand. A 42-foot racing/cruising sloop of cold-molded wood construction, designed by Peter Craddock. She carried VHF and SSB radios, a weatherfax, a GPS, a radar, a six-person life raft and two 121.5/243 MHz EPIRBs.

Crew and experience. Peter O'Neil (skipper): Extensive offshore racing and cruising experience over 20 years, including crossing the Tasman Sea and voyages to the Pacific islands. Murray O'Neil: Extensive sailing experience. New Zealand international yacht-racing representative. John McSherry: Crewed aboard *Silver Shadow* in offshore racing over previous three years, and had sailed on delivery voyages. Richard Jackson: Extensive sailing experience, including a great deal of offshore racing, and a number of delivery voyages.

Sofia

Registered in New Zealand. A 32-foot Thistle, designed by William Atkin, cutter-rigged and double-ended. She carried VHF and SSB radios, a four-person life raft, and a 121.5/243 MHz EPIRB.

Crew and experience. Keith Lewis Levy (skipper): Three offshore cruises and coastal sailing. Ursula Schmidt: Limited coastal sailing experience.

Waikiwi II

Registered in New Zealand. A 44-foot single-master, designed by Les Rolfe. Equipped with VHF and SSB radio, an eight-person life raft, a four-person life raft, an inflatable dinghy, a 121.5/406 MHz EPIRB and a 121.5/243 MHz EPIRB.

Crew and experience. John Hilhorst (skipper): Yachtmaster's certificates, Coastal and Ocean; commercial Launchmaster certificate. Extensive coastal experience under sail. Catherine Gilmour: Yachtmaster Coastal certificate and Boatmaster certificate. Some coastal sailing experience. Geoffrey Spearpoint: Boatmaster certificate. Some experience under sail as crew. Merve Bigden: Boatmaster certificate, harbor sailing. Shirley Bigden: Royal Yachting Association's Watch Leader and Boatmaster certificates. Ocean-passage experience.

NEW ZEALAND MARITIME SAFETY
AUTHORITY REPORT

≋≋≋

NEW ZEALAND'S MARITIME SAFETY AUTHORITY, WHICH IS charged with the task of maintaining safety at sea, investigated the dramatic events that took place in the South Pacific during the first week of June 1994. The following are excerpts from its report:

The ferocity of the Queen's Birthday storm could not have been predicted, and once within its fury there was little the yachts could do. Again, the issue of total preparedness for any event must be emphasized. One of the yachts in difficulty was not carrying essential lifesaving equipment, and it was totally by chance that the vessel was found.

Of particular note is the role played by the EPIRB and also the radio equipment. Its [the EPIRB's] value in "taking the search out of search-and-rescue" by allowing precise fixing of a distressed vessel's position, cannot be underestimated. In the case of radio, many of the vessels received both practical and emotional support via the radio during those harrowing days at sea.

The role played by the search-and-rescue teams, aircraft crews, and surface vessels that came willingly to the aid of the yachts, undoubtedly at great personal risk to themselves, is also gratefully acknowledged.

This maritime drama will be indelibly etched on the memories of those who survived, and the families and friends of those who lost their lives. The sea knows no friends, still less does it pamper mariners. To prepare for the worst will always be the best precaution.

Weather. There has been some criticism of the New Zealand Meteorological Service in not giving warning of the storm early enough for yachts in the South Pacific, particularly for that area to the north of New Zealand and up to Fiji and Tonga.

The storm center was difficult to find in the satellite pictures received. Judging by the information given in their warnings, Nadi (Fiji) and Wellington had different positions for the center.

Nadi has responsibility for issuing warnings when a storm center is above 25° south, and Wellington (New Zealand) has responsibility south of 25° south. Each issuing office is obliged to describe all winds of gale force and above affecting both areas, and this was certainly done by Nadi. It is also customary for Wellington forecasters to issue warnings to cover the area south of 25° south affected by gales while the storm center is still in the Nadi area, which was done on this occasion.

The subtropic area covers the seas between 25° south and 40° south from the Australian coast to 170° west. Forecasts are issued twice daily at about 0800 and 2000 New Zealand Standard Time (NZST). They are broadcast through [station] ZKLF in Auckland at 2230 and 0830 UTC respectively. The forecasts are also broadcast through [station] ZLM at 0903 and 2033 UTC daily.

The yacht fleet was caught out by a tropical depression, rather than a tropical cyclone. This depression started to form near Fiji on June 3. When it moved south, it deepened rapidly, dropping more than 10 mb [15 mb according to some observations—Ed.] in 24 hours. As it started, the depression entrained very cold air brought from the far south by an anticyclone over New Zealand.

When cold air meets warm air, a convergence zone is formed along which the surface pressure can sometimes drop rapidly. Consequently, with the high pressure to the south, the depression formed a "squash zone," resulting in very strong winds in the southern sector of the depression. Such rapid developments made it impossible for the yachts to avoid the storm's path.

It is of interest to note that with the exception of *Ramtha* and

Mary T, all the yachts that got into difficulties were in the southern hemisphere of the storm.

Lifesaving Appliances

All New Zealand yachts proceeding overseas are required to meet the Category 1 safety requirements of the New Zealand Yachting Federation (NZYF). These state:

" . . . yachts must be completely self-sufficient for extended periods of time, capable of withstanding heavy storms, and prepared to meet serious emergencies without the expectation of outside assistance."

Inspections were carried out on those yachts that fell into the above category by Honorary Yacht Inspectors approved by the NZYF. For each vessel, such inspections were carried out by two yacht inspectors.

The inspection consists of a thorough and detailed inspection of hull, rigging, safety and emergency equipment, provisions, water, and medical equipment. An assessment is made of the vessel's stability and suitability for offshore racing, and the qualifications and experience of the skipper and crew are also assessed.

There has been an assurance that these inspections were carried out in a thorough and reliable manner, and there has been no evidence or suggestion to the contrary.

Indeed, for those vessels taking part in the Tonga Regatta (*Silver Shadow, Quartermaster, Waikiwi II,* and *Ramtha*) the emphasis was on the safety of the yachts and personnel taking part.

The regatta organizers arranged a full-day "Preparation Seminar" and a full-day "Bluewater Safety Seminar" prior to sailing. The latter covered all aspects of bluewater safety, heavy-weather sailing, first aid, onboard systems, and general preparatory subjects. In addition, regular newsletters provided comprehensive advice and suggestions as to where and how skippers and crew could receive further tuition and advice.

The City of Sails Maritime School (and other similar organizations) provided excellent offshore sailing tuition; for example: celestial navigation, ocean medicine, GPS use and understanding, weather reading and understanding, and general seagoing safety measures. Attendance was available to all regatta participants. The issue of a Category 1 license is mandatory for New Zealand yachts, and was a regatta requirement.

While there was an official start time, actual sailing commenced at the discretion of each skipper, and the regatta rules called for a twice-daily radio schedule.

With regard to the other vessels affected by the adverse weather, the New Zealand vessels were required to go through a Category 1 inspection. All the other vessels involved (*Destiny*, *Heart Light*, *Pilot*, and *Mary T*) were foreign vessels, and there was no obligation for them to go through a Category 1 inspection.

Nevertheless they all appeared well-found, with the exception of *Pilot*, which had no life raft, EPIRB, or radio, except a handheld VHF that did not work.

Had *Pilot* been sailing on its own, and not involved with a large fleet of yachts leaving New Zealand, the chances of finding the vessel would have been very remote. From the information given in the 10-minute form (a document containing information about the boat, crew, experience, equipment, next of kin, and destination), which all boats departing New Zealand are expected to file, the earliest any search would have commenced would have been after their estimated arrival time at Tongtapu or Vava'u, which was given as 15 June. This is assuming they had someone expecting them, and there is no indication of this on the 10-minute form. The problems facing the search-and-rescue team would have been enormous, as the last known position would have been their departure point from New Zealand.

The aircraft that found them did so by luck, as the vessel did not show up on radar. They were found only because the aircraft was searching for another yacht.

Life Rafts

Life rafts are an important part of a vessel's safety equipment. Four of the vessels that got into difficulty lost their life rafts when the yachts rolled, however. This meant they had no choice but to stay with the vessel until a rescue could be undertaken.

One of the skippers rescued indicated that the weather was such, he would have been reluctant to attempt getting into his life raft, for fear it would capsize, unless the vessel was sinking beneath him.

Life raft from Quartermaster. Two reports have been received from experts in the care and servicing of such equipment. Both of the experts who examined the life raft came to similar conclusions, outlined below.

At some time, the *Quartermaster* must have suffered a serious knockdown and the life raft case was broken (a small piece of the case was still attached to the painter), possibly by the collapsing mast. Thus the crew needed to manually inflate the life raft.

It is known that the vessel's EPIRB was tied into the life raft, together with the lid of what is thought to be the remains of a grab-bag container. In these circumstances, the decision was made to abandon the vessel. One can only speculate as to why this was done, having regard to the weather conditions at the time. It may well have been that they had no choice because the vessel was so severely damaged that the life raft was their only alternative.

Inspections after the life raft was recovered showed there is clear evidence that the crew were at some time in the life raft. The canopy entrance had been closed, the boarding ladder released, and the observation port was tied down to the internal lifelines. While only supposition, it would appear that the crew were subsequently washed out of the life raft and presumed drowned.

Conclusions and Recommendations

Inspections. Before leaving New Zealand, all New Zealand registered yachts are required to go through a Category 1 inspection carried out by two Honorary Yacht Inspectors. This is to ensure it is up to the necessary standard with regard to the vessel, its equipment, and the ability of the crew.

This provision is not a requirement for foreign yachts but serious consideration should be given to making it so. [Subsequent to this report, New Zealand has initiated controversial inspection requirements for departing foreign yachts; see Appendix IV—Ed.]

The 10-Minute Form. Yachts leaving New Zealand are required to complete what is known as the "10-Minute Form." This form comprises an essential part of the information available to the search-and-rescue organization (SAR) when it is necessary to mount an operation. Yacht skippers should therefore spend adequate time in completing the forms so that SAR have adequate details from which to operate.

Consideration should also be given to amending the document to provide additional information on the material used in the construction of each vessel, for example, fiberglass, steel, et cetera. This would assist searchers where a radar search is required.

Similarly, some yacht skippers, when asked to give information regarding lifesaving equipment, wrote: "Surveyed to Category 1 requirements." Full details must be given, particularly with regard to the number, type, and color of flares carried.

Finally, full details of next of kin, including addresses and telephone numbers, would assist the police representative in contacting next of kin quickly, prior to information being broadcast by the media.

Sea anchors/drogues. Consideration should be given to amending the requirements of the Category 1 survey to provide for appropriately sized drogues or sea anchors to be carried on yachts. At present there is no such provision.

Heaving-to. Each vessel varies in terms of the best method for heaving-to, and it is difficult to lay down hard and fast guidelines. Nevertheless, it is essential that before going offshore, yacht skippers are aware of the best way of heaving-to their particular vessel, so that it lies better to the weather.

Security of equipment. There is no doubt that the storm encountered by the yachts was very fierce, with heavy and confused seas, which probably led to the large number of yachts being rolled. All crews who were rolled reported equipment being flung around the cabin. It is essential that all cupboards have a second latch on them and that every open compartment has a lee-cloth over it. Top-opening lids must have twist-button locks; floorboards must be secured; the galley and stove must be secured; and heavy items must be restrained. Failure to do this means possible loss or damage to medical supplies and lifesaving appliances such as flashlights and flares, as well as serious injury to the occupants.

Crewing. While the idea of several yachts leaving to sail offshore around the same time can lead to a feeling of safety in numbers, the fact remains that once things start to go wrong, the crew of an individual yacht are on their own.

Cruising yachts often go offshore with only two crew, for example, a husband and wife. In those circumstances there may be only one person competent to handle the vessel, and bad conditions and fatigue and/or injury can place the venture in jeopardy. Skippers should give consideration to the adequate crewing of their vessel for the run to the Pacific Islands. It is not enough to say: "I have made the passage often without difficulty and it will not happen to me."

The storm encountered was unusual, but yachts have been caught out before. In 1983, several yachts got into difficulties when returning to New Zealand following the Auckland to Suva race, with the loss of *Lionheart* and its crew of seven, and the loss of another yacht and one crewmember. Indeed, that tragedy occurred at the same time of year, June 4 to 7, 1983.

Self-steering. Yachtsmen must be aware of the problems associated with the use of an automatic pilot or windvane self-steering system in extreme weather. Any form of automatic steering cannot be expected to steer and control a small vessel adequately or safely in conditions of high wind, coupled with heavy confused seas. Yacht skippers should ensure that their vessels are adequately manned, so that manual steering can be maintained during extended periods of adverse weather.

Life rafts. Inflatable rafts are the last resort of safety when a vessel is sinking. It is therefore essential that skippers and crews are familiar with their operation and launching. For many skippers, and particularly crew, often all they have seen of a life raft is the sealed canister or valise on deck. It is suggested that courses be run for yacht crews to familiarize them with life raft operation.

The importance of having the correct size of life raft for the number of crew must also be emphasized. A great deal of research has been carried out by manufacturers and approval authorities with regard to buoyancy, ballast, crew configuration, proximity for support, and hypothermia reduction within the appropriate-size raft.

Had there been eight people in the life raft of the *Quartermaster*, they would have been tightly wedged. By having only three crewmembers in an eight-man raft, the ballast was reduced, therefore making the life raft lighter than it was designed for. Fewer people also means the crew may be thrown around inside the life raft, upsetting the balance and equal distribution of weight.

NEW ZEALAND MARITIME SAFETY REGULATIONS

≋≋≋

AFTER THE STORM, THE NEW ZEALAND GOVERNMENT INTRODUCED regulations that set standards for boats, local and foreign, leaving New Zealand. Introduction of the regulations caused considerable controversy among foreign cruisers who considered them an over-reaction to the June storm by the New Zealand Maritime Safety Authority.

Although the enactment of the regulations occurred after the storm, they actually had little to do with it. They originally appeared in the first draft of the Transport Reform Bill, 1993, long before the storm. They were intended to replace New Zealand Yachting Federation standards for offshore racing yachts.

The new regulations require all yachts departing New Zealand to meet the following minimum requirements:

Safety Equipment

- A functional EPIRB
- Life jackets in good condition, suitable for all crewmembers
- A minimum of two suitable safety harnesses
- A communication transceiver (at least VHF); must have maritime distress capability
- Suitable equipment to support crew in an emergency (e.g., life raft, lifeboat)
- A medical kit
- Suitable flares

Fitted Systems

- Suitable bilge pumping equipment
- Sufficient fresh water
- Suitable fire extinguishers
- Suitable anchoring system
- Suitable navigation system and equipment
- Basic tools and spare parts

Yacht inspectors, who charge a fee, can withhold a certificate of inspection if any other equipment or the condition of the vessel is inadequate and may compromise the safety of the crew and vessel.

These regulations are being reviewed (July 1995) due to the objections voiced by foreign visitors to New Zealand.

COMMENDATIONS

MEMBERS OF THE RESCUE TEAMS RECEIVED CONSIDERABLE recognition for their efforts. Among those who paid tribute to them was the Republican senator for Maine, William S. Cohen, who stated in the United States Senate on July 21, 1994:

> *Madam President, each year hundreds of United States citizens visit the waters of New Zealand by yacht to escape the cyclone season in the South Pacific region. In return, the people of New Zealand generously extend their protection and watchful eye to voyagers of all nations. This was evident when two constituents from Maine were caught in a violent and deadly South Pacific storm.*
>
> *During the first week of June, 1994, Barbara Parks and Greg Forbes, of South Harpswell, were voyaging across the South Pacific Ocean from New Zealand to the island of Tonga. Though initial weather reports indicated good sailing conditions, two days into the trip their yacht suddenly sailed into a tropical depression with winds exceeding 103 mph. Although Greg and Barbara were qualified sailors who could handle adverse weather conditions, there was little that could be done against this treacherous storm.*
>
> *As time progressed, and the storm strengthened, Barbara and Greg's yacht was slowly being decimated. Greg at this time was in the early stages of hypothermia and was losing strength. Fortunately, the Royal New Zealand Air Force had, by this time, been on a search-and-rescue mission.*

As the storm began to dwindle somewhat, Barbara was able to notice an Orion P3 plane that was passing by overhead. She sent two parachute flares into the sky but the Orion crew did not notice them. Barbara proceeded to put on a searchlight, which the plane was able to locate. Members of the plane crew proceeded to contact the Royal New Zealand Navy and notify them of the whereabouts of the destroyed yacht. While the Navy was on their way to rescue Barbara and Greg, the Orion plane flew above making sure that they did not lose sight of the boat. Eventually the naval ship located the yacht and escorted Barbara and Greg aboard, where they received food and medical attention.

Madam President, both Greg and Barbara are extremely grateful to the New Zealand Royal Air Force and Navy for rescuing them from a near-fatal boating trip. I would like to pay tribute to these heroic men and women who saved these lives and offer my deepest appreciation for their commitment to others.

Queen Elizabeth II also recognized the defense personnel's efforts. Flt. Lt. Bruce Craies was awarded the highest tribute, the Air Force Cross, and Sqd. Ldr. Mike Yardley received the Queen's Commendation for Valuable Service in the Air.

Queen Elizabeth II also recognized the work of Jon and Maureen Cullen, who toiled selflessly throughout the storm, offering advice and comfort to the people fighting for survival. They both received Queen's Service Medals for community service.

The Royal New Zealand Navy awarded Maritime Commander's Commendations to Leading Seaman Abraham Whata, Able Seaman Linton Hemopo, and Leading Medical Assistant Michael Wiig for the bravery they displayed in rescuing the crews of *Silver Shadow* and *Pilot*.

The commendation to Leading Seaman Whata read:

Throughout the combined search-and-rescue efforts, in atrocious seas and strong winds, Leading Seaman Whata was instrumental as RHIB [Rigid-Hulled Inflatable Boat] Coxswain, in maneuvering during the recoveries of the stricken crews. Leading Seaman Whata displayed seamanship skills which were of a high order and led the RHIB crew by his calm example. All personnel and the RHIB were ultimately recovered safely, although the crew were in considerable danger on many occasions.

In a team effort whose focus was the saving of lives, Leading Seaman Whata's actions stand out for his sense of duty and courage. His efforts and professionalism under very difficult circumstances are a fine example to all.

In his commendation to Able Seaman Hemopo, the Maritime Commander stated:

. . . [he] was instrumental in maintaining the safety of the RHIB and ensuring the crews from both yachts, Pilot and Silver Shadow, were recovered safely in the extreme conditions experienced. The RHIB crew were in considerable danger on a number of occasions.

In a team effort whose focus was the saving of lives, Able Seaman Hemopo's actions stand out for his sense of duty, diligence and the calm conduct of his professional duties. His selfless efforts are a fine example to us all.

Of Leading Medical Assistant Wiig, the Maritime Commander said:

. . . [he] boarded the yacht [Silver Shadow] which was moving violently in the heavy seas, and provided medical aid to Mr. O'Neil. Leading Medical Assistant Wiig then secured him to a stretcher and assisted the rescue team and the remaining crew to safely transfer him on to the RHIB.

The RHIB then returned to the ship, and once again Leading Medical Assistant Wiig was instrumental in Mr. O'Neil's safe transfer, by davit, on board HMNZS Monowai. During the rescue efforts, Leading Medical Assistant Wiig's actions exceeded those expected of him in his normal course of duty and were an example of courage and selflessness in extreme conditions.

The tributes did not end there. Cmdr. Larry Robbins of the *Monowai* was awarded the Order of the British Empire by Queen Elizabeth II. Prior to that he and the ship's company were awarded a commendation from the Chief of Naval Staff. It read:

> Over the period June 4 to 7, 1994, a large-scale search-and-rescue operation was conducted in the South Pacific, centered on position 25° south, 178° east. The operation involved the distress of 11 vessels and rescue of 21 people in storm-force weather conditions.
>
> HMNZS Monowai was in the vicinity of the search area when the first distress call was received, and consequently diverted to assist three yachts and rescue eight people. The most difficult rescue was conducted in 10-meter [33-foot] seas with the wind gusting to 70 knots and the ship rolling through 35 degrees.
>
> The highly professional manner in which these rescues were conducted amidst extremely uncomfortable and often dangerous conditions reflects the very best traditions of the Service. The Commanding Officer, officers, and ship's company performed with distinction under challenging and arduous circumstances.
>
> Monowai's achievements during the search-and-rescue operation have brought great credit to the RNZN, for which the Commanding Officer, officers and ship's company are commended.
> Well done.

INDEX

≡≡≡

official report of storm, 248–255
regulations for equipment and
systems, 256–257
10-minute form, 251, 253
New Zealand Meteorological Service (MetService), xvi–xvii
analysis of storm, 239–243
New Zealand National Rescue
Coordination Centre
(RCC/NRCC), 3, 32, 47,
64–66, 118, 121–124,
126–127, 171, 174, 226
Nomadic Duchess (Norwegian
freighter), 207–212, 238
Norman, Paul, 2
Norseman 447. *See Destiny*
North Atlantic
weather bombs in, frequency of,
58–59

O
Obsession, 75
O'Neil, Murray, 140–157, 246,
260, 261
O'Neil, Peter, 12–13, 122,
140–157, 233–234, 246
orange rescue cloth (distress
sheet), 39, 167, 210, 238
Orion P3. *See* Royal New Zealand
Air Force

P
Pacific Ocean. *See* South Pacific
parachute sea anchors. *See*
drogues (and sea anchors),
used as storm tactic

Parks, Barbara, 10, 130–139, 169,
236–237, 245, 258–259
Perry, Robert, design by. *See Destiny*
Pilot, xv, 9–10, 130–139, 169, 219,
228, 236–237, 245, 251
piloting skills
maneuvering catamaran using
engines, 111, 184, 192
maneuvering large rescue ship
alongside disabled yacht,
82–83, 86–88, 90, 92, 108,
110–111, 153, 208–209,
221–222
pitchpoling
Destiny, 24
Waikiwi II, 194, 195
*Pleiades Child. See Heart Light
(ex-Pleiades Child)*
portlights
broken, blocking, 204
flexing of, 188
possessions. *See* gear and belongings
Powell, Sqd. Ldr. David, 61, 63,
66, 149
preparation for hurricane-force
storm, x, 57–58, 71, 197, 231,
248
emergency planning/survival
training, 25, 250–251
mental and spiritual preparation, 103, 233, 236
yacht inspections, 250–253, 257
pressure drop. *See* barometer/baro-
graph readings, during storm
preventer, 16
pump. *See* bilge pump

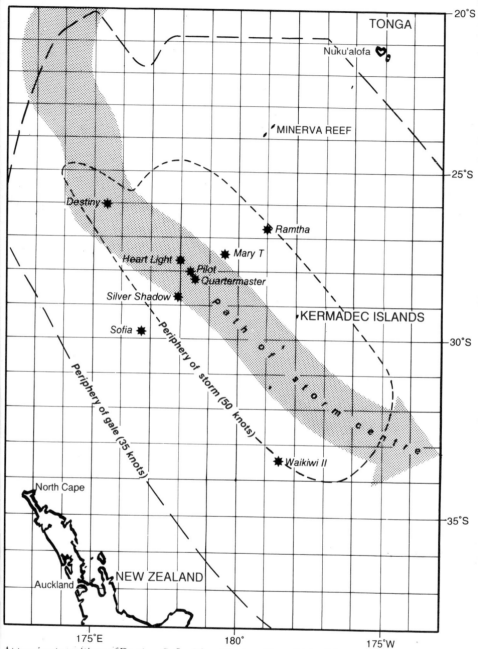

Approximate positions of Destiny, Sofia, Silver Shadow, Heart Light, Pilot, Ramtha, *and* Waikiwi II *when rescued. Position of* Mary T *upon issuing Pan call. Last known position of* Quartermaster. *(Courtesy of Graeme Cooper, Consultus NZ Ltd., based on New Zealand Meteorological Service information)*